MEAT IS MURDER!

CREDITS

Meat Is Murder!
An Illustrated Guide To Cannibal Culture
by: Mikita Brottman
CREATION CINEMA COLLECTION 8
ISBN 1 84068 040 7
© Mikita Brottman 1997, 2001
■■■■■
First published 1998 by:
Creation Books International
London • New York
New updated edition published 2001
www.creationbooks.com
Design/layout/typesetting:
PCP International, Bradley Davis
The Creation Cinema Collection – a periodical series.
A Bondagebest Production
■■■■■
Copyright acknowledgements:
Acknowledgments to BFI stills, posters and designs & United Artists Corporation for the reproduction of stills. All other stills from the Jack Hunter Collection, by courtesy of the film distributors.
Earlier sections of chapter six first appeared in: *Cinéfantastique*, February 1996 under the title "Stories Of Childhood And Chainsaws: The Texas Chain Saw Massacre As An Inverted Fairy Tale"; *Necronomicon 1* (Creation Books, London 1996) under the title "Once Upon A Time In Texas"; and Mikita Brottman, *Offensive Films: Toward An Anthropology Of Cinema Vomitif*, (Greenwood Press, Westport, CT: 1997). An early section of chapter eight first appeared in *Continuum 1: 1996* (Edith Cowan University, Australia) under the title "There Never Was A Party Like This! Blood Feast And The Primal Act Of Cannibalism" and in Mikita Brottman, *Offensive Films*. Parts of chapter seven also first appeared in Mikita Brottman, *Offensive Films* under the title "Exophagy And Exchange: Giving And Taking In The Green Inferno". Acknowledgments are gratefully extended to all editors concerned for courtesy copyright permissions.
■■■■■
Author's acknowledgements
Thanks to Richard Molyneux for the generous loan of films, David Bilton, Philip Simpson, James Williamson at Creation Books, and finally to my husband David, who knows exactly what is cooking in the pot.
■■■■■
Creation Books
"Popular books for popular people"

CONTENTS

"Out of the eater came forth meat"
—Judges, xiv. 4

PART ONE

CANNIBAL CULTURE, CANNIBAL CRIMES

chapter one:
the anthropology of anthropophagy

SOME form of cannibalism has been practised at some time or another in every corner of the ancient and modern world. Cannibalism is a regular and commonplace human activity – one of the age-old practises of mankind. Men have been eating each other all over the world from ancient times to the present day, and few other species have pursued the practise as long or as systematically as we have. Although rabbits, chipmunks, chimps, hyaenas and lions are known to eat their own, in many animal species a repugnance against cannibalism is innate and does not have to be learned, as it does in mankind. This is a book about people who eat other people, about when they do so and why, and for what reasons. It is also a book about the stories that are told about cannibals in myth, folklore and fairy tales, in fiction and literature in anthropological studies, in mondo films, "shockumentaries", and in horror movies.

Into the contemporary image of the cannibal are projected all those aspects of being human by which the self is traumatized – the forbidden drives, the revolting, deeply repressed desires of the individual, the anti-social aspects of human behaviour which the child has been taught to reject in the process of socialization. Cannibalism, therefore, is an immensely complex phenomenon with a wide variety of meanings. As a practise, it may represent simply a response to famine or a transformation and social formulation of psychic energy. As a ritual, it may represent the enactment of a cultural tendency for humans to regulate desire and to govern their social order. Depicted as a symbol, it represents all that must be repressed, regulated and controlled in the establishment of a stable social order. And of course, these various significances merge and intertwine in a variety of complicated ways.

The etymology of the word "cannibal" dates back to the European expansion of the sixteenth century. The word "Caniba", an Arawak variant on the word "Carib" used as an ethnic term to describe natives of the Caribbean Islands in the West Indies, became "Canib", plural "Canibales". The Caribs were believed by European explorers to have been anthropophages, from whom the word "cannibal" was subsequently extended as a descriptive term.

DIETARY CANNIBALISM

As anthropology has testified, there is nothing intrinsically bizarre, taboo or forbidden about cannibalism, particularly *exophagy* – the eating of members of a foreign or enemy tribe (as opposed to *endophagy*, the eating of one's own family members or tribal group). The most simple and easily explicable form of this practise is what is known as *gastronomic* or *dietary* cannibalism. Throughout the history of human culture, there have been many societies in different parts of the world for whom cannibalism is simply an important part of their dietary regime. Evidence of dietary cannibalism extends back at least five hundred years. Some of the skulls of Peking Man were discovered to have been smashed at the base, probably to provide access to the brains. This is a common practise amongst dietary cannibals, many of whom regard brains as a delicacy. In Britain, a recent archaeological discovery – the 1987 Cheddar Cave dig in Somerset – appeared to indicate that Britain's Stone Age population was cannibalistic.[1] In fact, it seems that there are few places on earth untouched by cannibalism.

Early man indulged in exophagy as a preferred form of protein consumption, eating human marrow and brains without much more compunction than he ate deer, otter or wild sheep. Hunters in some parts of the world were accustomed, after killing their human prey, to eat its most perishable parts raw – the heart, the liver, the fat behind the eyeballs – before they got down to the task of carving up the carcass into easily transportable pieces (see Tannahil 1975:7). Other tribes practised dietary cannibalism mainly during times of warfare, when a premium is placed on high-energy-providing protein consumption. The Tupinamba Indians of north west Brazil, for example – amongst whom war was endemic – made it a practise, during battle, to devour all enemies they could lay their hands on, and an enemy killed in the course of battle was eaten on the spot without ceremony. In other cultures, blood ingestion may have been necessary for dietary or immunological purposes.

But this kind of dietary cannibalism soon became extremely rare. When men learned to cultivate the soil, settled down and became farmers or pastoral nomads, the need for supplementary food began to diminish, and, as law and religion developed and became institutionalized, there gradually grew up a climate of opinion that was opposed to the casual eating of human flesh (see Tannahil 1975:29). The Eurasian state religions prohibited anthropophagy, and although this proscription was not always sufficient to prevent sporadic outbreaks of cannibalism during times of hunger brought on by sieges or crop failures, such lapses tended to be discouraged, and often severely punished. Cannibalism for dietary and protein reasons in human cultures today, except in times of war and famine, is so rare as to be virtually obsolete.

There is still a debate in academic archaeology and anthropology, however, as to whether dietary cannibalism actually ever existed at all. Although Christy Turner and several other published U.S. archaeologists working on the remains and ruins left by the Anasazi Indians have been convinced that cannibalism is "95 per cent" proven, their findings began to be attacked in the late 1970s by scholars who debunked stories of dietary cannibalism as colonial myth-making. Travellers' tales from the seventeenth century were derided as a means of proving the superiority of Western culture. These attacks were led by anthropology professor William Arens, at the State University of New York, in his book *The Man Eating Myth: Anthropology And Anthropophagy*. In this book, Arens accused figures like the seventeenth century German explorer Hans Staden of planting the classic scenario of cannibals popping humans in the cooking pot in the European mindset. But Arens goes much further than simply suggesting the early explorers embellished their stories. He claims that cannibalism glibly ascribed to "savages" is a convenient and fearful fiction, and nothing more. "I attacked the romanticists who saw cannibals everywhere," he claimed in a recent interview. "I think it is a reasonable question 'do people eat one another?', and I think the answer is 'no'. But I also think it is a reasonable question, 'why do people *think* other people eat each other'? That is more in the historical record than cannibalism itself. The major historical phenomenon is the *idea* that people eat each other, not the *fact*."

One of the main opponents of Arens's theories is the Nobel prize winner

Carleton Gajdusek, a physician and paediatric specialist who travelled to Papua New Guinea in 1957 to study child development in primitive cultures. Gajdusek's interest, however, was rapidly diverted to a brain disease, *kuru*, known as "laughing death". He set out to prove that *kuru* was a slow-acting virus infection – a discovery that shed light on Alzheimer's, AIDS, and BSE. Central to his research was the theory that *kuru* was transmitted amongst highland tribes by widespread acts of cannibalism: either the eating of a dead person's brain itself, or the handling of it by women and young children. "We believe that contamination during the cannibalistic ritual was the sole source of transmission of *kuru* from man to man," said Gajdusek in his Nobel Prize lecture.

In a recent ironic twist to the tale, however, Gajdusek has recently begun a prison term for child sex abuse. It turned out that he had been driven to Papua New Guinea by his sexual proclivities, and he chronicled in his diaries the homosexual freedoms of the young native boys. It was suggested that Gajdusek, the scholar-adventurer, defended until recently by close colleagues as a generous provider for the youths in his care, was in fact a compulsive paedophile who named several boys in his household with whom he had had sex, and said he had gone "to the ends of the earth" to find partners. "I did it with younger kids in cultures in which they're doing it all the time with adults anyway," he claimed.

Since Gajdusek's disgrace, Arens and his followers have claimed that the criminal passions of Gajdusek's personal life raise a number of questions over his academic work, particularly the exotic territory of his claimed encounters with cannibalism in Papua New Guinea. Arens suggests that if Gajdusek's sexual proclivities drew him to the country, this may have in the very least blinded Gajdusek to the possible sexual transmission of *kuru*. Lyle Steadman, an anthropologist at the University of Arizona, visited remote areas of Papua New Guinea in 1966 and became convinced that cannibalism was an excuse to kill people said to be cannibals, but that cannibalism was never actually practised. "I never saw a whiff of evidence of cannibalism," he said.

In 1982, Steadman published an attack on Gajdusek's field work, claiming that the scholar's taste for the exotic slanted his views. He questioned the lack of photographs. Gajdusek, in the past, had claimed to have photographs of cannibalism, and to have shown them to small scientific audiences, but described them as too sensitive for general distribution. Steadman says he is convinced that Gajdusek "may never really have discovered cannibals".[2]

SYMBOLIC CANNIBALISM

"Cannibalism is always 'symbolic' even when it is real."
                    —M. Sahlins, "Raw Women, Cooked Men"

Far more common, even today, is symbolic cannibalism: eating one another for ritualistic purposes. In order to fully understand such behaviour it would be necessary to explore the territories of anthropology, folklore, mythology, art and theology – a detour too far afield for this necessarily brief introduction. Like dietary cannibalism, symbolic cannibalism is an equally ancient practise. According to René Girard, trustworthy witnesses testify that as early as the fourth century, religious ceremonies on Mount Lyceum in Arcadia included such acts. And although this kind of cannibalism is also frequently recorded amongst societies whose protein resources were somewhat scarce, such as the ancient Aztecs, it was always accompanied by some kind of ritualistic significance. The Aztecs consumed the limbs, blood, organs, brains and living heart of their prisoners of war as part of a ceremony of human sacrifice, retaining their skulls for exhibition and display. Apparently, the priest would lay the living victim on a stone altar spread-eagle, plunge an obsidian knife into his chest cavity, rapidly make an incision, and tear the still-beating heart out of the body to eat fresh and raw. The eating of the heart symbolized the reinvigorating of the powers of the world and the transfer of the "life force", bestowed originally by the sun, to the priest, who was also a magician. Eating the hearts of victims, many of whom were warriors captured in battle, would give the priest-magician sufficient occult energy to perform the rituals necessary to keep the sun god himself from dying. The shrines that Cortez cleansed were devoted to the worship of gods who lived on the transfigured energy of human hearts torn from the living body in solemn sacrifice. It is now know, however, that the Aztecs adapted the practise from the Mayans, who were previously thought to be a culture of benign and peaceful scholars governed by astrologer kings.

More developed spirituality involved the belief that one could ingest the character and attributes of a respected foe by eating parts of him, and as full-blown religions evolved, so did the idea that one could become spiritual oneself by literally eating the godhead, as in the mystic ritual of the communion service in Christian liturgy.[3] In other early societies, symbolic cannibalism was morally sanctioned for a number of different magico-religious reasons – to facilitate conception, for example, or to absorb the virtues of others. Exophagic rituals for the symbolic purpose of absorbing the strength of others have been recorded amongst the Aborigines of Australia, the Maoris of New Zealand, the Hurons and Iroquois of North America, the Ashanti of Africa and the Uscoehi of the Balkans (Tannahil 1975:5). Australian aborigines indulged in exophagy and endophagy for a different number of symbolic reasons. It was a sacrificial ritual, it was good magic, a symbol of revenge, a sign of respect for the dead; it gave strength and courage, and some tribes are said to have believed that it was a necessary precursor to conception, since the life of the dead man passed into the woman's body, from which it was born again (Roheim 1925:391). The Iroquois of eastern North America practised torture followed by cannibalism in order to appease the appetites of the war god, who demanded that captives be taken and eaten, as well as to avenge the death of the family members they were replacing. Some were allowed to live and assume the rights and duties of the family members lost in war; others were tortured to death and eaten. As Sanday points out, in a fundamental sense it did not matter to the Iroquois whether the victim was allowed to live or was tortured to death, because in either case the victim was physically incorporated into the community (see Sanday, 1986:125). However, if it was decided that the victim was going to die, he then gave a farewell feast to which all tribesmen would be invited, including members of other villages, who would be invited to join in the torture and cannibalism of the body of the host.

The Basuto tribesmen cut out the heart of a slain enemy and ate it immediately, thinking to inherit his valour. Some of the tribes of South America ate the hearts of invading Spaniards, and the Sioux Indians used to reduce the hearts of their conquerors to powder and swallow it. Some head-hunting tribes ate or sucked out the brains, and the Zulus used to think that by eating the forehead and eyebrow of their enemy they could acquire the ability to look unflinchingly in the face of adversity. If a New Zealand warrior killed a chieftain, he would gouge out the eyes and swallow them, believing thereby to pass the soul of the chief into his own body. Other cultures, such as the Kwakiutl Indians, have developed rituals like the Kwakiutl Cannibal Dance, which avoids cannibalism by celebrating the cannibalistic desires of human beings before taming them and integrating them into the personality (Sanday 1986:41). In the Cannibal Dance, cannibalism is expressed and then controlled in a communal performance, providing an example of people taking responsibility for their own actions by admitting them. Similarly, in Lapland, early symbolic ceremonies surrounding death included naming a reindeer after the dead person (choosing an animal of a similar age and sex to the deceased), then ceremoniously killing and eating it.

The Tibetans were said to practise only symbolic endophagy. When any tribesman's father was about to die, all the relatives met together to feast on the dead body. In other cultures, if a person fails to eat the corpse of his or her same-sex parent, it is feared that the crops, children and animals belonging to that person will be weakened, having foregone their rightful inheritance of vitality (Sanday 1986:65). Amongst the Gimi of Melanesia, cannibalism – before it was abandoned in the early 1960s – was regarded as a practise that was invented by women and in which women especially were prone to engage. Adult males who ate human flesh were known as "nothing men" and were considered to have the same low status in their society as women (see Sanday 1986:73). In Madagascar, the ceremony of the *famidihana* is designed to enable the dead to give to the living the meaning of life. It involves the immediate family removing the dead from their burial places, removing the shroud from the corpse, then those seeking a blessing and happiness dip their hands in the decomposed matter and eat it, or smear it on their faces. Such ideas as these, combined with a belief that the soul possessed a life essence as transferable as blood, help to illuminate both the practise of headhunting and the cult of skulls (Tannahil 1975:24). Such practises also make psychological sense. The victim is restored inside the ego, where his characteristics are assumed. As Sanday points out, the cultural superego – the source of restrictions and morality, the very foundation of the social order – is thus internalized in each individual in the most literal sense: by eating.

The work of Lévi-Strauss and his followers has done much to try to elucidate the complex nature of such beliefs and the variations in myths, customs and the patterns of these manifold institutional beliefs in a wide range of cultures. Other interpretations of symbolic cannibalism in early societies rely heavily on the Freudian tradition which claims that torture, sacrifice and cannibalism are expressions of a condensation of love and aggression, which purportedly explains why many victims of cannibalism are treated with great kindness prior to their murder. According to Eli Sagan for example, cannibalism is the most fundamental form of human aggression, since it involves a compromise between loving the victim (in the form of eating him) and killing him (because he frustrates you). In other words, the cannibal is symbolically re-enacting his love-hate relationship with his father (Harris 1977:116).

In his study of a relatively modern cannibalistic society – the Tupinamba Indians of north west Brazil – anthropologist and philosopher René Girard provides a rather more subtle examination of the functions of symbolic cannibalism. According to Girard, this ritual form of cannibalism was reserved for enemies of the Tupinamba who were brought alive to the village. These prisoners lived for months and sometimes years on intimate terms with the men who would one day devour them. They participated in their captors' daily activities and married into their families; much the same relationship existed for a while between themselves and their captors, according to Girard, as their captors maintained amongst themselves.

Girard speculates that the main function of this kind of symbolic cannibalism is generative violence. The sacrifice of the scapegoat helps to bring about communal cohesion not just in psychological terms – to satisfy a neurosis or appease a guilt complex – but to bring about real, solid, concrete results. Ritual torture and cannibalism are used amongst the Tupinamba to re-enact an "original event", with the sacrifice playing the role of the "primordial victim", both vilified insofar as he "polarized the as yet untransformed violence", and revered insofar as he "transformed the violence and set in motion the unifying mechanism of the surrogate victim" (Girard 1974:276). The transference of communal violence onto the sacrificial victim of cannibalism is induced by the victim's sufficient resemblance to the "natural", direct target of violence (that is, the other members of the community) to make him an attractive sacrificial object, whilst at the same time he remains sufficiently "other" for his death not to risk plunging the community into a cycle of revenge. As Girard demonstrates, the victim drawn from outside social boundaries becomes the surrogate target for the expression of impulses that might otherwise be directed within. Sanday points out that in torture, violence is expressed; in cannibalism, violence is ritually devoured: "the whole affair is the means by which maleficent violence is transformed into a beneficent substance, a source of peace, political strength, and fecundity" (Sanday 1986:148).

Nineteenth and twentieth century missionaries and explorers furnished us with much of our information about tribal cannibalism in places like Africa. Over recent decades, tyrannical African leaders Idi Amin and Emperor Bokassa have both been found guilty of eating their human captives. In Papua New Guinea, cannibalism was widely practised until fifty years ago – Japanese soldiers were said to have been captured and eaten during the Second World War. In one South American tribe, slave-women were impregnated in order that their captors could eat their babies. On other occasions, conscious victims had limbs removed and were made to watch while they were cooked and eaten. Sometimes, to underline the contempt felt for them, they were offered some. Odd instances of cannibalism as both a literal and symbolic form of revenge are scattered throughout history until even comparatively recent times. For example, trapper John Johnson, who lived in the mountains of Montana in the 1880s, maintained a private war with the Crow Indians who had murdered his Indian wife and child. Whenever he came across a Crow camp, he would attack it single-handedly, kill the Indians, butcher their corpses and eat their livers. "Liver-Eating Johnson", as he came to be known, rather than being ostracized for his somewhat over-zealous law-keeping, later became a sheriff in Coulson, Montana, maintaining law and order for several years before vanishing into the mountains.

In 1955, artist and anthropologist Tobias Schneebaum left Mexico, where he was making a living as a teacher and artist, and travelled to Peru on a Fulbright fellowship in order to forego all contact with civilization. When he finally located a remote village settlement, Schneebaum spent months living as a brother with the Akarambas, a primitive and cannibalistic Peruvian tribe. During his time with the Akarambas, Schneebaum painted his body as a warrior, hunted with stone-age weapons, and observed – and eventually participated in – the murder of rival tribesmen and the ritual eating of human flesh. One night, Schneebaum and his Akaramba brothers initiated a violent assault on the village of a local tribe, saving the flesh of their victims to feast on later. In his personal account of his time amongst the Akaramba, Schneebaum describes the incident:

"...We ran into a fire-lit hut and animal arrows in front of my eyes were used as spears, and axes split into skulls. ...No time was passing, but seven men lay there dead, bellies and chests open, still pouring out hot blood, heads crushed and dripping brain... The bowels of the men had opened and their feces oozed out and mixed with their blood... Michii looked up at the moon and showed it to the heart. He bit into it as if it were an apple, taking a large bite, almost half the heart, and chewed down several times, spit it into a hand, separated the meat into six sections and placed some into the mouths of each of us. We chewed and swallowed."

—Schneebaum 1969:102–7

Earlier, when spending time in the Piqual Mission compound, Schneebaum meets a Spanish ex-missionary named Manolo who is living at the mission partly to help the locals with his skills in pharmacy, and partly to indulge his insatiable appetite for homosexual experiences with tribesmen and young native boys. Unbeknownst to Schneebaum, Manolo falls desperately in love with him. When Schneebaum sets out to find and live with the Akarambas, Manolo, left behind at Piqual, decides to commit a bizarre, homoerotic style of suicide by turning himself over to a tribe of local cannibals to be eaten. After eating his body, the cannibals plant Manolo's head on a stake and leave it standing right in the middle of their village. When Schneebaum returns to Piqual, he discovers a letter left for him by Manolo, who describes his suicidal fantasies of his forthcoming death, focusing on the excitement of being eaten alive by other men:

"I have myself and I have an end, but it's the road to that end that's giving me trouble. I've had dreams of my body being eaten by men and it thrilled me in such an indescribable way that I had an orgasm before I realized what was going on inside of me. I wonder if such a dream or thought ever passed your way?"

—Schneebaum, 1969:149-50

However, despite Schneebaum's relatively recent experiences, the ritualistic nature of symbolic cannibalism – in both primitive and modern societies – means that it is, by necessity, a special and comparatively rare occurrence. The main function of this type of ritual is to work as a kind of communal "safety-valve" to restore and reinforce order, control, cohesion and social taboos. Participants in the ritual are required to perform a number of actions that are normally forbidden: real or symbolic acts of sexual aggression, stealing, the eating of proscribed foods. In many societies, cannibalism, prohibited at all other times, provides the symbolic essence of the communal ritual. Outside the community and its laws there is no place for ritual. Inside the community, ritualistic violence, however horrific, ensures that undifferentiated mayhem can never hold sway (see Girard 1972:274).

HUNGER CANNIBALISM

A third identifiable type of cannibalism is that which occurs as a result of sheer necessity and utter desperation, generally in times of famine and warfare or during plane crashes, shipwrecks and other human disasters. At such times, there is always talk of the breaking of "man's oldest taboo", but in fact, the taboo on eating human flesh is by no means the oldest taboo in the world – others, such as the taboos surrounding incest, child-murder and necrophilia, are equally ancient. Cannibalism is simply one of the main prohibitions of those religions which have exerted the most influence on the attitudes and ideologies of the wealthier nations of the Western world.

Hunger cannibalism was witnessed in England and Ireland during the famines of 1588 and 1601, and in Scotland three hundred years later, for the same reason. Famine regularly led to bouts of cannibalism during the Dark Ages. There were cases in medieval Italy, England and Scotland, and when Henry IV besieged Paris in 1594, he discovered that bread was being made using ground-up bones from the charnel houses. In China, a frequent victim of periodic famine, human flesh was sold openly in markets, and human-meat restaurants thrived during the tenth century. Dishes made from the flesh of old men, women, girls and children apparently had distinct flavours. And when the fourth-century ruler of Northern China Shih Hu was entertaining, he used to have one of his harem cooked and served to guests while the uncooked head was passed round on a platter.

One of the most infamous cannibals in British history was Sawney Bean, who with his wife – "a woman as viciously inclined as himself", according to chronicler John Nicholson – and his numerous offspring, dwelt in a cave in Galloway, Scotland, during the sixteenth century. He abandoned his trade as a hedger and ditcher, and opted instead to prey upon other people for his food. The family cave was close to the sea and they lived by highway robbery: ambushing, killing and then eating passers-by. Any parts of the body which they were not able to eat were at once pickled in brine or hung up in their cave to be smoked. There were no obvious sexual or mystical motives for the actions of the Bean family – they murdered people purely to eat them as food.

In the eighteenth century, it became almost routine for sailors to resort to cannibalism when food ran out after a shipwreck. Known as the "custom of the sea", cannibalism was considered legitimate as long as straws were drawn to determine who was going to be eaten. Nevertheless, it was usually the cabin boy who ended up on the menu; in fact, the captain would normally take the cabin boy on board his lifeboat when a ship was abandoned to ensure there would be adequate provisions. Two famous shipwrecks led to celebrated incidents of human cannibalism at sea. The hunger and suffering witnessed by the survivors of the *Medusa* is captured in horrifying detail in Gericault's 1819 painting, *The Raft Of The Medusa*. The well-known shipwreck of the *Alignonette* led its survivors to feed upon the body of the weakest of their crew, the cabin boy, Richard Parker. When Parker became ill after having drunk sea water, Captain Thomas Dudley killed him and the surviving six men stayed alive by eating Parker's body. When they were rescued, Dudley freely admitted this. The six men were sentenced to death, but this was later commuted to six months' imprisonment. In an eerie coincidence, the cabin boy Richard Parker shares his name with the cabin boy in Poe's story *The Narrative Of Arthur Gordon Pym*, who is also eaten alive by his hungry crew-mates when their ship is destroyed.

During the bitter winter of 1846, pioneer George Donner led his party of westward immigrants out of Springfield, Illinois across Indian territory as far as Fort Laramie. Unadvisedly, the group turned off the normal route to try a short-cut across the Sierra Nevada. About 2,500 miles and seven months later, the party was prevented by bitter weather from crossing into safety by one day. With virtually no food or supplies left, the group of eighty-one (out of an original eighty-seven) made camp. Some tried to leave and various rescue parties were launched, but as the area's worst ever winter set in, people began to die, and many of the starving survivors were reduced to eating their friends' bodies. There

Géricault, *The Raft Of The Medusa*

were also a number of alleged murders committed by Lewis Keseberg, a German by birth. These murders began when Keseberg took a small boy to bed with him one night and presented his body in the morning for butchering. The others were convinced Keseberg had murdered the child. Similar deaths continued to occur until April, when the forty-six remaining survivors were rescued. Keseberg was regarded as a murdering cannibal by his fellow-men, but at his trial he claimed that, like the other members of the party, he had only resorted to cannibalism as an act of despair. He was freed by the court and within a few years he embarked upon a new career running a steakhouse. The story of the Donner party has since become one of the most gruesomely fascinating chapters in American history, questioning every individual's potential behaviour under such adverse circumstances.

Twenty-three years later, in the winter of 1874, an American gold prospector named Alferd Packer led a group of five men on a quest for gold in the Colorado Rockies. When he returned early, alone, he claimed he had been abandoned in the bad weather. However, he looked far too fat and healthy for the ordeals he said he had endured. Months after Packer arrived in Sagauche, Colorado, the mutilated bodies of the remainder of his party were discovered near Lake Fort Gunnison, their skulls crushed and skeletons stripped of flesh. Packer denied that he killed the men, and placed the blame on one of the other party members, Wilson Shannon Bell. He claims to have killed Bell in self-defense, and resorted to cannibalism only as a means of survival during the unusually harsh winter conditions. Packer was given a forty-year prison sentence for his crime, thereby gaining the dubious status of the only man in America ever to have been convicted of cannibalism. In 1995, a light-hearted musical was based on the events of the Packer expedition – Trey Parker's *Alferd Packer – The Musical* ("romance, adventure and campfire songs have never been so tasteless" – see chapter 4).

In a survey of outbreaks of hunger cannibalism occurring this century, anthropologist and historian Reay Tannahil draws attention to a number of well-documented examples. Instances of human cannibalism were recorded in parts of Germany along the banks of the Volga during the troubled years after the 1914–18 war, as well as the years following Stalin's collectivization of the Ukraine. From September 1941 until January 1944, Leningrad was under siege and some of those who survived did so because they forced themselves to eat the dead. Incidents of cannibalism were also reported at Stalingrad, and again in the Ukraine in 1947. In the ghettos of Warsaw and elsewhere during the Second World War, incidents of hunger cannibalism were recorded, and the eating of human flesh was not unknown in the concentration camps of Belsen, Buchenwald and Auschwitz. In Belsen, for example, a former British internee engaged in clearing away dead bodies gave evidence that "as many as one in ten had a piece cut from the thigh or other part of the body... On my very next visit to the mortuary I actually saw a prisoner whip out a knife, cut a portion out of the leg of a dead body and put it quickly into his mouth" (Hilberg 1961:172).

Chinese history has been witness to a number of terrible famines which have often led to the desperate act of human cannibalism. The great famine of 1959–61 saw numberless incidents of cannibalism, and in Guang Xi, the violent struggles that marked the height of the cultural revolution in 1966–68 were accompanied by many episodes of cannibalism. Zheng Yi, a prominent Chinese novelist and journalist, recounts incidents of livers and hearts being cut out of living victims – incidents which have been documented by reference to local party investigative reports and personal interviews with observers and even participants, some quite unrepentant. Still other stories are undocumented, such as the description of "a few elderly men who made a speciality of eating the human brain... they would kneel on the ground and suck out the brain through [a] pipe". However, Zheng Yi's estimate of the number of people who engaged in cannibalism during the Guang Xi famine, based on the estimated account of edible flesh per victim and the assumed amount eaten per consumer, runs to the total of 10,000–20,000 cannibals, an estimate that surely needs to be taken with a pinch of salt (see Zheng Yi, 1996).

Over the last five decades, the world has experienced a number of serious famines, particularly in the under-resourced countries of Africa and Asia. During such periods of necessity, incidents of human cannibalism have not been unknown, but have rarely been followed up with detailed press reports. For various reasons which will be examined later on in this book, the consumption of human flesh is considered far more shocking, sensational and unnatural when it is recorded as occurring amongst European or American peoples.

Tannahil draws attention to two recent examples of hunger cannibalism as a result of a human disaster. The best known of these is the Andes air crash of 1972 when a plane carrying fifteen young Uruguayan rugby players and twenty-five of their friends and relations crashed among the peaks of the Andes due to violent turbulence in the weather. Thirty-two of the passengers and crew survived, but two of these died during the first night, two more during the succeeding days, another nine in an avalanche that struck the fuselage on the sixteenth day of the ordeal, and three more before rescue finally came. For the first few days the survivors managed on a daily ration of a few pieces of chocolate, a capful of wine and a teaspoonful of jam, but as they became steadily weaker and supplies became more scarce, it soon became apparent that the time was approaching when it would become necessary to eat the dead. The survivors passed from revulsion to acceptance of their diet of human flesh, and lived off the bodies of their dead friends and colleagues until two of the men succeeded in fighting their way down the mountains to reach an inhabited valley and restore contact with the outside world. When their story came to be told, most commentators – including a spokesman for the Catholic church – expressed sympathetic understanding of extremes of desperation and necessity to which their quest for survival had taken them. Their seventy-two day ordeal, described in Piers Paul Read's book *Alive! The Story Of The Andes Survivors*, was subsequently replayed in the 1993 film **Alive!** (see chapter 5).

A second air crash that led to human cannibalism – this time in the Arctic – occurred coincidentally, during the same period in which the Andes survivors were undergoing their terrible ordeal. On November 8th 1972, a pilot carrying an English nurse and two Eskimo patients crashed into a hillside in the north-west territory of Alaska. The nurse died instantly, the Eskimo woman a few hours later, leaving the pilot and a 14-year-old Eskimo boy as the only survivors. The boy died after twenty days, refusing to eat the bodies of the women. The pilot survived for nine more days – until his rescue – by eating the flesh of the nurse. After his rescue, the pilot refused to speak about his ordeal (see Tannahil 1975:308).

Cannibalism is not at all remote from modern times, therefore, and there have been some notable recent examples. In 1988, some South Vietnamese refugees, helplessly adrift in a leaking and disabled boat, began to kill and eat each other to avoid starvation. Four people, including two children of eleven and fourteen years old, were beheaded and dismembered, and their cooked flesh distributed to others on the boat.

The *Fortean Times* keeps a record of all examples of cannibalism reported in the world's press on an annual basis, listing up to nine or ten every year, although the reliability of the news reports is sometimes questionable. In 1994, for example, seven notable examples of hunger cannibalism were reported in the world's press. In January, Gretchen Steinfurt was jailed for life in Germany for killing and dismembering her husband Hermann then serving him up to her boyfriend, Conrad Krueger, in hamburger soup (*Europa Times*, January 1994). On the 8th of April, Yuri Lukin, a doorman at the railway hospital in the Russian town of Saratov, was arrested and jailed for raiding the local hospital refrigerator, stealing the body parts and selling them as cooking meat at a local market to raise money for drink (*Reuters*, 8th April 1994). Also in April, starving slum dwellers in the city of Olinda in the north east of Brazil were recorded to have been regularly eating human remains taken from murder victims or hospital waste at the city's main open-air rubbish dump (*Reuters*, 19th April 1994; *Associated Press*, 18th April 1994; *Lancet* 18th April 1994). On the 19th April in Kazakhstan, five hungry convicts in a prison apparently killed their cellmate, skinned the body and cut it into pieces, which they boiled in a kettle and ate (*Reuters*, 19th April 1994). On the 2nd June in Buenos Aires, a pizza delivery boy named Carlo Sanchez was apparently murdered and eaten by a group of Satanists in an abandoned factory (*Wolverhampton Express And Star*, 1st June 1994; *Today*, 2nd June 1994); and on the 9th June, a drinking binge in the eastern Siberian town of Artyom turned into a night of cannibalism in which one reveller was cooked and eaten by his companions (*Reuters*, 9th June 1994).

In 1995, the world's press recorded six examples of hunger cannibalism in the former USSR alone. In February, a man in the Siberian town of Kemerovo confessed to killing a well-known criminal and using his flesh as the filling for *pelmeni*, a Russian version of ravioli, which he shared with two drinking companions (*Associated Press*, 8th February 1995; *Reuters* 9th February 1995). In March, a man who ate his son and a drinking companion was committed to an asylum by a court in the Tula region of Moscow (*Hong Kong Eastern Express*, 4th March 1996). In June, two Ukrainian brothers were convicted of beating up a homeless man, beheading him with an axe, cutting flesh from the corpse, frying and eating it (*Associated Press*, 5th and 9th June 1995). In July, two prisoners in Rubtsovsk in the Alta region of Siberia strangled another inmate, cut out his organs and cooked them in a washbowl over a blazing blanket (*Associated Press*, 5th and 9th July 1995), and one of the prisoners was caught repeating this same cannibalistic routine on a second cellmate in May of 1996 (*Reuters*, 9th May 1996). On the 23rd August 1995, when a schizophrenic murderer was seized in his one-room flat in St. Petersburg, there were two legs and arms in the hall, and a casserole by the oven containing human bones, picked clean. A plastic bag hanging outside the window was filled with human flesh and onions, and a shopping bag contained dried ears and other body parts, while there were many jars of pickled flesh which the police referred to as "winter supplies" (*Reuters*, 2nd September; *Sunday Times* 10th September 1995). In October, in Kaliningrad, outside Moscow, a 76-year-old widow was arrested on suspicion of killing her husband then eating and canning his remains. Cans of human flesh were found in her fridge (*Associated Press*, 3rd October 1995).

This litany of unholy feasts show us two rather significant facts. Firstly, not only is cannibalism a far more common practise than most of us would perhaps like to assume, but even cannibalistic mass-murderers like Ed Gein and Jeffrey Dahmer are not nearly or uniquely as monstrous as the Western media would like to have us believe. In fact, such seemingly bizarre behaviour appears to be a somewhat regular occurrence in the countries of South America and the former USSR – especially in the more remote areas which sometimes have very little media coverage of their own – and amongst people whose lives are, for reasons that will be later discussed, of little interest to the Western press. Secondly, this ghoulish selection of cannibal anecdotes highlights some of the many difficulties involved in any kind of classification or categorization of such unusual practises. At what point, for example, does hunger cannibalism become dietary cannibalism, and vice versa? Can cannibalism really be considered to be taking place solely for reasons of *hunger* in an environment where alternative food sources, however scarce, are available, such as a prison or a war-torn village? Can we still describe a situation as *hunger* cannibalism in which a victim is killed and then eaten merely as an afterthought, or killed specifically to be eaten, as opposed to being eaten because they are already dead, as in the Andes and Arctic air disasters? Can any type of cannibalism, whether it takes place for reasons of diet or of hunger, take place without any kind of symbolic or ritualistic undertones, and – by the same token – would symbolic or ritual cannibalism still take place amongst societies with adequate alternative sources of protein? In fact, many of the incidents listed above, however hungry their perpetrators, may be attributed at least partly to a fourth, terrifying kind of cannibalism – that induced by derangement or psychosis.

CANNIBAL COMPULSIONS

"A census taker tried to quantify me once. I ate his liver with some fava beans and a big Amarone."
—Hannibal Lecter in Thomas Harris, *The Silence Of The Lambs*

Most cultures, whether consciously or unconsciously, share in the belief that cannibalism is a natural evil basic to the character of all human beings, and must therefore be regulated, controlled and transformed by the moral and jural rules of society. People who do not observe these fundamental rules are considered to be less than human: the starving, the possessed, tricksters, witches, sorcerers or – as they are currently known in Western society – the criminally insane. Every culture throughout history has seen a scattering of deviant individuals who obtain sexual gratification from acts of cannibalism.

The psychotic cannibal's murder, mutilation and consumption of other human beings takes place for reasons neither of protein lack, nor as the result of extreme necessity, nor for morally sanctioned symbolic or ritualistic magico-religious reasons. The following chapter provides a series of case-studies of the most infamous and deranged psychotic cannibals. Suffice it to say for now that psychotic cannibalism is the extreme and terrifying reaction of a society or an individual whose moral boundaries have been forced to collapse, whose moral foundations have been shaken to the core, and whose basic human needs have been exploited and abused.

Psychotic cannibalism in whole societies, resulting from the collapse of social and moral boundaries, is far from unknown. Certain North American Indian tribes, particularly in Canada, suffer from a bizarre mental disorder known as the *wiitiko* or *windigo* psychosis – an acute anxiety state marked first by melancholy, then by a distaste for ordinary food, and finally by an obsessive desire for human flesh that invariably ends in homicidal cannibalism (Parker 1960:603–623). The chief characteristic of the psychosis – a compulsive desire to eat human flesh – has its origins in a form of demonic possession. If an individual becomes possessed by the spirit of the *windigo* – an insatiable, omnipresent ravenous monster with a heart of ice – he will be compelled to kill and eat his fellow men; and since there is a harsh tribal taboo against cannibalism, the possessed man is considered to be an enemy of his own kind, to be ostracized and despised (Masters 1993:279). Under these circumstances, the individual can be transformed into a cannibal monster with an addiction to human flesh. However, it needs to be pointed out that anthropologists appear to disagree as to the actual extent of this particular phenomenon.[4]

In 1879 a Kree Indian named Katist Chen, who was also known as Swift Runner, claimed to have been visited by the *windigo* when he murdered and ate his mother, wife, brother and six children during a hunting expedition the previous year. His earlier claims that the family had starved to death were dismissed, and he was found guilty of murder. Later he confessed to a priest about the *windigo*, and said that the spirit had visited him in his cell to make him confess. Only this way, Swift Runner claimed, could he banish the spirit. Sanday points out that the monster with a "heart of ice" conveys the image of an individual who has mastered dangerous forces at the expense of his own humanity. She also points out that this "heart of ice" may refer to the fact that most reports of *windigo* behaviour are associated with the winter period, when food is scarce. Other anthropologists argue that *windigo* belief determines *windigo* behaviour, and from behaviour exhibited in the plight of famine an image like that of the *windigo* monster is constituted. Still others argue that these images of person-like animals who eat animal-like people are a logical transformation of the economic fact that people must eat animals in order to live.

In individuals, as the following chapter amply demonstrates, a number of conditions must be in place before psychotic cannibalism is allowed to occur. One of these conditions is the inability to experience a profound and instinctive revulsion when faced with things that everybody possessing a contemporary Western sensibility would find disgusting (such as the sight and smell of putrefying corpses, disembowelment, the dismemberment of the human body, the sight and taste of brains, inner organs, intestines, and so on). This kind of profound and instinctive repulsion is caused by general features of the human relationship to the rest of the world, a consciousness of the dignity of the human body, of selfhood, individual privacy, the violation of bodily boundaries, and so on. The element of fear in disgust has the violation of moral taboos as its object and the violation of taboos in the individual leads, on a large scale, to the collapse and disintegration of human society.

Philosophers have argued that this profound and instinctive repulsion at such acts as the eating of human flesh represents a natural revulsion at those acts which subvert the moral foundation of a society by breaking and flouting its taboos. The acts of the men described in the next chapter damaged not only their immediate victims and the families of those victims, but the society whose identity-conferring rules are thereby called into question. These are violations that threaten society's conception of civilized life, and we know that we – at least – are civilized, by our capacity to be disgusted and revolted simply by thinking about such acts, and what they might involve.

NOTES

1.   Anthropologist Christy Turner has identified five minimum criteria for proving cannibalism through skeletal remains: evidence of cutting with stone tools; breakage of bones around the time of death to expose bone marrow; burning; "anvil abrasions", which can occur only if someone has defleshed the bone; and unusual missing vertebrae, apparently crushed to get the marrow out. Other researchers have reported "pot polish" on bones that were boiled.

2.   This controversial revival over the issue of cannibalism was the subject of a recent documentary on American television and a long article in the American academic magazine *Lingua Franca.* Next year (1998), Cambridge University Press is due to publish a collection of papers on cannibalism and colonialism, *Cannibalism And The Colonial World*, edited by Peter Hulme at Essex University.

3.   However, the doctrine of transubstantiation explicitly states that the wafer and the wine are, at the moment of Holy Communion, quite literally the body of Christ: the bread and wine turn into Christ's body and blood, rather than standing as a mere symbolic substitute.

4.   There are reports of the *windigo, wihtigo, whillco, wihtico* or *wiitiko* psychosis having been observed amongst various North American Indian groups such as the Algonkians, the Kree, the Salteaux and the Ojibwa. "Such manifestations as have been reported on seem to occur most in areas of great privation and hunger in which depressive reactions may be quite likely, accompanied by delusional beliefs. It would certainly seem difficult to classify it clearly within any western psychiatric typologies since it has features of hysteria, depression and syndromes related to sensory deprivation disorder. It could also be seen as having tenuous links with other manifestations of human flesh consumption such as vampirism and necrophagia" (Prins, 1990:58). Further examples of cannibal-related psychosis are not unknown. The Beaver Indians of North America (or "boreal forest Athapaskans", as they are sometimes known) describe a phenomenon known as the *Wechuge* monster, which dominates any individual whose animal-spirit-friend has been improperly treated by another (usually an outsider). The *Wechuge* monster dominates the individual whose animal-spirit-friend has received this treatment, and then turns to consuming others (see Sanday, 1986:39, 102). The Kwakiutl Indians of the Northwest Coast of North America describe a similar monster known simply as the Man Eater. Sanday speculates that fear of the cannibal monster in the form of animal-man beings is probably a cultural universal, appearing in all societies in response to concerns about the anti-social power of hunger.

chapter two:

cannibal criminals

"That I could drink thy veins like wine, and eat
Thy breasts like honey! that from face to face
Thy body were abolished and consumed,
And in my flesh thy very flesh entombed!"

—Swinburne, *Anactoria*, 108–114

I NCIDENTS of psychotic cannibalism in non-primitive Western cultures in the twentieth century are far less rare than most people commonly assume, and associated with a complex of pathological neuroses closely bound up with the nature and origins of aggression and violence, with childhood impulses and repetition compulsions, and with sexual instincts. The psychiatrist Anthony Storr has undertaken an intensive study into the origins of all human destructiveness, drawing our attention to the fact that the human instinct towards aggression is very closely linked to self-presentation, self-assertion, and self-affirmation. Storr points out that an aggressive attack upon another individual involving the use of physical force is a crude, extreme example of self-assertion at the expense of another. Human aggression is in many ways, according to Storr, a very extreme form of the assertion of individual identity, and those who tend to behave in an aggressive manner also tend to be those who have been neglected and disparaged, and thereby develop a particularly strong compensatory need to assert themselves (Storr, 1991:12). This may help to explain why some of the most violent aggressors – men like Ed Gein and Jeffrey Dahmer – appear to be so ordinary and inoffensive that they often made very little impression on those who met them.

But Gein and Dahmer are examples not of just unusually aggressive people, but violent murderers, serial killers, necrophiles and cannibals. Obviously, to understand the motives compelling such inhuman acts calls for an investigation into seriously abnormal behaviour, including abnormal psychology, psychiatry, forensic medicine, toxicology and pathology, much of which we will have to bypass in this necessarily brief introduction. However, as has been suggested by Freud and others, it is evident that such violently pathological behaviour originates from the same urges that lead patients suffering from traumatic neuroses (brought on by accidents or shock, for example) to repeat the unpleasant event – in dreams, fantasy, narratives or childhood games – in disguised form. Freud concluded that neurotics who had been exposed to trauma, children who had suffered distress, psychotics and other sociopaths were often subject to the tendency to attempt to master their traumatic experiences by repeating them compulsively, whether in dream, play, narratives, or in real-life acts. This led Freud to revise his theory of the pleasure-principle – the idea that human behaviour is primarily governed by the desire to obtain pleasure and to avoid pain – and to conclude that such impulses are counterbalanced by what he referred to as the repetition-compulsion. It is this repetition-compulsion, an instinct described by Freud as "an urge inherent in organic life to restore an earlier stage of things" and which most healthily acculturated individuals have been obliged to abandon under the pressure of external disturbing forces, that forms the wellspring of all psychotic and pathological impulses.

Some have claimed that there is nothing essentially "unnatural" about this animal instinct towards cannibalism. Calhoun's famous experiments with rats suggest the truth of Freud's conclusion that the repetition-compulsion is an urge inherent in organic life to return to an earlier stage of things, which the living entity has been obliged to abandon under the pressure of external forces. Calhoun proved that overcrowding is one cause of stress which tends to convert competitive aggression into violence in some animal societies. Calhoun's rats, placed in conditions of acute overcrowding, become not only violent, but also suffered from many other behavioral disturbances, including cannibalism. Some make the argument that these experiments suggest that our revulsion to cannibalism is an acquired response, rather than a "natural" one, and that – give the right set of circumstances – any one of us could become a cannibal.

CANNIBALISM AS PARAPHILIA

In humans, as any parent knows, the oral stage of childhood is particularly marked; children at this stage of development love games involving biting and devouring. The child's notions of eating and loving are inextricably bound together, and both love and power are transmitted through the mouth. Some children go through a more sadistic oral weaning stage, which finds expression in such actions as scratching, biting, pinching and so on, where the cruel tendencies are linked up with excitation of the mouth. These children may also experience exciting erotic sensations when brutally treating or killing animals; others may show similarly cruel tendencies at an early age – destroying property, breaking up their toys, and lighting fires (see De River, 1950:19). Psychologists have drawn attention to a fusion of complexes at this stage of childhood: the cutting of the child's teeth, the realization that teeth can inflict pain, and the (male) child's unconscious fear of castration. This infantile phase is never entirely forgotten, and sometimes is carried through into adult life. Indeed, many people have described the incorporation of the lover in penetrative sexual intercourse as a kind of symbolic and ritualized cannibalism.

The adult who finds it impossible to rid himself of infantile erotic fixations is described as a paraphiliac[1]. The paraphiliac is "stuck" in an early stage of sexual desire, and cannot pass on from this stage in order to develop more free expressions. Common examples of paraphilias include paedophilia (the sexual love of children), exhibitionism (the desire to expose oneself in public), frotteurism (the desire to rub one's body against a stranger in a crowded place), and fetishism (the sexual fixation upon an object). Psychiatrist Wilhelm Stekel concluded that such immature gratifications are more prone to repeat because they need to rediscover the euphoria of the first time, like an infantile regression. Stekel classified paraphilia as a disease, describing it as "a spiritual parasite which incapacitates its host for any other form of mental endeavour". The condition also has close associations with schizophreniform disorders, hysteria, severe personality disorders, and mental retardation.

Some psychoanalytic writers suggest a number of connections between homosexuality and the oral (or "cannibal") phase of infantile development. Like homosexuality, cannibalism is something forbidden, but it has a special status amongst forbidden things, perhaps because of its extreme rarity. Not only is it rarer than other forbidden sexual or sex-related activities such as incest and murder, but it is fraught with a stronger and more mysterious weight of interdiction because it is so rare as to be unlisted in our usual directories of classified transgression. Cannibalism has all the enormity of murder without that crime's associated disadvantage of risking undue recognition of commonly accepted rules through the very process of violating them. Cannibalism, as an act of total degradation, invites the indignity of a pariah.

Psychotic cannibalism seems to be an acute form of paraphilia where the psychotic finds it impossible to rid himself of the infantile erotic fixations of the oral weaning stage, projected into sadistic adult activities such as biting, nipping, licking, sucking, fellatio and cunnilingus, closely followed by murder, torture, vampirism, sadism and necrophilia. In other words, the urge to sniff, kiss, lick, suck and nibble is followed swiftly – and not surprisingly – by the urge to bite, tear, gnaw, chew and swallow. Some of the psychotic cannibals analyzed by criminal psychiatrist Paul De River reported other unusual fixations. One admitted that in his sexual practises with men he had obtained pleasure out of "sucking tongues". He also admitted that he entertained the idea of destroying his wife, and the urge to destroy women had been with him for four years (De River, 1950:110). Another criminal admitted that he bit off the nipple of one of his victims, and might have swallowed it, though he could not be sure (De River, 1950:156). In one case, the patient sought above all else the satisfaction of his urge to kill and eat a woman who had rejected him sexually, who was once symbolic of love but soon became a symbol of pain, rejection, humiliation and maltreatment (De River, 1950:142). In a similar case, a patient reported on his fixation to kill, consume, and incorporate some of the body of his victim as his very own, an urge which De River interpreted as simply a sublimated return to the primary instinct of hunger (De River, 1950:133). De River's perhaps most extreme example was of a mortuary attendant who became fixated on the corpse of a 15-year-old girl. After drinking some of her blood, he became so sexually excited that he put a rubber tube up into the urethra and sucked the urine from her bladder. Finally, his urge to go further got stronger and stronger, and he started to feel that if only he could devour her and even chew parts of her body, it would give him satisfaction. "He was unable," reports De River, "to resist this desire." (De River, 1950:155-6).

TWENTIETH CENTURY CANNIBALS

Powerful and charismatic killers like Manson, Brady and Hindley, and the Reverend Jim Jones are regularly analyzed in relation to Nietzsche's "will to power", Durkheim's notion of the transcendence of anomie through communal bonding, or similar philosophical or psychoanalytic paradigms. The charisma of such individuals is often regarded as a threat to the rational social order, since charismatic relationships can offer the promise of an existence more central and unitary than that of the divided self. What is particularly interesting about the following selection of cannibal killers is that many of them – particularly Fish, Gein, Dahmer and the young Sagawa – display personal characteristics that are anything but charismatic, being described by family and colleagues as awkward, asocial, neurotic, unpopular or chronically shy. Figures like Gein and Dahmer have been diagnosed as suffering from an unstable ego relating to the lack of a socially-based continuity of identity, a complex which, as often testified, can create an appetite for symbolic substitutes for the transcendence of self.

In the nineteenth century, the diagnosis for such personality disorders tended towards hysteria; the early twentieth century favoured schizophrenia; contemporary versions are diagnosed as narcissistic. The hysteric, the schizophrenic and the narcissist are all driven to seek out intensities of experience, existence, feelings and fusions without the accompanying fears of personality disintegration. The narcissistic personality often gravitates towards the quasi-psychotic, charismatic personality who seems to be acting out the raging intensity of self which they themselves tend to lack. In its most extreme form, however, the narcissistic personality becomes a borderline pathology seeking the ecstasy of boundary loss – the blur between self and other – through the ancient practise of cannibalism.

The kinds of narcissistic personalities whose psychotic tendencies are liable to slip over into pathological cannibalism are those – like Fish, Gein and Dahmer – who suffer from an inadequate sense of stable identity. In some ways, it could be argued that pathological cannibalism is a side-effect of the twentieth century. Increasingly, the twentieth century tends to encourage responses to the modern world that result in the formation of selves unable to contain the basis of a stable sense of identity. Such tendencies include the economic ideology of individual competitiveness, the technological organization of society, mass-mediated forms of cultural representation, the intrusion of the market place into family life, the disintegration of the traditional bases of communities, alliances and affiliations, and the proliferation of fragmented, disconnected, specialized roles. These and other modern social tendencies all help to decompose the sense of a stable, coherent self and identity. Such personalities, encouraged by the contemporary ideology of "self-fulfilment" into attempting to attain that sense of self through conformist channels, go round and round in a confused circle of failed erotic liaisons, compulsive commodity acquisition and display, or workaholism, none of which can ever provide enough stability to provide the absent sense of self. Indeed, the changing dynamics of the labour-market, the transience of erotic attachments and the changing market of goods in contemporary society make it necessary to seek out constantly renewed criteria of values. The new, postmodern personal values become qualities like adaptability, pliability, and a general willingness to surrender to the situational. Yet this emerging postmodern validation of the conceptual fluidity of identity and interactive role-playing is in many ways merely a cover for the creative production of a series of situation-determined, sequential, borderline-pathological selves.

Such individuals, when they become parents, are often the kinds of parents who are overly in need of excessive love from their children. Consequently, they are liable to fail to express necessary admonitions or prohibitions to them. Those children who grow up unable to internalize parental admonitions often fail to evolve a stable and coherent superego, and are likely to grow up themselves with narcissistic personalities similar to those of their parents. Twentieth century society encourages the evolution of these kinds of individuals, both on a conscious and an unconscious level, since, after all, the unstable, incoherent borderline personality makes both a better worker and a better consumer. Unstable personalities are more mobile, more flexible, and more open to change.

The psychologically repressed borderline personality will often, therefore, develop its own primal, image-bound, myth-based, magical ways of thinking similar to those of childhood. The borderline personality who seeks an outlet in cannibalism is indulging in precisely this kind of magical thinking. To the psychotic cannibal, consumption of the other obliterates the boundaries between self and non-self in a blissful, transforming union which effects a complete withdrawal from society into a self-fulfilling mutuality of experience. The magical act of cannibalism is an expressive, actualizing practise leading to a safe loss of selfhood through the complete corporeal merging of self and other. In the cannibal's apocalyptic way of thinking, he is enacting, personifying and living out the repressed rage and desire of his lack of selfhood, and the vital energy generated by cannibal acts is seen as an index of heightened significance. As long as the daily world of the twentieth century continues to lose its enchantment – that is, to become more controlled and rationalized – we will continue to breed psychotic cannibals, driven to seek out increasingly solipsistic ways of re-enchanting their own barren worlds.

There are at least forty named paraphilias in the latest edition of the America Psychiatric Association's *Diagnostic And Statistical Manual Of Mental Disorders*, the manual used in the legal classification of the criminally insane. The eight listed by name include *#302.84: Sexual Sadism*, which incorporates paraphiliac rape (raptophilia or biastophilia) and lust murder (erotophonophilia) (see Money, 1990:26). Cannibalism is not mentioned in the manual, and belongs under *#302.90: Paraphilia Not Otherwise Specified*. But many rapists and lust murderers are alleged to have indulged in necrophile activity, thus confirming how difficult it is to place criminal behaviour into the discrete categories implied by the neat and systematic structures of the APA-DSM. For the sake of clarity, therefore, I have imposed a number of limitations on what, for the purposes of this chapter at least, counts as "genuine" psychotic cannibalism.

Firstly, there appear to be quite well documented accounts of what today might be regarded as psychotic cannibalistic behaviour dating from the fifteenth century, from Gilles de Rais of Cevci to Gamier, Leger, Sergeant Bertrand, and so on. For the reasons just explained, the following discussion of selected cannibal killers will be restricted to those whose crimes occurred during the twentieth century, from Fritz Haarman to Jeffrey Dahmer. My working definition of cannibalism excludes *necrophagy* – the consumption of human flesh that is already dead, as opposed to the murder of living human beings for the specific purposes of consumption (as in the case of Walter Krone, a German necrophage who went to jail for seven years in 1980 for eating parts of a girl who had been killed in a road accident). Neither have I included what might be called "single episode" psychotic cannibalism (except in the exceptional case of Issei Sagawa), as in the example of Dean Baker, who in 1970 confessed to a California patrolman: "I have a problem: I'm a cannibal", whereupon he pulled from his pocket a man's severed fingers and admitted killing someone and eating his heart raw. Or the case of Albert Fentress, a history teacher in New York, who invited an 18-year-old boy into his house then shot him, cut up his body and ate parts of it, before being committed to a mental institution indefinitely in 1979. Or the case of Anna Zimmermann, a female cannibal from Monchen-Gladbach in Germany, who in 1981 murdered her lover, cut him into manageable, pan-sized steaks, and, after saving them together with a finger, an ear and his penis in the freezer, fed them to her two children aged six and four – something she had previously done with the family pets.

I have also excluded quasi-cannibals like Richard Chase, the so-called "Vampire of Sacramento", who consumed the viscera of pigs and rabbits (mixed together in a blender), but not those of human beings. Other notable vampires that have escaped the confines of this study include Tracey Wigginton, who murdered a man she met at a Brisbane dance in 1989 and, according to the friends who were with her, feasted on his blood. Mark Heggie, aged 23, drank the blood of his victim after trying to kill her in North London in 1992. He told detectives he often drank animals' blood and obtained work in abattoirs to satisfy his cravings. And Marcelo Costa de Andrade, who was arrested in Rio in December 1991, confessed to killing fourteen boys, aged from six to thirteen and drinking their blood "to become young and pretty like them" during the previous eight months. Similarly excluded from the final selection are those suffering from the allied conditions of necrophilia, clinical vampirism (habitual blood ingestion), and "occupational" or "incidental" cannibalism, as in the case of the lust murderer who gets carried away in his frenzy and swallows flesh from his victim's mouth, buttocks or genitalia.

I. FRITZ HAARMAN – "THE BUTCHER OF HANOVER"

"I have my tastes, after all."

It is particularly unusual that Germany, a small country in comparison with the USA, has produced at least three psychotic cannibals this century, with all of them operating at the same time, between the wars, during the 1920s.

Born into a bitter, unhappy family in the depressing climate of post-war Germany, Fritz Haarman was devoted to his mother, who had been incapacitated after his birth and remained a lifelong invalid, and filled with hatred for his father Olle, a railway worker whose beatings made Haarman's childhood desperately unhappy. Before his three sisters drifted into prostitution, Fritz used to enjoy dressing up in their clothes. It soon became apparent that his IQ was lower than average and, when he showed dangerous signs of uncontrolled violence, his father tried to have him committed to an institution, but the directors declared him to be safe and refused Herr Haarman's request. Fritz eventually escaped from home to join the army, but was soon dismissed as "undesirable", and it was at that point that he devoted himself to a career of theft and sex attacks.

Haarman also became well-versed in the crafts of stealing, picking pockets and indecently assaulting small children, for which he served a series of short jail sentences ending with a five-year sentence imposed in 1913, when he was 34, for fraud and theft. Upon his release from prison in 1918, Haarman moved into a third-floor apartment in a Hanover slum with his homosexual lover, Hans Grans. It was here, in the ghettos of Hanover, that Haarman embarked upon a new series of crimes to complement his inglorious career: murder and cannibalism. His victims were nameless, untraceable vagrant youths he picked up at the railway station. After persuading them to accompany him back to his apartment, he would attack them, use their bodies for his own sexual gratification, then kill them by tearing out their throats with his teeth, after which he would drink their blood and indulge in necrophile activities. He would then drag the cannibalized body up to the attic of his grimy apartment, whose walls were encrusted with dried blood. Then, sometimes alone, sometimes with the help of Grans, he would dismember the body, slice it up and transfer the edible flesh into buckets, which he then took to sell (as horse-meat) at his stall in Hanover's market-place, where he also did a thriving trade in selling second-hand clothes. Haarman's meat business was particularly successful since his prices were lower than those of anyone else, and the local police, for who Haarman had worked for many years as an occasional informer, turned a blind eye to his black market trade.

Haarman's disguise as a butcher and meat-trader satisfied the curiosity of his neighbours, who were intrigued by chopping noises, bloodstains in the halls, and buckets of blood being carried up and down stairs late at night. Some of the

Fritz Haarman under arrest

neighbours were even the grateful recipients of Haarman's surplus bones, which he gave them to make soup with. One customer who bought some meat from Haarman's market stall was so worried about it that she went to the police to ask them what it was, only to be told that it was pork. Finally, public concern about the number of missing children in Hanover, coupled with the discovery of child-sized skulls and bones washed up by the River Leine, led the chief of police to have Haarman watched. He was observed attempting to pick up a boy at the railway station and to sexually molest him. At this point Haarman was arrested, and, with him in custody, officers went to search his apartment. They discovered the bloodstained room and piles of clothes, but it was the mother of a missing boy, who spotted her son's coat being worn by one of Haarman's neighbours, that prompted his full confession. Haarman instantly implicated Grans in the murders.

At their trial on the 4th December 1925, Haarman, now forty-five, was declared mentally sound by two psychiatrists, found guilty of twenty-four murders (though this was believed to be a gross underestimate), and beheaded. Grans, aged twenty-five, was sentenced to life imprisonment but released after only twelve years. There are great similarities between the Haarman case and that of Georg Karl Grossmann (the "Butcher of Berlin"), arrested in 1921.

In **The Mad Butcher** (aka **Meat Is Meat** aka **The Strangler Of Vienna**, John Zuru, 1972), Victor Buono plays a Haarman-style character who turns his victims into sausages. In 1973, Fassbinder disciple Ulli Lommel directed **Zaerlichkeit Der Voelfe** (aka **Tenderness Of Wolves**), based directly on the Haarman case. Although the film features plenty of graphic blood-drinking, actual cannibalism is omitted. **Totmacher** (a.k.a. **Deathmaker**, dir. Romuald Karmaker, 1995) is a filmed intimate play based on the original interrogation files of the Haarman case.

II. JOACHIM KROLL – "UNCLE JOACHIM"

"I wouldn't use the lavatory if I were you – it's stopped up."

Like his compatriot Fritz Haarman, the unimposing Joachim Kroll was considered as a youngster to be mentally defective, evidenced by his lack of schooling and his inability to read. Kroll blamed his perverse appetites on an incident which happened in his childhood when he witnessed some pigs being butchered, and the scene awakened his sex drive[2]. When he was in his teens his mother, a widow, moved with her five children to west Germany. When she died, the brothers and sisters went their separate ways, and eventually lost contact with Joachim.

A soft-voiced, small, unremarkable and insignificant little man, Kroll kept company only with other men, and was unable to achieve a normal sexual relationship with a woman. He was, however, highly sexed, albeit a deviant, admitting to the police that after several of his regular bouts of carnage, during which he ejaculated twice on some occasions, he would return to his room and seek yet more gratification with a much-used rubber sex doll. He also kept a large hoard of children's dolls used as bait for little girls he would befriend, and also used as practise for strangling children. Occasionally Kroll would masturbate with one hand while strangling a doll with the other.

Kroll's first murder took place when he was about 22, in 1955, when he attacked 19-year-old Irmgard Srehl in a village just north of the Ruhr district. Her naked body was found with its abdomen ripped up and evidence of frenzied rape, but lack of bruising around the genital area proved that the rape had not been inflicted on the girl while she was still alive, and this was the case with all Kroll's female victims. Four years later, he murdered a 24-year-old woman named Klara Tesmer in Rhinehausen, and it was during this killing that Kroll is first known to have practised cannibalism. Klara's body was found with pieces hacked from the buttocks and thighs, which Kroll wrapped up and took home for his supper. Another man, Heinrich Ott, was charged with the murder, and hung himself in his cell while awaiting trial. A month later, Kroll murdered Manuela Knodt, aged 16, in Bredeney.

In April 1962, Kroll abducted and murdered 13-year-old Petra Giese on her way home from a carnival. Her body was found to have been raped and mutilated, with pieces of flesh cut from her buttocks and thighs. Two months later, the body of 12-year-old Monika Tafel was discovered in an identical condition. A 52-year-old man was arrested for the murder of Petra Giese, and a 34-year-old man for that of Monika Tafel. Then in August 1965, an attack in Grossenbaum on Marion Veen went badly wrong, and Kroll ended up killing Marion's fiancé, Herman Schmitz, while Marion got away, but was unable to identify her attacker. Kroll's next killing, that of 20-year-old Ursula Rohling in Marl in September 1966, led to another police bungle which ended in the arrest of Ursula's fiancé, Adolf Schickel, who was also driven to suicide by this false accusation.

Kroll's final murder, and the one which led to his arrest and capture, was that of his youngest victim, a 5-year-old girl named Ilona Harke who lived in Bredeney. After killing and raping the child, Kroll cut large quantities of flesh from her buttocks and shoulders, wrapped them in greaseproof paper and took them home with him to eat. That night, a man was on his way to use the shared lavatory on the top floor of his apartment building in Friesen Street, Laar, north of Duisberg, West Germany, when he bumped into his neighbour, "Uncle Joachim", who advised him not to use the toilet because it was "blocked up". When the neighbour asked what it was blocked up with, Kroll replied "with guts". One look into the toilet bowl was enough to alert the police, whom Kroll later told that he only cannibalized those victims whom he considered to be young and tender. In total, Kroll confessed to 14 murders which could be accounted for, from the slaying of a 61-year-old widow to the mutilation of a 5-year-old child. However, there are undoubtedly other sex killings which were committed by Kroll during this period (1955–66), which remain officially unsolved.

III. KARL DENKE – THE CANNIBAL LANDLORD

Born in the 1920s, Denke was the landlord of a cheap boarding house at Munsterberg in Silesia (now Ziebice in Poland), and organist at his local church. During the lean years following the end of the First World War, Denke had apparently fallen into a systematic routine of murder and cannibalism, killing a long succession of guests – mainly travellers, tramps and beggars – who were offered free accommodation during the dire years between 1918 and 1924, taken into Denke's boarding house, and never emerged. Known as "Papa" by his friends and tenants, Denke was regarded as a God-fearing man whose kindness to the homeless was much admired.

Since most of his tenants were vagrants about whom no-one asked any questions, they made easy prey for Denke. Between 1921 and 1924 he killed at least thirty strangers, both male and female, in order to pickle their flesh bit by bit. After each murder, he methodically entered the victims' names, weight, date of arrival at the boarding house and date of death in his neatly-kept ledger. Towards the end of December 1924, the inhospitable landlord was interrupted in the process of murdering a young traveller who had been lodging with him over night. Denke's upstairs neighbour heard terrible screams from the lower floor and rushed downstairs to find a young man bleeding profusely from a hatchet wound to the back of his head. The man lost consciousness, but before doing so he managed to say that Denke had attacked him from behind.

During their search of the premises, police came across a bag full of various identity papers and an assortment of clothing. The cellar contained even more surprises, including two pots filled with pickled human cutlets, several tubs of human dripping and a collection of bones from thirty different men and women who had been served up by Denke as supper for his more fortunate residents. With evidence like this in front of him, Denke had no choice but to admit to his crimes, and claimed that he had eaten nothing but human flesh for the last three years. Soon after his arrest in 1924, the unfriendly innkeeper hanged himself by his braces in his prison cell whilst awaiting trial.

IV. ALBERT FISH – THE "GENTLE CANNIBAL"

"I have had children in every State."

Born Hamilton Fish in Washington DC in 1870, Albert came from a family troubled by a history of insanity and misfortune. His father died when Albert was five, and he was subsequently placed in an orphanage from which he regularly absconded. When he was fifteen, he was apprenticed to a painter and decorator, and at eighteen he married. Throughout the early years of his marriage he was known as a meek, gentle, retiring man, a good Christian and a fond father to his six children. It was only after the breakup of his marriage nineteen years later that his bizarre behaviour first made itself known.

Initially Fish became recognized by the police as simply a minor nuisance – a petty swindler and eccentric pervert. He was arrested in December 1930 for writing obscene letters to lonely widows who had placed advertisements in personal columns of newspapers and magazines, or who had lodged their names with marriage agencies. The letters, which were sent over a period of years, led Fish to serve several short stints in prison and mental hospital. During this period, he became obsessed with the notion of atonement through self-punishment, and engaged in savage bouts of self-flagellation, burning himself, eating his own excrement and inserting needles into his pubic region and scrotum. When he was arrested, X-rays revealed the presence of twenty-nine needles in his scrotum, some of which had been there so long that they had begun to corrode. He also began to be obsessed with flesh-eating, serving raw meat to his children on nights when the moon was full, and collecting newspaper articles on cannibalism, which he carried around with him until they turned into yellow crumbs in his pockets.

When he finally turned to murder and necrophilia, Fish's preferred victims were children. He was responsible for over a hundred violent assaults on young girls, and the murder of twelve of them. "I have had children in every State," he bragged when he was finally arrested, and the authorities suspected that Fish's figure of one hundred was an underestimate. He was finally brought to trial on the 12th March 1935, when he was sixty-five, for the murder of 12-year-old Grace Budd, whose flesh he had cut into thin strips, boiled, then eaten in a stew with cabbage and potatoes.

On the 3rd June 1928, Fish, calling himself "Frank Howard", had arrived at the doorstep of the Budds' apartment in New York City in response to an advertisement placed in the newspaper by Grace's father, Paul, who was looking for work. Fish, appearing to all intents and purposes like a kindly old gentleman, offered Paul Budd a job on his Long Island farm, and volunteered to take his young daughter Grace to a children's party while her father was packing. She was never seen alive again. Five months later, however, the Budds received a letter describing, in some detail, what had been done to their daughter ("It took me 9 days to eat her entire body"). Although Fish ended the letter by taking great pains to point out that he had not attacked Grace sexually ("I did not fuck her tho I could of had I wished to. She died a virgin"), he later confessed to a psychiatrist that this was a lie. From an imperfectly erased address on the back of the envelope, the police traced Fish to a seedy hotel room in a New York boarding house, and began their investigation into his long and bizarre career of assault, abduction, murder, necrophilia and cannibalism. Apart from Grace Budd's murder, Fish also confessed to murdering a man in 1910, to mutilating and torturing to death a mentally retarded boy in New York in 1919 and another boy in Washington in the same year, to killing and eating 4-year-old William Gaffney in 1927, and 5-year-old Francis McDonal in 1934. The police suspected him of many more murders, but they began the process of charging him with the killing of Grace Budd. Then they handed him over to the psychiatrists.

At his trial, Fish's defense attorney fought hard to prove his client's

Albert Fish

insanity, backed up by the testimony of the famous psychiatrist Dr. Frederic Wertham. After his first interview with the harmless looking, frail old man, Wertham commented that "He looked like a meek and innocuous little old man, gentle and benevolent, friendly and polite... If you wanted someone to entrust your children to, he would be the one you would choose". After further interviews, however, Wertham came to the conclusion that "this man is not only incurable and unreformable but unpunishable. There is no known perversion that he did not practise, and practise frequently. In his own distorted mind he is looking forward to the electric chair as the final experience of true pain" ("What a thrill it will be if I have to die in the electric chair!", claimed Fish, "It will be the supreme thrill – the only one I haven't tried"). Wertham made a detailed study of Fish and listed eighteen sexual perversions in which he indulged, including sado-masochism, exhibitionism, coprophagia (the eating of faeces), undinism (sexual acts involving urination), fetishism (he liked to insert roses into his penis, and then eat the roses), and cannibalism. Nevertheless, despite his obvious insanity, Fish was found guilty of murder; one of the jury later confided that "I thought he was insane, but he deserved to be electrocuted anyway".

On the 16th January 1936 at Sing Sing, Fish took his seat in the electric chair and eagerly helped the electrocutioner to fix the electrodes on to his legs. He smiled as other electrodes were placed on his head, and as 3,000 volts shot through his body, he laughed. But the "gentle cannibal" proved a difficult Fish to fry. By a perverse twist of fate, the electric current was caused to short circuit by the collection of metal needles nestling deep inside his scrotum, and a second charge of electricity had to be pumped through his body before he was finally declared dead.

V. EDWARD GEIN – "WEIRD OLD EDDIE"

"I had a compulsion to do it."

Born at the turn of the century into the small farming community of Plainfield, Wisconsin, Gein lived a repressive and solitary life on his family homestead with a weak, ineffectual brother and domineering mother who taught him from an early age that sex was a sinful thing. Eddie ran the family's 160-acre farm on the outskirts of Plainfield until his brother Henry died in 1944 and his mother in 1945. Thanks to federal subsidies, Gein no longer needed to farm his land, and he abandoned it to do odd jobs here and there for the Plainfield residents, to earn him a little extra cash. But he remained alone in the enormous farmhouse, haunted by the ghost of his overbearing mother, whose bedroom he kept locked and undisturbed, exactly as it had been when she was alive. He also sealed off the drawing room and five more upstairs rooms, living only in one downstairs room and the kitchen.

"Weird old Eddie", as the local community know him, had begun to develop a deeply unhealthy interest in the intimate anatomy of the female body – and interest that was fed by medical encyclopedias, books on anatomy, pulp horror novels and pornographic magazines. He became particularly interested in the atrocities committed by the Nazis during the Second World War and the medical experiments performed on Jews in the concentration camps. Soon he graduated on to the real thing by digging up decaying female corpses by night in far-flung Wisconsin cemeteries. These he would dissect and keep some parts – heads, sex organs, livers, hearts and intestines. Then he would flay the skin from the body, draping it over a tailor's dummy or even wearing it himself to dance and cavort around the homestead – a practise that apparently gave him intense gratification. On other occasions, Gein took only the body parts that particularly interested him. He was especially fascinated by the excised female genitalia, which he would fondle and play with, sometimes stuffing them into a pair of women's panties which he would then wear around the house. Not surprisingly, he quickly became a recluse in the community, discouraging any visitors from coming near his by now neglected and decaying farm.

Gein's fascination with the female body eventually led him to seek out fresher samples. His victims, usually women of his mother's age, included 54-year-old Mary Hogan, who disappeared from the tavern she ran in December 1954, and Bernice Worden, a woman in her late fifties who ran the local hardware store, who disappeared on the 16th November 1957. Mrs. Worden's son Frank was also the sheriff's deputy, and upon learning that weird old Eddie Gein had been spotted in town on the day of his mother's disappearance, Frank Worden and the sheriff went to check out the old Gein place, already infamous amongst the local children as a haunted house.

There, the gruesome evidence proved that Gein's bizarre obsessions had finally exploded into murder, and much, much worse. In the woodshed of the farm was the naked, headless body of Bernice Worden, hanging upside down from a meat hook and slit open down the front. Her head and intestines were discovered in a box, and her heart on a plate in the dining-room. The skins from ten human heads were found preserved, and another skin taken from the upper

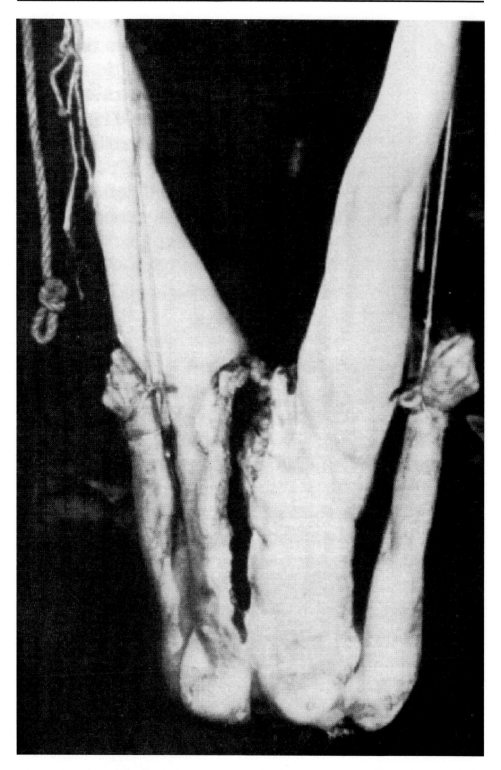

Victim: Bernice Worden

Ed Gein

torso of a woman was rolled up on the floor. There was a belt fashioned from carved-off nipples, a chair upholstered in human skin, the crown of a skull used as a soup-bowl, lampshades covered in flesh pulled taut, a table propped up by human shinbones, and a refrigerator stocked full with human organs. The four posts on Gein's bed were topped with skulls and a human head hung on the wall alongside nine death-masks – the skinned faces of women – and decorative bracelets made out of human skin.

The scattered remains of an estimated fifteen bodies were found at the farmhouse when Gein was eventually arrested, but he could not remember how many murders he had actually committed. Although considered fit to stand trial, Eddie was found guilty, but criminally insane. He was first committed to the Central State Hospital at Waupon, and then in 1978 he was moved to the Mendota Mental Health Institute where he died in the geriatric ward in 1984, aged seventy-seven. It is said he was always a model prisoner – gentle, polite and discreet.

There is a certain amount of debate over the extent to which cannibalism played a part in Gein's crimes. An early police statement to the press, based on the fact that much of the evidence was found in Gein's refrigerator, reported that "the crimes almost certainly seem to involve cannibalism"; some, however, feel that this storage of bodily parts is not in itself evidence of cannibalism, and this element of Gein's crimes has been blown all out of proportion. Others, including Moira Martingale, claim that Gein confessed to feeding on the dead flesh of corpses (see Martingale 1993:78). Robert Bloch, discussing his interest in the Gein case when working on his novel *Psycho*, referred to Gein's indulgences in "necrophilia, cannibalism, and a few other 'isms' that weren't in the province of my character – and wouldn't have been very popular with readers in the fifties", and some feel that Bloch's references to the case have helped to paint a picture of Gein as a necrophile and cannibal instead of simply a murderous, flesh-wearing grave robber.

There are some obvious similarities between Hitchcock's reclusive Norman Bates and the apparently inoffensive but secretly deranged, mother-fixated Gein. Hitchcock's **Psycho** led on, of course, to a plethora of pale imitators: **Psycho 2**, written by Tom Holland and directed by Richard Franklin, **Psycho III** (1986), written by Charles Edward Pogue and directed by Anthony Perkins, and Mick Garris's **Psycho IV: The Beginning** (1990), which was made for cable TV, and went straight to video in Europe. The Gein case also provided a basis for the 1967 monster movie **It**, ostensibly based on the mythical Jewish folk demon, the Golem, in which mad curator Roddy McDowall carries on conversations with the rotten corpse of his mother, which he keeps at home in her bed.

"The Texas Chain Saw Massacre... What happened is true! Now the movie that's just as real!", screamed the posters for Tobe Hooper's 1974 classic of independent cinema. Whilst not a literal rendition of the Gein case, the terrible house in **Chain Saw**, with its bizarre artifacts made out of human detritus – armchairs that bear human arms, lamps made out of human hands – resembles the Gein homestead in many of its particulars, and the crazy Leatherface, who hangs up his victims alive on meat hooks, also sports a grotesque mask fashioned from stitched together pieces of human skin. In Joseph Ellison's 1980 study of psychopathic child-abuse **Don't Go In The House**, Donny (Dan Grimaldi) keeps the corpse of his religious fanatic mother in his apartment, and, as a consequence of her nasty habit of burning his arms when he misbehaved as a child, enjoys nothing better than bringing a young woman home and frying her up alive. And in William Lustig's **Maniac** (1980), the eponymous Oedipal killer indulges in garroting, decapitation, shooting and scalping, with the murderer's scalp collection adorning a row of tailor's mannequins.

Gein's fondness for wearing human flesh resurfaced again in 1991 as one

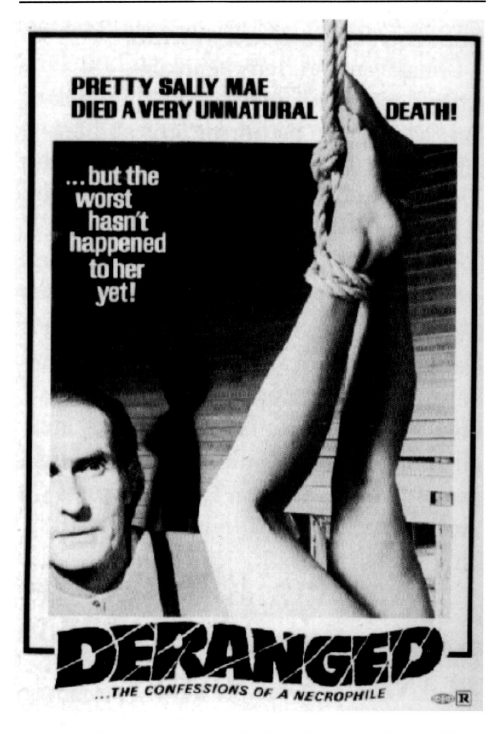

PRETTY SALLY MAE
DIED A VERY UNNATURAL DEATH!

...but the
worst
hasn't
happened
to her
yet!

DERANGED
...THE CONFESSIONS OF A NECROPHILE

of the inspirations for the character of Buffalo Bill in Jonathan Demme's **Silence Of The Lambs,** the homosexual psycho killer so named because he likes to "skin his humps". Gein was also the inspiration for the psycho-biopic **Deranged,** a 1974 offering from American-International Pictures, co-written and co-directed by Alan

Ormsby, and the lesser known but equally reverential **Three On A Meathook** (1973), directed by small-time auteur William Girdler and filmed in Louisville, Kentucky. It also seems likely that Jörg Buttgereit, a self-confessed "Geinophile", was influenced by Eddie's predilections whilst making his paeans to necrophilia, **Nekromantik** (1988) and **Nekromantik 2** (1991).

VI. EDMUND EMIL KEMPER – "THE CO-ED KILLER"

"I just wondered how it would feel to shoot Grandma."

Born into an apparently "normal" family, the second of three children, Kemper exhibited rather spooky childhood behaviour at an unusually early age. His crush on his schoolteacher seemed normal, until he admitted standing outside her house one night, imagining what it would be like to kill her and then make love to her. He also admitted fantasies about killing his neighbours, having sex with corpses, and creeping into his mother's bedroom carrying a weapon, thinking about killing her. Fun and games with his two sisters involved staging pretend executions, and cutting the head and hands off their dolls – something he would do later to his victims.

Kemper's parents separated when he was seven, and his mother moved from California to Montana. He saw very little of his father, and claims his mother frequently ridiculed and punished him, subjecting him to a strict regime of discipline which included moving him into the family's cellar, which could only be reached through a trapdoor under the kitchen table. The reason for this somewhat harsh removal, according to Kemper's mother, was that her huge son's bulky presence was making his two sisters feel very uncomfortable[3].

In his early teens Kemper – like Jeffrey Dahmer some years later – began demonstrating grave cruelty to animals, killing the neighbourhood cats, sometimes burying them alive, then putting their heads on the tops of poles and muttering incantations over his "trophies". Once he sliced off the top of a cat's head with a machete; at other times he kept animal body parts in his wardrobe. Such unsavoury habits turned him into something of a loner, sitting at home reading books about the occult, playing with his guns and knives, and indulging in a violent fantasy life which sometimes spilled over into reality. By this time, Mrs. Kemper was finding her oversized son increasingly difficult to handle, and decided to send him to live with his grandparents, who owned an isolated ranch in northern California, where Ed could keep out of trouble.

One day, about a year after he was sent to California, Kemper took a .22 calibre rifle when his grandfather was out in the fields, shot his grandmother three times in the back of the head, then stabbed her dead body over and over again in a murderous frenzy. When his grandfather returned home, Kemper shot him as well, then phoned his mother and told her what he had done. When she asked him why he did it, he replied "I just wondered how it would feel to shoot Grandma". Kemper was handed over firstly to the California Youth Authority, then transferred to Atascadero maximum security hospital where he spent four of the next five years. When he was twenty-one, the parole board claimed he was cured, ordered his release, and sent him back home to live with his mother, who was now living in Santa Cruz and working as an administrative assistant at the University of California. A psychiatrist declared him "a very well-adjusted young man who had initiative, intelligence and who was free of any psychiatric illness".

After obtaining a university parking sticker, developing a collection of favourite knives and adapting his car so that the passenger door was impossible to open from the inside, Kemper was soon back in action, hanging around campus and looking for hitch-hiking co-eds to pick up. His first crime was the double murder of two college girls, Anita Luchese and Mary Anne Pesce, whose bodies he took home with him where he decapitated and dissected the corpses, had sex with them and – again like Dahmer a decade or so later – took Polaroids during the process. His next victim four months later was 15-year-old Aiko Koo, whom he picked up as she was hitch-hiking to a dance class, suffocated to death, then raped. Then he took the teenager's body home and mutilated it as he had his previous victims, keeping the decapitated head in the car with him for several days.

The following year, Kemper attacked and murdered three young women, aged between fifteen and twenty-three, in the same way. After killing his chosen victim by shooting or stabbing – an act which, itself alone, often induced orgasm – Kemper would take the body home, remove the head and hands, then have sex with the lifeless torso, often eating parts of the flesh before chopping up the rest of the body and burying the pieces in the mountains the next day. The act of decapitation in particular caused him great sexual excitement, and he would wrap the heads of his victims in cellophane and keep them in his closet to perform sex acts on when he felt the urge. Once he buried a head in his back garden facing his bedroom, so he could imagine it looking at him, and he could talk to it at night.

Kemper's reign of murder reached its climatic finale on the 21st April 1973, when he bludgeoned his mother to death with a hammer, then slashed her throat, decapitated her, removed her larynx and flushed it down the waste disposal unit. He then propped her head on a hatbox and used it as a dartboard before sexually attacking her headless corpse and dumping the body in a closet. Still unsatisfied, he next telephoned his mother's best friend Sarah Hallett and invited her round for a "surprise party" for his mother. When she arrived, he strangled and decapitated her before driving into Santa Cruz the next morning and giving himself up.

In his confession, Kemper admitted cannibalizing two of his victims. He confessed to taking flesh from the womens' legs and freezing it, later using it as part of a casserole. He also admitted retaining other "keepsakes" of his victims, including teeth and pieces of skin. In an interview with FBI man Robert Ressler, Kemper claimed that "what I needed was to have a particular experience with a person, and to possess them in the way I wanted to, I had to evict them from their human bodies". He told one women reporter that whenever he saw a pretty girl, "...one side of me says, 'Wow, what an attractive chick, I'd like to talk to her'... The other side of me says, "I wonder how her head would look on a stick?'". "The Co-Ed Killer" was found guilty and legally sane, and despite his request for execution, was instead sentenced to life imprisonment. At present he is in the California Medical Faculty at Vacaville, and makes a brief cameo appearance in the neo-mondo documentary **The Killing Of America** (see chapter 4).

VII. CARROLL EDWARD ("KING") COLE

"I think I kill my mother through them."

Old "King" Cole's reign of violent killing came to an end in December 1980, when he was arrested in Dallas, Texas and confessed to the murders of thirty-five "loose women" whom he killed, or so he claimed, because they reminded him of his mother. Police matched up only seven of Cole's alleged thirty-five killings, but this was more than enough to earn him an execution.

In San Diego in 1971, Cole strangled Essie Louie Buck to death in his car. No charges were ever brought against him for this murder, although he was questioned about the crime by police. Then in Las Vegas in 1977, he strangled Kathryn Blum in a parking lot, returned to San Diego, and in the summer of 1979 strangled Bonnie O'Neil on the street. He then went back to Las Vegas, and, in the same year, strangled 51-year-old Marnie Cushman in a hotel room. Next he travelled to Dallas, where on the 11th November 1980 he strangled Dorothy King in her home. On the following night, he strangled Wanda Faye Roberts in a parking lot before returning to the home of Dorothy King where he slept in Dorothy's bed with her corpse. Later in the same month, he strangled 39-year-old Sally Thompson in her apartment, but made such a noise doing so that her neighbours called the police. The police arrived, arrested Cole, took him into custody, questioned him and released him, before re-arresting him again, at which point he finally confessed to his serious of heinous murders.

Because his known offenses took place in two different States, Cole was sentenced to one trial in Dallas and another one in Las Vegas. At both trials, Cole pleaded insanity, repeating his claim – and not without some evidence – to have killed thirty-five times in all, in States as diverse at California, Texas, Wyoming, Nevada and Oklahoma. He gave a substantial account of cannibalizing the body of his victim in Oklahoma before dismembering her and dumping her remains in a trash can, although some suspect this story may have been fabricated to enhance Cole's plea of insanity or help him to get the death penalty, since he was desperate to be executed. At the Texas trial he was convicted of three counts of murder, but at the penalty hearing the jury voted against the death penalty and sentenced Cole to three life terms. However, at the second trial in Las Vegas, where he was – upon request – given a non-jury hearing, Cole was sentenced to death for the murder of Marnie Cushman. "King" Cole was executed by lethal injection in Carson City, Nevada, on the 6th December 1985.

VIII. TED BUNDY – THE CHARISMATIC KILLER

A handsome man of exceptional charm and charisma, Bundy was also more intelligent and better educated than your run-of-the-mill cannibal killer. After winning a scholarship in Chinese Studies at Stanford University, Bundy went on to receive a B.Sc. in psychology in 1972 and was first employed, ironically, as an assistant director of the local Seattle crime commission. His appointment coincided with a mysterious spate of killings in Washington State. The victims, all attractive young girls aged between sixteen and twenty-three, were killed on a monthly or twice-monthly basis throughout the whole of 1974. The murders were usually accompanied by extreme violence, rape, sexual mutilation, and, on occasion, incidents of cannibalism. In the unstoppable frenzy of his murderous psychosis, Bundy was known to bite and swallow chunks out of the buttocks and thighs of his female victims.

Later, when Bundy gained a place at the University of Utah to study law, his move away from Washington coincided with a new wave of sexual killings of

Ted Bundy

young girls in the Salt Lake area. Eventually, he was arrested and imprisoned for kidnapping an 18-year-old named Carol DaRonch. At the same time, officers investigating the murder of Caryn Campbell, a 23-year-old who disappeared on the 12th of January 1975, began to take an interest in the charming and handsome law student, eventually proving that Bundy had been at the location of Caryn's death on the day she was killed. An extradition order was issued, and Bundy removed to Colorado to face a charge of murder. In June 1977, while awaiting trial, he escaped, but was recaptured almost immediately. Six months later he escaped again, this time climbing through the ceiling of his cell, and carried out the killings of Lisa Levy, 20, Margaret Bowman, 21, and Kimberley Leach, 12. Later in the month that Kimberley Leach was murdered, February 1978, Bundy was finally recaptured by officers investigating a minor traffic violation. Under interrogation, Bundy confessed to over one hundred killings, though later withdrew the confession. At his subsequent trial, during which he was convicted of forty murders in a four-year period over five States, Utah State Prison psychologist Dr. Al Carlisle concluded that "I feel that Mr. Bundy is a man who has no problems, or is smart enough or clever enough to appear close to the edge of 'normal'". Bundy was sentenced to death, though the American system of appeals allowed him to remain on Death Row for a further ten years, until his execution on January 24th, 1989.

One of the most interesting and unusual elements of the Bundy case is the fact that Bundy's handsome appearance, wit and charm made him a highly attractive companion, and he experienced no difficulty in establishing relationships with women. Much was made by various representative factions of the women's movement of the fact that, during his time on death row, Bundy confessed to being an avid user of pornography, and blamed this habit for his compulsive sexual violence towards women. His case was used, in part, for the inspiration behind the characterizations of the two serial killers Buffalo Bill and

Hannibal Lecter in Thomas Harris's *Red Dragon* and Jonathan Demme's film **The Silence Of The Lambs**. Bundy's preferred *modus operandi* was to loiter around college campuses with his arm in a fake sling, struggling to carry a heavy stack of books to his nearby car. Like Buffalo Bill, he would regularly attract the assistance of a helpful co-ed, who would help him carry the books to his car, thereby trapping his potential victims with hardly any difficulty at all.

Like Hannibal Lecter, who also initiated a daring escape through the ceiling, Bundy came to be regarded, over the years, as something of an authority on the personality of the serial killer, and some of his insight found its way into the FBI Behavioral Research Unit's stock of profiling clues to be used by police officers and psychiatrists. Asserting that he gained his evidence from years of incarceration with such serial killers as Ottis Toole and Gerald Stano, Bundy claimed that most killers were like himself – intelligent people capable of exercising reason and making rational decisions in relation to their crimes. Ironically, however, although Bundy was able to diagnose the classic characteristics of most serial killer profiles, he was unable to recognize the same traits when they manifested themselves in his own character.

The Deliberate Stranger (Marvin Chomsky, 1986) is based directly on the Bundy case, but any details of his cannibalistic attacks are omitted.

IX. ANDREI CHIKATILO – THE "ROSTOV RIPPER"

"I am a freak of nature, a wild beast."

As in so many similar non-Western cases, very little information has been recorded in the Western media about the case of the "Rostov Ripper" except for the usual hyperbolic and retrospective accounts of his grotesque and violent crimes. In this case, however, the absence of publicity was partly a strategic decision motivated by a mixture of the customary Soviet secrecy and the desire not to cause panic. The media, still controlled by the authorities, dutifully obeyed, and kept quiet about the news that Rostov had on its streets a sadistic murderer who picked up people at random and slaughtered them in the most unspeakable of ways. It is fairly clear, however, that Chikatilo's fifty-five known victims make him the worst individual serial killer the modern world has known so far. As an adult, Chikatilo trained and worked as a teacher, then later became Head of Supplies in the Rostov locomotive repair shop. The only known accounts of his youth come from Chikatilo himself, who during his trial insisted on addressing the court, and drew its attention to the early privations of his home life, giving a long, self-pitying account of his "dreadful" childhood.

Between 1978 and 1990, the inhabitants of the normally quiet town of Rostov – a busy port in the south-east of what was at that time the U.S.S.R – were terrorized by a series of violent murders – at the worst stage, there were eight deaths in a single month. The killer's approach was always the same. He always picked on the weak and vulnerable people at the edges of society, trawling the streets and railway stations for homeless tramps and drifters who were unlikely to be missed, or singling out solitary children on their way to and from school. The first known victim, in 1978, was a teenage girl whose body was found murdered and mutilated in a wood. The police, initially blaming the crime on a known sex offender, had the man executed by firing squad. On another occasion, a different suspect committed suicide while in prison awaiting his trial, but it was not long before further bodies were found. Despite an exhaustive manhunt that extended from Rostov to Siberia, the carnage continued for the next ten years, spreading into the neighbouring States of Ukraine and Uzbekistan. In just two months in the summer of 1984, the Ripper murdered ten people – more than one a week. But at the end of 1984, with more than thirty murders on their hands, the police were no nearer to catching him.

The murderer would bite off victims' tongues and breasts and eat them, cut off noses and lips, slice off boys' genitals – or remove the testes, leaving the empty scrotal sac – and, like Eddie Gein, excise girls' reproductive organs, then devour them on the spot, sometimes cooking them over a rough fire he built at a nearby spot in the forest. In court, he described how he boiled and ate the sawn-off testicles or nipples of his victims, or carved slits in some corpses to use for his own brand of necrophile sex, often not bothering to kill his trussed-up victims before the spree of carnage began. So vicious was his butchery that a number of policemen broke down and requested to be removed from the case. Some investigators even theorized that the murders had been committed by Satanists or a gang collecting testicles for transplants (see Martingale 1993:130). In his peculiar pleasures, Chikatilo seems to have had much in common with another, earlier child-eater, Albert Fish.

Andrei Chikatilo was arrested on three separate occasions on suspicion of the Rostov killings before finally being taken into custody. In 1979 he was picked up after being found lurking suspiciously in an isolated, wooded area, but after being questioned by police he was released and allowed to go on his way. Five years later, in 1984, he was picked up close to a murder scene carrying a length of rope and a knife in his briefcase. After tests proved that his blood group differed from the semen samples taken from the bodies of some of his victims, he was released without charge. Unbeknown to the Russian police, however, Chikatilo was one of those individuals whose different bodily secretions have different serological groupings, which is probably the main reason why he managed to escape detection for so long. In November 1990 he was picked up in the street when a policeman spotted bloodstains on his face. Again he was released, but this time the police kept him under surveillance until the 20th November when he was spotted approaching a young boy at a railway station. After being taken into custody, Chikatilo readily confessed to an unbelievable fifty-five brutal murders, although, as he was the first to admit, "there may be more". The two volume indictment read out at his trial listed the murders of eleven young boys, eighteen young girls, and six adults.

After his arrest, Chikatilo was subjected to extensive psychiatric evaluation. His examiners concluded that, although he fell broadly into the category of "lust killers", the basic requirement for sex had been interwoven with all kinds of other needs and fixations, including murder, mutilation and cannibalism. He was brought to trial on the 14th of April 1992, and chained up inside an iron-barred cage that had been built around the dock, where he was surrounded by the baying crowds of his victims' families, screaming for his blood. It took three days for Judge Leonid Akubzhanov to read out the evidence to a packed courtroom; his testimony was frequently interrupted as relatives of the victims and other spectators repeatedly erupted into outbursts of anger, tears and abuse. Chikatilo concluded his graphically detailed confession, which led police searchers to various forest locations where many of the mutilated bodies of his victims still lay buried, with the words "I am a freak of nature, a wild beast".

In court, Chikatilo gave a highly vivid description of an incident that

Andrei Chikatilo

happened to his brother Stepan a few years before he himself had been born, in 1936. Stalin's collectivization of private farmland had caused widespread famine amongst Soviet citizens in the southern republics. The people of Chikatilo's village, Yablochnoye in the Ukraine, were hit by the famine even harder than the rest of the Soviet Union, and one day the young Stepan, having wandered too far from home, was captured, set upon and eaten by a group of starving Ukrainian peasants[4]. It is claimed by Moira Martingale (1993:143), however, that authorities could find no record or documents confirming the birth of a Stepan Chikatilo in Yablochnoye, and that none of the villagers remembered this boy, still less the terrifying fate which was claimed to have befallen him.

Chikatilo was found sane at the time of his killings, and therefore guilty. However, his lawyer, Marat Khabibulin, has rejected the court's findings, arguing that his client's mental health has not been properly evaluated, and has announced that he will appeal to the Supreme Court of the Russian Federation of Moscow against the verdict. If this appeal fails, Chikatilo faces execution by firing squad, but his death sentence has to be confirmed by the President's Commission on Pardoning, which in 1992 was still considering death sentences handed down in 1989. Until that decision is made, Chikatilo spends his days in a special cage, isolated from other prisoners, who would probably kill him if they could. The father of one of his victims works at Novocherkassk prison, where he is currently held.

In 1995, Chris Gerolmo directed **Citizen X**, a film based directly on Chikatilo. The film features Stephen Rea, Donald Sutherland and Max Von Sydow – but no cannibalism.

Other Soviet cannibals – about whom even less is documented – include Ilshat Kuzikov, arrested in St Petersburg in 1995, and Nikolai Dzhumagaliev (a.k.a. "Metal Fang"), whose reign of terror lasted throughout 1980 in the republic of Kazakhstan.

X. SPREITZER, KOKORALEIS, KOKORALEIS AND GECHT – THE "CHICAGO RIPPERS"

The gang of sexual psychopaths that terrorized Chicago during 1981 and 1982 was a close-knit, youthful, family-based affair consisting of 21-year-old Edward Spreitzer, his 19-year-old best friend Andrew Kokoraleis, Andrew's younger brother 18-year-old Thomas Kokoraleis, and Robin Gecht, who denied any involvement in the crimes. Bizarrely enough, it turned out that Gecht had once worked for another of Chicago's notorious serial killers, John Wayne Gacy.

The series of attacks by the mystery killers rapidly dubbed the "Chicago Rippers" began in May 1981, when Linda Sutton was gang-raped and stabbed to death by three men, who left her mutilated body missing its left breast, a sign that soon came to be recognized as the killers' grisly trademark. Just over a year later, in 1982, Lorraine Borowski and Shul Mak went missing from their homes: their mutilated bodies were not discovered until September. In August 1982 the mutilated body of Sandra Delaware was found in the north tributary of the Chicago River. Delaware had been strangled, and her body was missing its left breast. Next, in the Gold Coast district, the body of Mrs. Rose Beck Davis was discovered lying between two apartment blocks. She had been raped, bludgeoned, axed, stabbed and strangled, and both breasts had been mutilated. Finally in September of the same year, an 18-year-old prostitute was attacked, raped, slashed and left for dead beside the North Western railroad tracks. She survived her ordeal, and identified her attacker as the driver of a red van.

A few nights later, the police stopped a red van and took in three men for questioning. They were Edward Spreitzer, Andrew Kokoraleis and the owner of the van, Robin Gecht, who was recognized by the prostitute as the man who had tried to kill her and who – it turned out – had previous convictions for violence and sexual assault. Spreitzer and Kokoraleis eventually admitted their part in the series of killings, and, in the process, also implicated Thomas Kokoraleis, Andrew's younger brother. Under police questioning, Spreitzer and the Kokoraleis brothers admitted to taking part in performing a number of grotesque sadistic rituals upon the severed left breasts of each victim, in which cannibalism played a significant part. Gecht continued to deny involvement in either the rituals or the crimes.

Edward Spreitzer, indicted on six murder charges, was sentenced to die by lethal injection. Andrew Kokoraleis received four separate prison sentences. His younger brother Thomas plea-bargained a single sentence of seventy years imprisonment, and Robin Gecht, convicted of attempted murder and rape, was given a total of one hundred and twenty years imprisonment.

XI. ISSEI SAGAWA – "THE GODFATHER OF CANNIBALISM"

"Finally I was eating a beautiful white woman, and thought nothing was so delicious!"

Issei Sagawa, the son of a wealthy Japanese businessman, was convicted of only one incident of murder, but that was more than enough to make him into a well-known celebrity in Japan. The incident occurred in 1981, when Sagawa was thirty-two and putting the finishing touches to his doctoral thesis on Shakespeare's *The Tempest* in Paris at the Université Censier. Sagawa, "a clever and delicate young man", became obsessed with a fellow postgraduate student, a 25-year-old Dutch woman named Renée Hartevelt. On June 11th 1981, Sagawa invited Hartevelt, who seemed not uninterested in him, around to his apartment for dinner and a discussion about literature. After the discussion, Sagawa asked Hartevelt if she would have sex with him. After she declined, he requested that she read a poem into a tape recorder for him to work on his pronunciation. While she was doing so, Sagawa went to get his .22 calibre rifle and shot Hartevelt in the back of her head. He then had sex with her body, slept with it and ate portions of it raw. Two days later, he stuffed the remains of the body into a pair of suitcases which he dumped in the Bois de Boulogne, where they were soon discovered by the police.

When they raided Sagawa's small Paris apartment, police officers found pieces of red meat carefully wrapped in plastic bags, which were taken to the police laboratory. Forensic evidence established beyond any doubt that this was human flesh, cut from Hartevelt's arms, thighs and hips. Other pieces of human flesh in the refrigerator were eventually identified as coming from the victim's lips. These pieces matched the strange mutilations found on Renée Hartevelt's dismembered corpse.

Arrested and tried, Sagawa was found to be insane and committed to a French mental hospital. Apparently, while he was in La Santé prison awaiting the court's decision on whether or not he would be tried for murder, a fellow prisoner showed him a newspaper article about modern cannibalism in Africa. The article suggested that cannibalism had always been essentially ceremonial. Sagawa asked an Ethiopian inmate if this was true, and apparently the man replied that it was not true, that Africans indulged in cannibalism because they enjoy it. To Sagawa, this seemed proof of what he wanted to believe. In La Santé, he became the pen pal of several Japanese literary figures, who sent him a number of books about cannibalism. "I felt better after reading those books because I realized I was not so unusual", claimed Sagawa, who himself began working on a number of pieces of fiction. In May 1984 his father's company, Kurita Water Industries, signed an important business deal with the French chemical conglomerate Elf-Aquitaine, and, not accidentally, at the same time, Sagawa was transferred to a mental hospital in Japan. In August 1985 he was released from care, even though many doctors – including the hospital's deputy superintendent – considered Sagawa to be an untreatable psychotic.

During his time in confinement, Sagawa had time to reflect on the nature of his deed, and to consider where his fantasies of cannibalism might have come from. "I've always felt a sense of loss, a sense of being half-formed", he confessed. "I had no softness to me, I was all straight lines, fated to crave the substance I lack. ...I'm a weak, small, short, ugly man ... that's the plain truth". He remembered playing exciting games with his brother and uncle, in which they were both carried off by a man-eating giant to the "cannibal pot" to be baked alive. These games, claims Sagawa, led to a fascination with man-eating giants and devils, and this fascination, coupled with his feeling of incompleteness and his overwhelming desire to have the fleshy fullness he lacked, led to him being increasingly taken over by fantasies of cannibalism. "For me", he claimed, "eating is to fulfil the hunger for existence". In Paris, these fantasies turned into a compulsion. Shortly before the crime, Sagawa recollects fantasizing about finding the dead body of Jean Seberg, who had recently committed suicide in a Paris street, and taking it home with him to eat. In more general terms, he has also discussed the notion of "Japanese schizophrenia" – the image of the untouchable, "inscrutable Oriental" combined with the Japanese envy of white cultures as part of an inferiority complex emerging from their internalization of Western fears of the "yellow peril".

In the summer of 1986, Sagawa emerged from five years of confinement in prison and hospital, hoping to disappear anonymously into Japanese society. He changed his name to Shin Nakamoto, and moved into a small apartment, spending evenings with his family, who had remained supportive throughout the whole affair. However, the Japanese press maintained a constant interest in his case, and when Sagawa allowed himself to be interviewed and photographed for *Hanashi No Tokushu*, a highly respected Japanese literary magazine, his face and identity became too well known for privacy. "The ultimate taboo can be overcome," boasted the editor of *Hanashi No Tokushu*, "and Sagawa is the only man who can do it". A few years later, a French magazine presented him with a fleshy and voluptuous model and asked Sagawa if he would paint her while they interviewed him. More than happy to oblige, he was dismayed to discover that, when the magazine published his painting on its cover, a small painted knife and fork had been added to it. Ironically, whilst his crime has provided Sagawa with a meal-ticket to celebrity, there has been very little or no press interest in the victim, Renée Hartevelt, at the expense of a general fascination with the gruesome details of the crime.

Sagawa has since grown used to his notoriety and the press attention which has surrounded him ever since the murder. When a 27-year-old man named Tsutomu Miyazaki hit the headlines after having been arrested for killing four girls and eating parts of their bodies, Sagawa was only too glad to comply with the newspapers' demands for a quote. The Japanese press have since appointed him a kind of instant expert on the subject of cannibal and serial killers. He has now written four books, including *Kiri No Naka* (*In The Mist*, 1983), a loosely fictionalized account of his crime, that has already sold 200,000 copies in Japan, and was updated and completed in 1991 as *The Mirage* (see Chapter 3). In this book, he revels in the description of eating human flesh ("it looked like beef, red meat... a little came out and I put it into my mouth... it had no smell or taste, and melted in my mouth like raw tuna in a sushi restaurant"). Ironically, while *In The Mist* depicts the consumption of Hartevelt's body as a "delicious" experience, Sagawa has reported that he did not particularly enjoy the acting out of his fantasy, and in fact was rather revolted by it.

Writing, Sagawa claims, is for him a kind of self-confirmation, a re-experiencing of the event, a need to confirm his experience again and again, to go through the factors one by one and write them all down. He has written a book of short stories full of black humour called *Fantasies Of A Cannibal* (1992), a book about his time in Paris called *Paris En Fleur* (1986), a book dealing with his experiences in a psychiatric institution called *Santé* (1990), the novel *Excuse Me For Living* (1991) – also used as the title for a 1993 Channel 4 "Witness" documentary about Sagawa made by Colin Wilson – and a recent book called *House Of The Gaijin* (1994). His latest work presents a detailed fantasy involving a return to his mother's womb.

A well-known celebrity in Japan, he often appears on television and writes a weekly column for a Japanese tabloid. He claims, not without some pride, that "the public has made me the godfather of cannibalism, and I am happy about that. I will always look at the world through the eyes of a cannibal". His ambition is to achieve "personal salvation" by being eaten by a young woman. "That," he says, "is the only way I can be saved." In 1989 he announced his intention to open a vegetarian restaurant; by 1992 he was planning his autobiographical film with Juro Kara, and wondering who to choose to play the victim.[5] In the same year there was much outrage – particularly from the Netherlands embassy in Tokyo – when the Japanese authorities issued Sagawa with a passport enabling him to travel to Germany to appear on a chat show and talk about how he killed and ate Renée Hartevelt. Sagawa has stated that he now feels that he is the food on which the media and the public are indulging their appetite for transgression.

Films directly inspired by Sagawa's case include **Adoration** (1987) and **Love Ritual** (1990) [see chapter 8].

XII. CONSTANZO AND ALDRETE – THE "GODFATHER" AND THE "HIGH PRIESTESS"

As in the case of Andrei Chikatilo and other non-Western cannibals, there was considered to be something foreign-smelling about the case of Constanzo and Aldrete. For all the sheer horror the Matamoros slayings might have elicited in white middle-class America, the brutality had been dispatched *el otro lado*, across the border. The perpetrators themselves were Latinos. Many commentators suggested that the crimes could be traced to the remnants of barbaric rites that predated Columbus. It happened "down there", but it couldn't happen here.

In 1989, a police drug squad raid on the remote Rancho Santa Elena west of the Mexican border town of Matamoros unearthed secrets far worse than the large quantities of marijuana and cocaine that were found in an outbuilding. A prominently displayed severed goat's head dominated a makeshift altar, and the outbuilding itself was scattered with bloodstains, scraps of human hair and lumps of human brain pulp. Mexican and American law enforcement officials also uncovered voodoo paraphernalia, La Palma cigars, cheap rum, human body parts, animal bones, chicken and goat heads, thousands of pennies, gold beads, and an iron kettle filled with a mixture of blood and flesh. It was revealed by those detained in the drugs raid that the ranch was headquarters to a Satanic cult based loosely on Santeria and led by "The Godfather", Adolfo de Jesus Constanzo, and the "High Priestess", a Brownsville college student named Sara Maria Villareal Aldrete. Before Matamoros, the multiplying reports of "occult-related" crimes throughout the country were frequently met with suspicion and even ridicule by some authorities. After Matamoros, the climate changed considerably.

The main function of the cult was apparently to appease Satan in return for inviolability from police bullets, so the dealers would not be harmed in the event of a police shoot-out. The cult's rituals included kidnapping, slaughter, human sacrifice and cannibalism. In each Satanic celebration, the victim's heart,

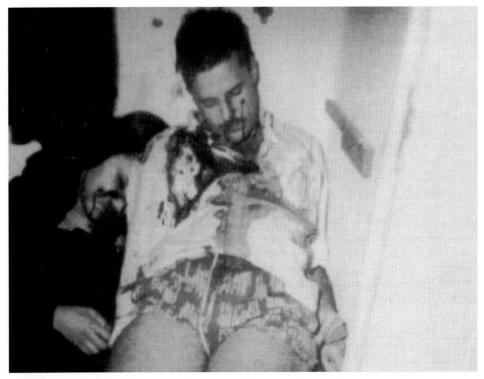

Adolfo de Jesus Constanzo shot dead by police

brains, lungs and testicles were ripped out, boiled up in an iron kettle with animal blood, then consumed by cult members to sanctify themselves in a kind of "cannibal communion". The cult believed that the blood and the energies of violence it contained would make them unconquerable soldiers in the war of evil. Detainees led the officers to the graves of at least fifteen men and boys, including a *gringo* from the University of Texas, Mark Kilroy, who disappeared on a spring vacation in Mexico. Other victims besides Kilroy included Ruben Vela Garcia, Jose Luis Garza Luna, Esquiel Rodriguez Luana, all agricultural workers; Ernesto Rivas Dias, a 23-year-old welder on vacation in Matamoros; and Jorge Valente del Fierro Gomez, a municipal policeman. Many of the bodies had been decapitated, and all of them extensively mutilated. Apparently, Aldrete was an honours college student by day, and a *narcotraficante* by night. At her home in Matamoros, police discovered a further assortment of voodoo paraphernalia, and another blood-splattered altar of sacrifice.

An active homosexual, Constanzo had also set up a male pornography ring which may have been his first serious link to the professional criminal underworld. When the *federales* raided Constanzo's apartment in the capital, they found numerous nude pictures of men. The Godfather and the High Priestess were traced to an apartment in Mexico City, which was laid siege on the 5th May 1989. Rather than being taken into custody, Constanzo had himself and his homosexual lover shot dead in a walk-in wardrobe by a third member of the cult, Mario de Leo Valdez. Valdez, Aldrete and two more of the cult's members were indicted on various charges, including murder and drug offenses, although they apparently denied all knowledge of Satanic activities. In August 1990, Sara Maria Aldrete was acquitted of Constanzo's murder but sentenced to six years imprisonment for criminal association, and currently awaits trial for the rest of the cult murders. Valdez was sentenced to thirty years for the murder of Constanzo and his lover, and the other cultists await trial for the ranch murders and an assortment of drug and firearm offenses. The cult has recently been linked to a string of gory homosexual killings in Mexico City's *Zona Rosa*.

XIII. JEFFREY DAHMER – THE "MILWAUKEE CANNIBAL"

"My consuming lust was to experience their bodies."

First child of a comfortable, middle-class Ohio family, Jeffrey Dahmer grew up as a healthy, quiet, somewhat shy child with an interest in wildlife and anatomy. During his late teens, when his parents began divorce proceedings, Jeffrey became increasingly sullen and introspective, spending afternoons when he should have been at school drinking cans of beer out of brown paper bags. His childhood interest in anatomy took on a bizarre twist when Dahmer began deliberately injuring dogs and cats, and bringing fresh "roadkill" back to the house to dissect in his bedroom. It was about this time that Jeffrey began to come to terms with his homosexuality, masturbating over pictures of the male torso, preferably prone and nude.

Dismissed from college, discharged from the army (where he served two years at Mainz in Germany), Dahmer committed the first of at least seventeen murders at his family home in Ohio, whilst his father and stepmother were away. One night, he was driving around when he spotted 18-year-old Stephen Hicks hitchhiking home from a rock concert. Hicks was not wearing his shirt, and Dahmer was excited by his body, especially his chest. Hicks agreed to accompany Jeffrey home for a couple of beers and a joint. According to Dahmer, they then got drunk and had sex, after which Hicks wanted to leave and Dahmer didn't want him to. Hicks was strangled, mutilated and decapitated, then dismembered with a kitchen knife, the body parts shoved in dustbin sacks and hidden deep in the crawl space under the house. Dahmer reported in court how he later retrieved the body and moved it to a safer place in a sewage duct, but not before taking the severed head into his bedroom and using it as a masturbation aid.

Sent to live with his grandmother in Milwaukee, Dahmer's sullenness and alcoholism were exacerbated, and he began hanging out in the homosexual clubs and bars of Chicago and Milwaukee. He also began to engage in a number of minor sexual offenses against children, including indecent exposure, for which he spent a short custodial sentence in 1989. When his son was released on probation, Dahmer's father Lionel repeatedly requested that the probation service provide his son with psychiatric help. But by this time the killings had already begun in earnest and it was too late, both for Dahmer and for those of his victims he had already murdered in his grandmother's basement, including Stephen Tuomi, James Doxtator, Richard Guerrero, Anthony Sears, Raymond Smith and Edward W. Smith.

Dahmer selected his victims at homosexual bars in Chicago and Milwaukee. He especially liked tall, good-looking, boyish men with a broad torso and well-defined chest muscles, features that Dahmer himself noticeably lacked[6]. According to his testimony, his usual *modus operandi* was to hang around the bars, drinking on his own until closing time, then, as the patrons were leaving, approach his target and offer him $50 to accompany him home for sex. Once home, Dahmer would ply his unfortunate guest with a special potion of sleeping tablets crushed into a strong glass of spirits. He was preoccupied with the horror film **The Exorcist III**, and would often play the video of it to his potential victims. After they were sedated, they were then either stabbed or strangled. Dahmer would then proceed to have anal and oral sex with the corpses and then dismember them, always doing this in the nude to avoid messing up his clothes. Before dismemberment, he would frequently wait until the bodies were stiff with *rigor mortis*, then he would stand them up, cut them open, and – like Ed Kemper – take Polaroids of their bodies. Sometimes, in a further twist of cruelty, Dahmer would anonymously telephone the families of his murder victims and tell them their sons were dead, and that he had killed them.

Things became a lot easier for him when Jeffrey finally moved out of his grandmother's apartment, got himself a steady (albeit monotonous) job working nights at the local chocolate factory, and moved into his own place, 213 Oxford Apartments, in a run-down district of Milwaukee. Throughout 1990 and 1991, his list of victims grew to include Ernest Miller, David Thomas, Curtis Straughter, Errol Lindsay, Tony Hughes, Konerak Sinthasomphone, Matt Turner, Jeremiah Weinburger, Oliver Lacy and Joseph Bradehoft. The fact that the murders were fairly "low-key" and no large-scale manhunt deployed was related to the fact that Dahmer's victims tended to be down-and-outs, hustlers, or smalltime rent boys of no fixed abode. Much was made at Dahmer's trial of the fact that nearly all his victims came from among the ethnic minorities. Members of the black and Hispanic communities felt that the police were less than rigorous when investigating reports of missing persons who happened to be from minority groups. The family of one victim even went as far as to file a $3 million lawsuit against the city of Milwaukee and its police force, charging them with racism and negligence.

In the hot summer of 1991, Dahmer's frenzy finally began to reach breaking point. Neighbours in the Oxford Apartments began to complain about sounds of scuffling and banging coming from room 213 in the middle of the night. The landlord complained about the foul smell coming from Dahmer's apartment, and the apparently "harmless", "quiet" young man explained that his freezer cabinet had broken and the meat was beginning to rot. In fact, what was rotting in Dahmer's apartment were nine severed heads – two in the refrigerator, seven in various stages of having the flesh boiled off to the skull – four male torsos wedged into a barrel, several pieces of male genitalia stored in a pot, and other scraps of human bodies and limbs. Also scattered around the apartment were videotapes and photographs of the victims in the process of being drugged, strangled and gradually dismembered, some still alive. Others were less lucky. Those of his victims that Dahmer particularly liked he cooked and ate. During the trial, he claimed to have eaten the bicep of one of his victims seasoned with salt, pepper, meat tenderizer and steak sauce, and claimed that it tasted like beef. He also admitted experimenting with various culinary seasonings in order to make the flesh taste better, and kept human-meat patties in the freezer. It was finally determined that he ate the flesh of three victims and performed sex acts on two of the severed heads.

Another young victim, Konerak Sinthasomphone, was the unfortunate victim of one of Dahmer's bizarre experiments. In May 1991, two months before the full horror of what had gone on in Jeffrey Dahmer's apartment was discovered, Sinthasomphone was drugged shortly after Dahmer had taken a number of provocative photographs of him. In an attempt to make his captive

Jeffrey Dahmer

into a zombie totally subject to his every whim, Dahmer then performed rudimentary brain surgery on his victim by boring a hole in his skull with an electric drill. Sinthasomphone managed to escape briefly, and the police received a telephone call from Sandra Smith, one of Dahmer's neighbours, who had spotted a naked boy, his legs covered with blood, running down the street, having escaped from Dahmer's apartment. Assuming some kind of homosexual quarrel, the police returned Sinthasomphone to Dahmer, who quickly finished him off and dismembered his body for disposal.

In mid-July 1991, police were called to 213 Oxford Apartments by a handcuffed teenager who had narrowly escaped being slaughtered by a dazed and confused Dahmer wielding a butcher's knife. On the 24th July, the story was picked up by the press. "The CANNIBAL", proclaimed one London daily tabloid, next to a mug-shot of Dahmer. "This is the face of cannibal killer Jeffrey Dahmer – the twisted beast who butchered, cooked and ate his victims". Anxious relatives of missing youngsters began a vigil outside the apartment block where the "cannibal" had lived.

The trial of Jeffrey Dahmer began on the 13th January 1992 at Milwaukee County Court. Dahmer pleaded guilty but insane to seventeen murders, including one in Ohio and one for which there was insufficient evidence to bring a charge. The jury, already warned by Dahmer's attorney, Gerald Boyle, to expect "graphic descriptions of human carnage, killing, cannibalism, mutilation, everything you can possibly imagine", sat through over three months of harrowing evidence testifying to Dahmer's drug-taking, paedophilia, cannibalism, necrophilia and dis-memberment fetishes. Two female jurors who couldn't endure the trial had to be excused. Afterwards, the remaining members of the jury were offered counselling to help them cope with the gruesome details they had heard. Boyle, hoping to solidify Dahmer's plea of insanity, explained how his client's appetite, never satisfied, hungered for new excesses and needed to experiment with different experiences such as opening up the corpse and masturbating into the viscera. The jury were in retirement for six hours, eventually returning with a majority verdict of ten to two, finding Dahmer guilty and sane.

On the 1st of May 1992, Jeffrey Dahmer was sentenced to life imprisonment sixteen times over. He began serving his sentence at Columbia Correctional Institution at Portage, about eighty miles north west of Milwaukee, in an isolated glass cage reminiscent of that which contained Hannibal Lecter in **Silence Of The Lambs**. The high-tech equipment and design are supposed to make it one of the most safe and secure prisons in the country. A year after his trial ended, Dahmer admitted publicly that he would kill again if he were ever released. In 1994, he was attacked in the prison latrines, and brutally beaten to death by a fellow prisoner. **The Secret Life** (David R Bowen, 1993) was a film portrayal of Dahmer's case, but again the cannibalism was glossed over.

NOTES

1.   Paraphilia, from the Greek para (meaning "beyond", "amiss" or "altered"), and philia (meaning "love") is a biomedical term first used by I.F. Krauss. It was adapted by Wilhelm Stekel, whose pupil, Benjamin Karpman, introduced it to American psychiatry in 1934. It was first used officially as a replacement for the legal term "perversion" in the American Psychiatric Association's *Diagnostic And Statistical Manual Of Mental Disorders*, 3rd edition.
2.   Interestingly enough, Ed Gein made a similar claim about his own sexuality - that he too was awakened sexually by witnessing the slaughter of pigs.
3.   Kemper was eventually to reach 6ft 9 inches, and to weigh over twenty stone.
4.   Which is almost exactly what happens in the plot of Tennessee Williams' psychodrama, *Suddenly One Summer* (see chapter 3).
5.   Sagawa eventually did appear on film in 1992, in the disturbing Japanese "pink" film **Shisenjo No Aria (An Aria Of Gazes** a.k.a. **The Bedroom,** directed by Sato Hisayasu).
6.   An interesting connection between Dahmer and Issei Sagawa, who also selected his potential victims according to the health, size and vitality of their bodies, attributes which Sagawa was acutely self-conscious of lacking.

chapter three:
cannibal chronicles

ANDREI Chikatilo's psychiatrist Aleksandr Bukhanovksy claims that the principal reason behind Chikatilo's deviant crimes was the fact that he was terrified in his childhood by a frightening story about his brother being eaten alive by a pack of starving Ukrainian peasants. Albert Fish claimed that he too had been alarmed by stories about cannibalism told to him in childhood, and Issei Sagawa attributed his fascination with eating human flesh to spine-tingling tales of a child-eating ogre acted out once a year by his brother and uncle.

Stories about people who eat one another have been told as a matter of course since the very beginnings of human civilization. Cannibalism is a regular practise in the myths and legends told and retold in both early and modern primitive societies. Many cultures share narratives of celestial beings who feed on human flesh, or heroes and heroines who have indulged in cannibalism, sometimes unknowingly, and sometimes for the purposes of revenge. Cannibalistic ogres threaten the heroes of countless primal myths, and the threat of being devoured provides the thrill and appeal of many similar modern narratives, especially for children. The cannibal in folklore is usually posited as an ogre, ogress, or other horrific parental figure, although Joseph Campbell has collected folkloristic examples of cannibal husbands, sons-in-law, mothers, and mothers-in-law (see Campbell, 1968). In his introduction to the science of mythology *The Raw And The Cooked* (1964), anthropologist Claude Lévi-Strauss discusses the various forms of cannibalism found in early myths, from tales of 'natural' cannibalism, where the flesh is eaten raw, to 'supernatural' cannibalism, where the flesh is cooked. According to Lévi-Strauss, the act of cannibalism plays a significant part in the science and structure of mythology, representing both a food category and a set of equivalencies connecting life and death (Lévi-Strauss, 1964:153). As such, it is often a feature of "founding" or "explanatory" myths. For example, a Paraguayan story explaining how certain cultures become carrion-eaters refers to a group of sorcerers who, as a punishment for attempted cannibalism, were doomed forever to feed on carcasses, with no respect for the fresh kill, and hence never to achieve a perfect life. A similar story explaining the origins of the jaguar tells of a woman who devoured her husband and children in the night, then ran away into the bush and was transformed into a large, fierce black cat (Lévi-Strauss, 1964:99, 140). The Fijians have a founding myth entitled "How The Fijians First Became Cannibals", which corresponds very closely to Freud's story of the primal horde controlled by the primal father. In the Fijian myth, the primal horde stands for primordial chaos; the hero comes as a terrible outside cannibal to a place where endophagy and incest reign, and teaches the Fijians how to regulate their culture by substituting endophagy for exophagy (see Sanday 1986:43).

Such myths and legends obviously reinforce the symbolic importance of cannibalism within a culture. Classic and recurrent themes include the ingestion by the enemy of the hero's virtues, and the need to exercise his power to harm.

Cannibalism in such stories stands as a symbolic process which presupposes magical influences, and may be based on the belief that particular parts of the dead man contain powers symbolically (or otherwise) appropriate to them, thereby differing in its imagined mode of operation from the chemical or psychological workings of our more customary diets.

FREUD AND FAIRY STORIES

The Western equivalents of such myths and legends are folk and fairy tales, which are equally rich in cannibalistic aggression, albeit often indirect. In fairy tales like "Little Red Riding Hood" and "Goldilocks And The Three Bears", the threat of cannibalism is modified into a threat of being devoured by humanesque characters in animal form. In others, like "Jack And The Beanstalk", "Tom Thumb", "Hansel And Gretel" and their Eastern European equivalents, such as the tales of Baba Yaga, cannibalism is threatened directly, though the threat is never carried out – at least, never on the tale's protagonists. Like many other forms of death and violence in the fairy tale, cannibalism is generally associated with regenerative functions: the killer takes the substance of his enemies in order to recharge his own strength and power. Sometimes the very act of killing gives the killer the power of his victim.

The recurrence of cannibalism as a universal theme in myths, folklore and legends is generally understood in psychoanalytic terms, usually with reference to "the dread of being eaten" – a phrase used by Freud to describe the fears that children have connected with mothers and fathers. For a tangled web of reasons, cannibalism in Western culture is generally traced back to anxieties rooted in the reality of aggressive parental behaviour, guilty fantasies projected on to fathers and mothers, the transformation of oral-aggressive tendencies or projected hostility towards the mother, who both nourishes the child and imposes a number of restrictions on him during the course of his development. There is a recurrent emphasis on orality in Freudian thought. Freud tends to regard fictive renditions of cannibalism as variations on the Oedipal situation, thereby associating it with incest. According to Freud, cannibalistic fantasies have to do with the "incorporation" of parental qualities, with "identification" with the parent, and with infantile sexuality and narcissism. Freudian readings of the fictive transgression of the cannibalistic taboo tend to speculate that such stories relate to the world from the child's point of view – hence the importance in fairy tales of food, the absence of food, consumption, privation, the indulging of gluttonous urges, oral satisfaction, pleasure, survival (eating or being eaten), and good and bad behaviour[1]. In traditional psychoanalytic terms, mythic, fictive and legendary instances of cannibalism are usually interpreted as a disfigured form of parental aggression or a projection of the protagonist's oral greed. For example, "Hansel And Gretel" – a tale in which the animistic gingerbread house attracts children for the witch to kill, cook and eat – is usually interpreted psychoanalytically as a cautionary tale wherein the satisfaction of oral urges brings to life fiends whose voracious appetites outpace those of even the most famished children[2]. Similarly, "Tom Thumb" – a story in which the giant plans to kill seven young boys and eat them with a "good sauce" – is most often considered to be a narrative that speaks to the child's guilty feelings about unrestrained oral greed and dependence (Tatar 1992:197). Bettelheim argues that these tales about the victims and perpetrators of oral aggression function as rites of passage, serving to acculturate the young

Gustave Doré, *Little Red Riding Hood*

child and help him to come to terms with loss, Oedipal conflicts, ambivalent emotions towards parent and sibling figures and his own fears and anxieties about being a child, and a human being.

Freud remarked on the connection between murder, cannibalism and incest, which seemed to him – as the most obvious and widespread cultural taboos – to be closely related to one another, as psychoanalytic readings of other folk and fairy tales, such as the Baba Yaga stories, seem to testify. Freud suggests that in most such stories, as in real life, cannibalism becomes enmeshed with a complex array of other pathological and psycho-sexual matters. The best example of this is his study of the patient he named the "Wolf Man" in *From The History Of An Infantile Neurosis* (*Standard Edition* XVI 1:7–122). In this remarkable case, Freud identifies the patient's fear of being eaten with a strong sexual excitation in the oral (or "cannibal") phase of childhood, with a homosexual-passive wish to be penetrated by the father, with strong anal preoccupations and with a complex interplay of homosexuality, masochism and castration fears.

THE TABOO AND THE PRIMAL DEED

Any story which tells of the transgression of a taboo can help us to understand and come to terms with the notion of the "primal deed". This concept is one of the most fundamental principles of psychoanalysis, whether it be – in Freudian terms – a reference to the incest and parricide of Oedipus, an infant's toilet training trauma or the patient's repressed recollections of parental sexual intercourse.[3] Western culture's narrative version of the primal scene is the well-known myth of Oedipus and its eponymous psychological anxieties and neuroses. The Oedipus story is usually considered to provide the basis for the two most essential taboos of totemism: incest and murder. But what of our culture's third elementary taboo – that of cannibalism? Where does this taboo find its primal deed?

According to Freud, human social structure originated in what he referred to as the form of the 'primal horde'. Each horde consisted of a large group of male members – brothers – with equal rights, including equal rights to the possession of the female members of the family, as may be observed in a number of ape species today. Adapting Darwin, Freud contended that the brothers who had been driven out of the primal horde bonded together to kill the patriarchal leader ("the father"), and to atone for their crime they created, out of a "filial sense of guilt", taboos against murder and incest, thereby laying down the foundations for the social organization and moral restrictions of Western culture today.

In many versions of the story of the primal horde, including that told by Freud, the brothers' killing of their father is followed by their devouring of the father's body: the totem meal. Consequently, the sacramental killing and communal eating of the totem meal, whose conception is forbidden on all other occasions, is an important feature of totemic religion. In support of this proposal, Freud cites three examples from the anthropologist Robertson Smith (the Aztec and Otawa, both of South America, and the Ainu of Japan), and three from the folklorist Frazer (the Zuri of California, the Aborigines of central Australia and the Bini of West Africa) of the ritualistic devouring of sacred animals in a totemic meal[4]. Although the taboo of cannibalism has not become enshrined for Western culture in a narrative reformulation of the "primal deed" as palatable as the myth of Oedipus is for modern psychoanalysis, cannibalism is at least as strong a taboo, at least as capable of inflaming our imagination, at least as shocking to modern culture as incest and murder. Murder and incest prohibitions are traceable, for the psychoanalyst at least, to contemporary narrative manifestations of the Oedipus myth, yet the prohibitions against cannibalism are also intact, although arcane in origin. As René Girard puts it, we are perhaps more distracted by incest than by cannibalism, but only because cannibalism has not yet found its Freud and been promoted to the status of a major contemporary myth (see Girard 1977:277).

As one of humankind's most significant taboos, cannibalism, in both its literal and figurative senses, is a recurring theme throughout the history of the narratives we tell about ourselves. Whether serving the function of metaphor, satirical trope, exotic background setting or central theme, cannibalism is a motif that recurs in world literature with a certain degree of regularity. To trace the entire literary history of cannibalism would require a book in its own right. This chapter, which is intended to give a brief outline of the most significant references to cannibalism in literature and how its relevance has altered over time, presents merely the bare bones of an argument, stripped clean of most of its flesh.

CLASSICAL CANNIBALS

Just like early myth and legend, classical literature is full of stories about people who have, at one time or another, sampled the taste of human flesh. Literary examples as far back as Homer show that eating the enemy can be considered a homage, but can also be viewed as an act of ultimate aggression and degradation. Ovid's *Metamorphoses* (6 fab. 9 & 10) regales us with the story of Philomena, who, after being brutally raped by her sister's husband Tereus, then had her hands and tongue cut off so she would never be able to reveal the name of her persecutor. But after conveying the truth to her sister Procne, Philomena devised an appropriate revenge. The two sisters murdered Procne's 6-year-old son Itylus, then served him up to his father baked in a pie. Tereus, in the middle of the meal, called for Itylus; Procne immediately informed him that he was feasting on his own son's flesh, and Philomena proved the point by bringing out the child's severed head[5]. Elsewhere in the *Metamorphoses* (3. v.725) we learn of the story of Pentheus, who was torn limb from limb and devoured by the Bacchanals, including his mother Agave and her two sisters, Ino and Autonoe. In Seneca (1. *Hist 18.* and elsewhere), Atreus serves up Thyestes the children he had by his sister-in-law the Queen Aerope. After the meal is finished, the arms and heads of the murdered children are produced, and the sun, according to Seneca, is said to have shrunk back in his course with horror at the sight. The practise of cannibalism also rears its head in the *Odyssey*, in the story of the cannibalistic ogre Polyphemus.

In Hesiod's *Theogany* (v.138, 209 and 460) and elsewhere, we are told the story of Saturn, who obtained his father's kingdom by the consent of his brothers, provided that he did not bring up any male children. Pursuant to this agreement, Saturn always devoured his sons as soon as they were born because he dreaded from them a retaliation of his unkindness towards his father. However, his wife Rhea, unwilling to see her children perish, concealed from her husband the birth of Jupiter, Neptune and Pluto and, instead of the children, gave him large stones to eat, which he immediately swallowed without perceiving the deceit. And

Juvenal, whose gross and extravagant style was intended to be particularly severe on the vices and dissipations of the age in which he lived, wrote about cannibalism in his *Satires*.

The motif of inter-familial cannibalism is not such a rare one in classical and mediaeval literature. The narrator of Dante's *Inferno* (1314) comes across two shades in hell, frozen together in the same hole, one of whom is gnawing the head of the other. The cannibal tells the narrator that he is Count Ugolino della Gherardesca, who during the Guelph civil conflicts was imprisoned with four of his sons and grandsons in a tower subsequently named "The Tower Of Famine". They remained in the tower until March 1289, when the tower was locked up and the keys thrown in the river. After eight days the tower was opened, and all the victims found dead of starvation. In the *Inferno*, Ugolino, wiping his mouth on the hair of the head he is currently chewing, describes the terrible days of starvation that eventually led him to feed off the dead body of one of his own children:

"'I took to fumbling them over:
two long days I groped there, calling on the dead:
Then famine did what sorrow could not do.'

He ceased, and rolled his eyes asquint, and sped
To plant his teeth, which, like a dog's were strong
Upon the bone, back in the wretched head"
—Dante, *Inferno*, ix, iii, 73–78

One of Montaigne's *Essaies* (1.xxxxi) is dedicated to the subject of "Des Cannibales". Montaigne argues that cannibalism, in a figurative sense, is an act of vital authenticity, of physical, emotional, and political self- realization. And in its literal sense, according to Montaigne, the temptation of cannibalism at a time of severe hunger represents the supreme test of civilized man, and the validity of his moral codes.

The practise of cannibalism shows up on several occasions in Shakespeare. The first is in *Titus Andronicus* (1594), Shakespeare's blood-soaked retelling of the Procne and Philomena story from Ovid's *Metamorphoses*. Shakespeare's version tells of the rape and mutilation of Titus's daughter Lavinia by Chiron and Demetrius, the two sons of the Empress Tamora, Queen of the Goths. In order to extract his revenge, Titus murders Chiron and Demetrius and serves them up to their mother unknowingly, baked in a pie. During the murder, he calls upon his mutilated daughter Lavinia to "receive the blood":

"... and when that they are dead,
Let me go grind their bones to powder small,
And with this hateful liquor temper it,
And in that paste let their vile heads be baked."
—Shakespeare, *Titus Andronicus*, V. iv, 197-200

In Shakespeare's *Othello* (1604), the Moor seduces Desdemona with his courageous stories of heroic adventures in foreign lands. Othello's encounter with the cannibals not only casts an interesting light on his own perceived otherness, but exemplifies the strange romance of cannibalism, its exotic and vaguely prurient fascinations. Othello tells stories of his seafaring adventures, and

"...of the Cannibals
that each other eat, The Anthropophagi,
and men whose heads grew beneath their shoulders..."
—Shakespeare, *Othello*, I, iii, 142–144

Similarly, traveller and historian Sir John Mandeville in "The Fable Of The Bees" (4th & 5th dialogues) uses the fascinating and outlandish exoticism of the cannibal process to suggest that men without masters are inevitable destined, metaphorically speaking, to devour one another[6].

EIGHTEENTH CENTURY CANNIBALS

Eighteenth century satire often evoked cannibalism as a metaphor, or referred to the custom in a figurative sense. At the very beginning of the century, Swift shocked his readers with his *Modest Proposal For Preventing The Children Of Poor People From Being A Burthern To Their Parents, Or The Country, And For Making Them Beneficial To The Public*. In this *Modest Proposal*, Swift employs his habitual pessimism as a weapon to scourge away the smug credulity of optimists, just as he employs a form of tortured reasoning to jolt us into a full understanding of the terrible possibilities inherent in human nature:

*"I have been assured by a very knowing **American** of my acquaintance in **London**, that a young healthy Child well Nursed is at a year Old a most delicious, nourishing, and wholesome food, whether **Stewed Roasted, Baked** or **Boiled**, and I make no doubt that it will equally serve in a **Fricassee**, or a **Ragoust.**"*
—Swift, *A Modest Proposal...*

This ironic strategy of proposing human cannibalism as an answer to economic poverty is a stark and extreme expression of righteous anger in the guise of a misanthropic outburst. And although this satirical rhetoric is not without its moments of occasional impishness, its levity does not conceal Swift's ultimate disgust at the human condition, and the extremes of indignity to which it drives us[7]. Another eighteenth century exponent of cannibalism – although to completely different ends – was the Marquis De Sade. In De Sade's pointedly sadistic imagination, all men and women have absolute, albeit temporary, rights over the bodies of all other men and women. *Ernestine* (1788) and *Justine* (1791) both involve cannibal-related acts and fantasies, subjecting women to sadistic tortures for the purposes of sexual gratification. De Sade indulges his cruel themes in obsessive detail, revelling in the vitalizing and highly charged sexual excitements of violence and murder. The four protagonists of De Sade's notorious *120 Days Of Sodom* (1785) also display an exuberant indulgence in the ideas of carnage, bloodshed, sexual obscenities and cannibalism, listing the details of its practise. In De Sade, violent sadism and orgiastic feasts of human flesh are part of a quest for the most extreme ways of attaining sexual gratification, including blood lust in the cannibal act.

Towards the end of the eighteenth century, the continental-influenced British Gothic novelists began to explore the sensual cruelties of the traditional horror story. Germanic-style narratives such as Horace Walpole's *The Castle Of Otranto* (1764), Emily Radcliffe's *The Mysteries Of Udolpho* (1794) and Matthew Gregory Lewis's *The Monk* (1796) all sent their protagonists on frightening journeys to investigate haunted houses, strange castles and distant abbeys – those terrifying, archetypal representations of the human unconscious, where things are not always what they seem to be. The Gothic novelists told stories of self-exploration, of deprivation, of perverse scenes of misery and slaughter. The very best of the second-generation British Gothic novels, Charles Robert Maturin's *Melmoth The Wanderer* (1820), presents the reader with a litany of cruel and bizarre episodes, including scenes of torture from the cells of the Spanish Inquisition, tension and repression in unrestful monastic retreats, gruesome supernatural mayhem, and – in one memorable scene – innocent people torn to pieces by a frenzied mob in the streets. In other episode, a pair of newly-wed lovers are locked up together in a prison dungeon, and it is not long before their tender devotion towards one another's bodies develops a distinctly cannibalistic propensity, and worse:

"All the horrible and loathsome excrutiations of famine had been undergone; the disunion of every tie of the heart, of passion, of nature, had commenced. In the agonies of their famished sickness they loathed each other – they could have cursed each other, if they had had breath to curse! It was on the fourth night that I heard the shriek of the wretched female, – her lover, in the agony of hunger, had fastened his teeth into her shoulder; – that bosom on which he had so often luxuriated, became a meal to him now."

—Maturin, *Melmoth The Wanderer*

NINETEENTH CENTURY CANNIBALS

This exploration into the dark extremes of the human condition continued into the nineteenth century, both in Britain and elsewhere. The custom of cannibalism was often addressed in the nineteenth century spirit of romantic irony. Nineteenth century travel literature and exotic adventure-writing also sometimes referred to cannibalism in order to make an ironic contrast between the "barbaric" lives of the cannibals and the supposedly "civilized" lifestyles of the European populations. Often displaced into exotic places and romantic climates, these investigations into the vital extremities of violence and murder regularly hinted at the perverse excesses which "civilized", bourgeois, Western individuals are capable of reaching. For example, in 1837, Edgar Allan Poe's *The Narrative Of Arthur Gordon Pym Of Nantucket* (which was translated into French by Baudelaire, who had a fascination with the narrative), tells the story of four shipwrecked men who after many days privation, drew lots to decide who should be killed and eaten, and who remain alive. The cabin boy Richard Parker drew the short straw:

"He made no resistance whatever and fell instantly dead when stabbed in the back... Having in some measure appeased the raging thirst that consumed them by drinking the blood of the victim, and having by common consent taken off the hands, feet and head, and throwing them, together with the entrails, into the sea, we devoured the rest of the body piecemeal...."

—Poe, *The Narrative Of Arthur Gordon Pym*

In America, as Poe's narrative amply illustrates, the geographical frontier was not the only boundary that was being pushed further and further back. The same could be said of the boundaries of moral behaviour separating man from beast, especially in extreme circumstances. This fascination with exploration found its literary equivalent in novels like Melville's *Typee* (1848), a semi-autobiographical account of life in the Marquesas islands in the 1840s. A blend of personal experience and the narratives of explorers and missionaries, it influenced many later writers on the Pacific, including Robert Louis Stevenson and Jack London. In *Typee*, the protagonist imagines the "unholy rites practised in exotic places" in his "strange visions of outlandish things... Cannibal banquets... savage woodlands guarded by horrible idols – heathenish rites and human sacrifices...". In *Typee*, the natives, although cannibals, are presented as far more gracious, far more polite and gentlemanly than "civilized" man, and yet the protagonist still feels unable to remain on the island. *Typee* is a novel about the impossibility – for modern man, at least – of achieving a state of placidity and calm. Some of the issues raised in *Typee* can also be found in Daniel Defoe's *Robinson Crusoe*, as well as in Melville's better known novel, *Moby Dick*. In *Moby Dick*, Ishmael is met at an inn by Queequeg, a Polynesian native and sometime cannibal covered from head to foot in tattoos. Of course, Queequeg turns out to be more polite, courteous and discreet even than the "civilized" Ishmael himself.

Flaubert's romantic faux-history *Salammbô* (1862), for which most of the material was gathered in Tunisia, has a similarly exotic selling – a remote time and place somewhere in antiquity. The narrative centres around obscure sacrificial doings at the heathen temple of Moloch, including gruesome cannibalistic sensualities, the taking of pleasure in cruelty, and the eating of raw human flesh. Implicitly, the narrator himself participates in vivid enactments of cannibal episodes which involve him treading in vomit and spilt entrails, committing murder, and shedding torrents of human blood. Whilst on the one hand *Salammbô* is a story of barbaric cruelties and repulsive sexual desires, it is also, on the other hand, a dramatic exposé of the depravities of human nature. Through the narrator's implication in savage and barbaric extremes of behaviour, we ourselves, through a subtle process of narrative self-identification, become personally involved in these perverse affinities, and ultimately responsible for scenes of misery and slaughter. In what has been described as his own "cannibal style", Flaubert analyzes his own anthropophagic appetite for scenes of human misery through *Salammbô*'s descriptions of the cannibal desolations of the battlefield, and the interior release of emotions that it elicits.

Another thoughtful exploration of the evidence of barbaric savageries in modern people is Tolstoy's novel *Resurrection* (1899), an indictment of the Russian prison system which also involves episodes of cannibalism. Like *Salammbô*, *Resurrection* is recounted with a carefully moralized impartiality, and a deep inwardness of personal dramatization. Finally, at the close of the century, H.G. Wells's seminal science fiction novel *The Time Machine* prefigures a future human civilization divided into two races. The hairy, cave-dwelling Morlocks have turned cannibalistic, and live on periodic feedings from the bodies of the healthy but unquestioning young Eloi, a race of blond, blue-eyed youngsters bred purely for human sacrifice:

"I tried to look at the thing in a scientific spirit. After all, they were less human and more remote than our cannibal ancestors of three or four thousand years ago... Why should I trouble myself?

These Eloi were mere fatted cattle, which the ant-like Morlocks preserved and preyed upon."

—H.G. Wells, *The Time Machine*

As Wells implies, some aggression is necessary in human beings for advancement and survival. Total passivity, as demonstrated by the Eloi, would ultimately result in our annihilation.

TWENTIETH CENTURY CANNIBALS

The movement towards modernism in the twentieth century was impelled partly by the publication in *Blackwood's Magazine* of Joseph Conrad's powerful novel *Heart Of Darkness* (1899), a story of exploration and self-discovery in the Belgian Congo. By following a series of obscure clues, including the phrase "Exterminate all the Brutes!" scrawled into a sailing log book, the narrator, Marlowe, falls upon his antithesis in the tyrannous Kurtz, a colonizer driven mad by the anarchy of total gratification. Cannibalism is not mentioned explicitly in *Heart Of Darkness*, but it forms an implicit part of the "unspeakable rites" in which Kurtz, the decadent representative of colonial exploitation, is driven to take part. Kurtz's last words ("The horror! The horror!"), spoken in the impulsive unconsciousness of delirium, bespeak the violent predilections for massacre amongst the colonizers, and the instinctive commonality of extermination urges. Kurtz's glimpse of "the horror" forms part of a central drama of self-discovery, with a specific bearing on the cannibal theme. *Heart Of Darkness* suggests an implicit relationship between racial primitivism and certain surviving instincts in the personal history of modern, "civilized" man. The narrative implies that there is a connection between the psychology of primitive peoples and that of infantile features in the mental life of neurotic patients in the modern, "civilized" world.

Heart Of Darkness is preoccupied with a commonplace of self-questioning, a general hankering for primitive vitality, for the "Africa within" and the cannibalistic horrors which lie beneath the surface in all of us. Whilst the novel is not specific about cannibal acts, there are certainly suggestions – sometimes all the more frightening for their unspokenness – that extreme experiences have been enacted in their totality. At the same time, a rich, non-committal irony is contained in Conrad's description of Marlowe's 'choice of nightmares', in that the teasing effect of sustaining unspoken suspicions leads to an energy of emotional commitment in the narrator, and a corresponding expectation of participatory response in the reader.

Prior to the twentieth century, literary evocations of cannibalism tended to hover on the outskirts of the story – both geographically, spiritually, and psychologically. In the twentieth century, however it is fairly true to say that cannibalism "came to consciousness" when Western culture began to shift from a representational to an expressive conception of art. The twentieth century brought in its wake a new orgiastic primitivism in which the previously distinctive realms of art and action, of primary impulses and secondary considerations, between interior and exterior worlds became confused. Cannibalism was no longer a barbaric fantasy on the margins of "civilized" existence, but came to represent some very central aspect of the human condition.

For example, in the "aesthetic terrorism" of the Theatre of Cruelty, instigated by the work of the French playwright Antonin Artaud, the spoken word is used as a sacramental language for materializing the unwanted demons of experience. It aims to provide the spectator with "the truthful precipitates of his dreams, in which his taste for crime, his erotic obsessions, his savagery, his fantasies, his utopian sense of life and of things, even his cannibalism, pour out on a level that is not counterfeit and illusory but internal" (Artaud 1976:244). As part of this aesthetic, Artaud published his decadently grand and gory neo-classical montage of bloodshed *Heliogabale, Où L'anarchist Couronné. Heliogabale* presents its readers with a catalogue of mutilation, human sacrifices, orgiastic cannibal feasts, carnage and butchery. This is not simply wholesale slaughter for its own sake, but an exposé of the essential interconnectedness of bestiality and mysticism, blood and excrement, splendour and filth. In Artaud's entire *Oeuvres Complètes*, in fact, emphasis is on the traditionally forbidden sexual and parasexual activities including murder and cannibalism, particularly the entranced energies of longing surrounding the original cannibal fantasy and the exhilaration surrounding anal experiences. In Artaud, self-realization comes about by way of the violent, orgiastic or cannibal act. Of course, there has always been an association between eating and sexual activity, as in the similar words "consummate" and "consume"[8], and in the similar vocabulary used to apply to both gastronomic and sexual appetitive indulgence[9]. Similar analogies are often made between cannibalism and sexual desire or an intense, all-consuming love.

Other erotic cannibal fantasies can be found in the works of Norman Mailer, who is always quick to introduce, with equal and related formulaic facility, the cannibal-exploitative theme. For Mailer, homosexuality in particular is often associated with exploitative cannibalism, which itself is often used as an image to refer to political or psycho-sexual self exploration, or both. He constantly returns to the theme of our own fears of the "cannibal within", whom we refuse to face. There are cannibals in all of us, according to Mailer, desiring both to eat and to be eaten. In *An American Dream*, the character Stephen Rojack indulges in a cannibal fantasy about the corpse of his wife. After killing his wife Deborah then having sex – including anal sex – with her maid Ruta, Rojack observes that "I had a desire to take Deborah to the bathroom, put her in the tub. Then Ruta and I would sit down to eat. The two of us would sup on Deborah's flesh, we would eat for days: the deepest poisons in us would be released from our cells" (Mailer, 1951:52). Rojack's exhilaration at the murder of his wife is repeatedly referred to in sexual terms, and sexual adventures are regularly described in connection with cannibal yearnings. This set of obscene and perverse images, however is always analogic in its implications – a diseased extension of "ordinary" images of sexual eating. Similarly, in his essay "The White Negro" in *Advertisements For Myself*, Mailer discusses the erotic nature of murder and violence, and the merger of aggression with sexuality. The entire experience is regarded as one of vitality liberated. Right and wrong never enter into it: the morality of free experience overcomes any kind of restraining imperatives.

Indeed, cannibalism sometimes seems to be an obsessive theme in Mailer. In *The Presidential Papers*, a novel woven around presidential fantasies and the Kennedy myth, cannibalism is listed as "among the topics a president ought to consider, and rarely does" (Mailer, 1968:18–19). In *Cannibals And Christians*, Mailer explores the political history of the century through cannibal images; the Nazi holocaust is identified with a kind of technologized cannibalism, an upside-down parody of primitive reversion. In *Barbary Shore* (1968), he analyses the technical horror of the concentration camps and an associated example of real cannibalism, involving holocaust victims attempting to eat one another in the gas chambers (1968:151–2). The practise of cannibalism also finds apposite use as a metaphor for certain kinds of American politics. It stands for either political or psychological exploration, or both, merging with specifically sexual manifestations of the cannibal motif. Cannibalism is also used in Mailer as a metaphor for imperialism.

Yet matters of conquest and mental domination are always associated with a vitalizing, primitive vigour. According to *The Presidential Papers*, cannibal urges in modern man should be neither denied or suppressed, but passed through, overcome, transcended, swallowed, and digested. These fierce personal energies of anger and aggression are part of Mailer's belief in the existential imperative of freewheeling exposure to unceasing variegations of sensations, and the enormous and terrible complexities of moral experience. This total openness, with its unlimited perspectives, leads to endlessly expanding realities of experience and endlessly receding limits, opening up all kinds of new possibilities, always associated with neither guilt nor innocence but with human vigour, life and vitality.

In Tennessee Williams's tense psychodrama *Suddenly Last Summer* (1958), cannibalism is the dreadful and secret ordeal witnessed by the traumatized Catherine "last summer" on La Playa San Sebastian at the Cabeza de Lobo. Catherine is considered deranged by the rest of her family who are unable to acknowledge the reality of her horrifying experience, recounted to her doctor at the climax of the play. Catherine recalls that her cousin Sebastian was pursued from the beach and into the streets by a band of naked street children who attacked and devoured him right in front of her eyes:

*"They had **devoured** parts of him... Torn or cut parts of him away with their hands or knives or maybe those jagged tin cans they made music with, they had torn bits of him away and stuffed them into those gobbling fierce little empty black mouths of theirs. There wasn't a sound any more, there was nothing to see but Sebastian, what was left of him, that looked like a big white-paper-wrapped bunch of red roses had been torn, thrown, **crushed!** – against that blazing white wall...."*

—Williams, 1958:158-159

Yukio Mishima, who committed ritual *seppuku* in 1970, was a homosexual sadist who was stimulated by the sight of blood and joined the army only to be able to observe blood, agony and death at first-hand. His dreams, according to his biographer Henry Scott Stokes, were of "bloodshed – massacring youths, preferably Circassian, on large marble tables, and eating parts of their bodies". Cannibal-style rituals form part of the gruesome pay-off in Mishima's *The Sailor Who Fell From Grace With The Sea* (1963). Similarly, the French poet Jean Genet, like William Burroughs in much of his later writing, envisages cannibalism as part of his homoerotic fantasies: both practises, indeed, could be described as the craving for one's own kind. In Genet, as in Burroughs, the violence and carnage of cannibalism are always bound up with a libidinous exhilaration, where delirious cruelty, as part of the socio-pathology of the battlefield and the besieged city, are revered as the ultimate experience of restless energy and passionate self-realization. The gruesome notion of human cannibalism is thereby enjoyed for its own sake, aesthetically, outside the domain of practical action.

In the work of Jean Genet and Monique Wittig, the cannibal theme becomes an uncompromising image of absolute separateness as well as a means of direct sexual expression and extreme otherness, as part of the search for a truly ignoble crime. Like Mailer, both Genet and Wittig celebrate the act of cannibalism as primitive, vitalizing, authenticating, restorative and liberating. Deeply taboo, the act of cannibalism is associated with all the honour of murderous grandeur.

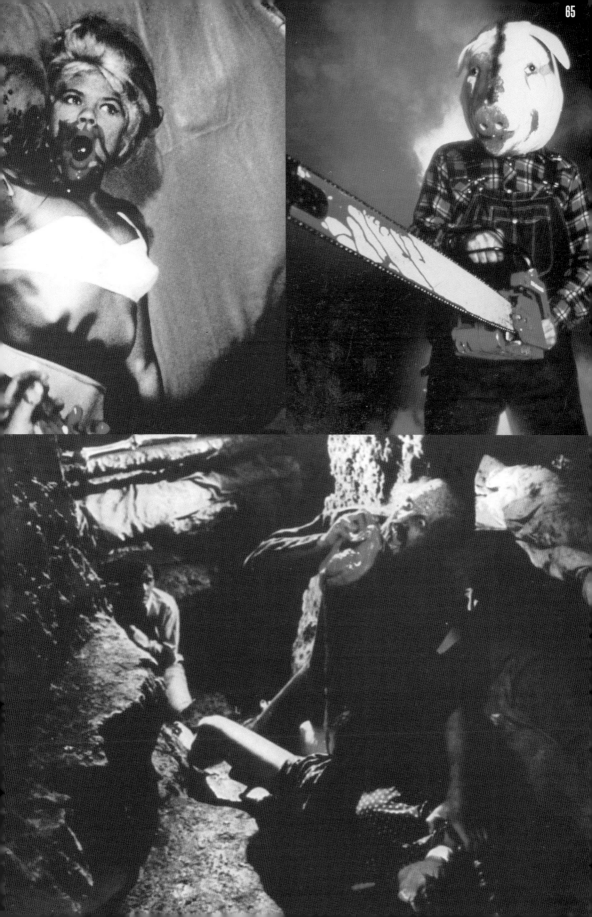

In *Pompes Funebres*, for example, Genet presents us with sexual cannibal fantasies with homosexual and anal erotic elements. Cannibalism in this case involves a dead sexual partner: death arouses sexual desire towards the deceased which takes on a cannibal form. Cannibal themes in Genet, as in Mailer, range from the metaphorical (with both political and sexual implications) to the literal, although – like Mailer – Genet ensures that the link between fantasy and enactment is unclear. His cannibal feelings and fantasies are more frequent and more extreme than Mailer's, and the idea of actual, physical cannibalism is much closer to the surface. Genet absorbs the dead hero in a totemic ritual of nourishment and is thereby reassimilated into the tribe that had rejected him, and that he had rejected. The poet's cannibal passages describe his eating of the body of his dead lover as an act of homage, and an act of love. Notions of incorporation, both literal and metaphorical, are attached to fantasies of tribal ritual, and it is never clear if the cannibal episodes in Genet are dreamed, experienced physically, remembered, or experienced metaphorically.

Cannibalism in feminist writer Monique Wittig's *Les Guérrillèrres* (1969) is a far more aggressive act. In *Le Corps Lesbien* (1973), for example, cannibalism is regarded solely as an aggressive-possessive mode of lesbian sexual gratification. *Le Corps Lesbien* features innumerable cannibal-dismemberment sequences. Cannibal routines, including mutual eviscerations, mutilations and visceral penetrations are performed on living people as well as corpses, and cannibalistic aggression becomes a direct expression of sexual love. Wittig's lesbians spend their time mutilating, dismembering and eviscerating one another, chewing on one another's sinews and vital organs, vomiting, decomposing, penetrating and being penetrated through every orifice and organ, fondling one another's innards, chewing up bits of lung and spitting them out, feeding one another with bodily parts, crunching and tearing one another apart piece by piece, muscle by muscle, vein by vein in the full sensuous expression of physical love. On Wittig's Sapphic island with its entirely female population, dead lovers return to life again, elaborate ritual meals of severed limbs are served with exotic sauces to the beloved, and vomit, curses and dismemberment are all part of the process of lovemaking. *Le Corps Lesbian* is a "literal fantasy" of mutilation and death, both of which are imagined with all their physical characteristics and consequences just as though there were happening, or had happened. In Wittig, as in Genet, the interplay between the literal and the metaphorical remains both a joke and an imaginative exploration of "possible" states. Both writers negotiate different degrees of "literalness" as well as an interplay between the literal and the metaphorical, so that cannibal acts are presented as part of the central vitality of sexual intercourse, with all the intensity it involves.

In March 1991, the 26-year-old Brett Easton Ellis published his controversial second novel *American Psycho*, the story of a wealthy young Wall Street broker with a taste for torture and murder[10]. Set in a world and an era recognizably our own, *American Psycho* prefigures a millennial apocalypse wherein our society is caught up in an insane confusion of materialism, cruelty, violence and madness. One afternoon, as his psychotic frenzy is approaching its most extreme stage, the narrator, Patrick Bateman, wakes up in his exclusive Manhattan apartment to discover, in the kitchen, the fresh corpse of a girl he has no memory of killing:

"I spent the next fifteen minutes beside myself, pulling out a bluish rope of intestine, most of it still connected to the body, and shoving it into my mouth,

choking on it, and it feels moist in my mouth and its filled with some kind of paste that smells bad... I want to drink this girl's blood as if it were champagne and I plunge my face down into what's left of her stomach, scratching my chomping jaw on a broken rib... In the kitchen I try to make meat loaf out of the girl but it becomes too frustrating a task and instead I spend the afternoon smearing her meat all over the walls, chewing on strips of skin I ripped from her body, then I rest by watching a tape of last week's new CBS sitcom, Murphy Brown."

—Ellis, *American Psycho*, 1991:344–5

Ellis's confusion of cannibalism with sex and pornography seems bizarre only until we recall the testimonies of psychotic cannibals like Ed Gein and Jeffrey Dahmer (see chapter 2), for whom cannibalism was a highly charged sexual act. The case histories of De River's sexual psychopaths testify to a number of similar examples. More disturbingly, perhaps, in his book *Alive: The Story Of The Andes Survivors* (1974), Piers Paul Read describes how a Chilean magazine, which usually specialized in pornography, devoted a double-page spread to photographs of what remained of the limbs and bodies of the cannibalized victims.

Human cannibalism continues to be a popular theme in contemporary fiction, especially science-fiction, evinced by the popular and critical success of short stories like H.P. Lovecraft's "The Picture In The House" and "The Rats In The Walls", Stephen King's "Survivor Type", Alice Sheldon's "Morality Meat", Sokyo Komatsu's "The Savage Mouth" and, perhaps the best-known of such fiction, Harry Harrison's *Soylent Green*. It also forms part of the plots of Robert A. Heinlein's *Farnham's Freehold*, and *Stranger In A Strange Land*, as well as many other science-fiction stories and novels, such as Tama Janowitz's latest offering, *A Cannibal In Manhattan*. In Poppy Z. Brite's 1995 novel *Exquisite Corpse*, mass-murderer Andrew Compton escapes life imprisonment in London and flees to America to resume a career of carnage and necrophilia. There he meets aristocratic playboy Jay, who indulges a penchant for cannibalism with vagrants picked up in New Orleans's French Quarter.

Red Dragon, to take another example, is the first of Thomas Harris's novels featuring the sociopathic genius and serial killer Hannibal "the Cannibal" Lecter, probably best known from his portrayal by Anthony Hopkins in Jonathan Demme's **The Silence Of The Lambs**. Cormac McCarthy's 1973 novel *Child Of God* tells the story of Lester Ballard, a Tennessee backwoodsman who, evicted from his family home, takes to living in a run-down shack, living off a diet of tasteless corn bread, with the stuffed animals he wins at a fairground rifle range as his only companions. With his shack burned out, he takes to living in a cave, shooting young women dead and robbing graves to procure bodies for sex. By the time he is eventually apprehended, his cave is populated by dead women in advanced stages of putrefaction. Committed to a state mental hospital, he spends the rest of his life in a cell next-door-but-one to a deranged cannibal who used to feed on his victims' brains with a spoon.

However, the ultimate in this century's cannibal fiction must be Issei Sagawa's *Kiri No Naka (In the Mist)*, published in 1983. *In The Mist* is a loosely "fictionalized" account of Sagawa's own murder and cannibalization of a 25-year-old Dutch student in 1981 (see chapter 2). Yet to be fully translated into English, the book has already sold 200,000 copies in Japan alone. In this scene, the day after the murder, the narrator sets out to devour the limbs of his beloved:

"I touch the cold body again and I wonder where I should start. I start to cut off all the meat before amputating the limbs. While I cut her calf I suddenly want to taste it. I see the beautiful red meat beneath the fat. I grasp her knee and her ankle, and tear it with my teeth.

It is tender. I slowly chew and savour it. After eating most of the calf I look at myself in the mirror. There is grease all over my face. And then I start to eat at random. I bite her little toe. It still smells of her feet. I stab the knife into her arch and see the red meat deep inside. I thrust my fingers inside and dig out the meat and put it in my mouth. It tastes okay. Then I stab the knife into her armpit. Ever since I saw it under her yellow sleeveless top I wondered how it would taste. I cut off the skin and bite. It is tender and melts in my mouth. I can still smell her body. I had no idea it would taste this good.

The wonderful taste cheers me up. I devour her underarm up to the elbow."

—Sagawa, *In The Mist*

BLOOD LIBEL

In order to respect and obey cultural taboos, we need to understand why those taboos are in place. To understand why those taboos are in place, we need to see what happens when they are broken. Therefore we break the rules in fantasy: in narratives, which are our acceptable and sometimes cathartic cultural versions of broken taboos. We keep to our taboos because we have seen what will happen if we don't.

Myth, legend and literature present us with a series of fictionalized morality tales: stories which tell us of the wrong way and the right way to behave ourselves in culture. When cultural taboos are broken, the horror and disgust experienced by those observing the consequences reinforce those basic taboos. Of course, this horror and disgust is sometimes lascivious and voyeuristic. The whole point of a taboo is that it is a sanction against human desire – against what we, as human beings, want and need – sometimes consciously, sometimes unconsciously. Lasciviousness and voyeurism are fundamental characteristics of the "unfettered" human being.

These cannibal narratives that different cultures tell themselves are not about racism, or colonial relationships, or exploitative cruelty, or explicit voyeurism, or sexual acts. These are stories about dissolving redundant relations, about shame, blame, courtesy, conduct, public and private rituals, behaviour and respect, about the rules of blood libel – libels not just against foreigners, but against mankind in general. The regular strategy of rejection, according to anthropology, starts with the libel, whether this be the simple food libel (the libelled group eats disgusting foods), the sex libel (the demeaned category is promiscuous, effeminate or incestuous), to the blood libel (the demeaned category is murderous and – ultimately – cannibalistic) (see Douglas 1992:86). Nevertheless, the majority of these narratives of blood libel are stories of resolution and restoration, reassuring us that mankind is not, in fact, "other" by nature (barbaric, murderous, a slave to his passions, sensual and ineducable), but rather amicable, restrained, equable, generous and humane.

There is a long tradition in Western culture of attributing to any individual that the establishment considers dangerous the most unattractive characteristics that could be imagined. Earlier individuals were (and still sometimes are) almost automatically accused of cannibalism. It is a very easy process for people to regress to these primal modes of magical and mythic thinking, including the perception of archetypal images and the acting out of primal myths on their own bodies, or the bodies of others – to literalize ancient stories, myths, legends and Biblical injunctions. Sometimes, these modes of thinking are used as techniques of rejection, as ways of dealing with marginal categories such as terrifying, "primitive" peoples – or those who tell stories about them.

The following study of filmic stories of human cannibalism is necessarily limited in its focus, cannibalism proving an enormously popular theme amongst horror (and other) film directors, especially those marketing to alternative, fringe and "underground" video markets. A number of perhaps rather significant films have thereby been omitted, by the necessities of time, space, and the demands of categorization. No vampire films have been included, for example, since I've elected to analyze only those films that deal with actual flesh-eating, as opposed to "mere" blood-drinking.

NOTES

1.   For examples, see Norman O. Brown, 1966:IX.
2.   For examples, see Marie Tatar, 1992:196.
3.   Both Klein and Lacan also look back to the early experiences of childhood, and to Jung, the conscious mind grows out of the unconscious psyche which is much older than it, and which goes on functioning together with it, or even in spite of it.
4.   Muensterberger points out, however, that Freud's list of examples is virtually exhaustive, and that there are plenty of other instances in which the sacramental meal is entirely absent. In fact, when the total ethnographic record is considered, the sacramental totemic meal is, according to Muensterberger, extremely rare indeed.
5.   Versions of the same story are also told by Virgil, Heraclitus, Catullus, Plutarch and Sophocles.
6.   A theme picked up, with only minor variations, in the nineteenth century work *Cannibals All, Or, Slaves Without Masters*, a pro-slavery document by American writer George Fitzhugh.
7.   Rochester's *Satyr Against Reason And Mankind* makes a similar point, although much less graphically, to the intent that man is not only more cannibalistic than beasts, but in a worse sense.
8.   Although the French, of course, go one better, using the verb *consommer* to refer to both meals and marriage.
9.   For example, "desire", "lust", "hunger", "devour", "satiation", "appetite" and such phrases as "a tasty dish", a "nice piece of flesh", and so on.
10.   *American Psycho* was made into a film in 1999, directed by Mary Harron (who also made the acclaimed **I Shot Andy Warhol**, 1996) and featuring Christian Bale as Patrick Bateman (after Leonardo DiCaprio backed out).

PART TWO

THE CANNIBAL CAMERA

chapter one:
anthropological and arthouse

T HE practise of human cannibalism appears on both the cinema and video screen in a whole variety of different forms and contexts. This chapter will be examining firstly what might be described as cannibal "documentaries", or as "anthropological" cannibal films (that is, films describing or depicting images of cannibalism for a purportedly educational, informative, academic, or natural-historic purpose), and secondly a selection of those unorthodox or eccentric avant-garde cannibal-themed movies limited to the arthouse, small theatre or film festival circuit.

CANNIBAL CURIOSITIES

"With the advent of jet air travel, Africa is only hours away. MEET YOUR NEW NEIGHBOURS! ...See Primitive Passion! See them drain the hot blood of their beasts and drink it down! See young men "coming of age", their front teeth knocked out with stones! See heretofore never-witnessed Rites of Human Mutilation dating from the Dawn of Civilization! See it all!
Uncut! Uncensored! Unclothes! Unashamed!"
—One-sheet copy, **Karamoja**, 1946

Back in 1945, a 66-minute short called **Karamoja**, an "anthropological study" of the Congo natives produced and directed by Ernest Gold, caused a stir not dissimilar to that surrounding the release of Ruggero Deodato's infamous **Cannibal Holocaust** in 1979. And, like the narrative within **Cannibal Holocaust**, the story behind **Karamoja** – "The Land Of The Lost People" – was one that seemed unlikely, to say the least. According to the advertising copy, a Californian dentist, Dr. Truetle, set off for Africa intending to hunt big game, but arriving in Nairobi fell in with an English lady conservationist who convinced him to photograph his expedition instead of killing animals. Armed only with a 16mm Bolex camera, Truetle and his companion travelled down the Belgian Congo to film a primitive native tribe almost unknown to white men, known as the Karamojans. Truetle apparently shot ten thousand feet of 16mm Kodachrome print documenting the "unspeakable rites and customs" of this savage tribe, including habitual nudity, blood-drinking, the dismemberment of a calf, the brewing of beer from animal urine, savages smearing one another all over with the dung of animals, punching holes through the lower lip, knocking out the front teeth of adolescent males with stones as a rite of passage, male circumcision, the carving of insignia on human bodies and – or so the press copy implied, at least – human cannibalism. And all perpetrated by savages "wearing nothing more than the wind".

The press copy, however, was written by the liberal pen of Kroger Babb, grand-daddy of the exploitation film and promoter of such high-grossing, sex-hygiene drive-in movie fodder as **Mom And Dad**, **The Devil's Weed**, and **One Too Many**. Ersatz-anthropological "documentaries" like **Karamoja** were nothing new in 1946 – in fact, a few years earlier, Andy Dietz's 16mm short **Slash Of The Knife God** also showed native male circumcision rituals, though not in the colour and close-up of **Karamoja**. The earliest such film was probably **Cannibals Of The South Seas** (1912), a popular exotic location documentary made by husband-and-wife filmmaking team Martin and Osa Johnson, who continued to shoot such films until Martin Johnson was killed in a plane crash. Other landmarks in the genre include the Johnsons' **Among The Cannibal Isles Of The South Pacific** (1918) and David F. Friedman's **Cannibal Island** (1956), an hour-long exploitation documentary about the pygmies of the South Pacific filmed with a "long-distance lens" to avoid the "dangers to man" of ordinary close-up photography.

However, none of these anthropological-exploitation movies actually showed human cannibalism, despite their graphic promises, and **Karamoja** – the story of the "world's lost tribe" – did not break with this hallowed tradition. The "unspeakable rites" promised in Babb's advertising copy were no more than natives drinking the blood of cattle from a vein in the cows' necks, and then stitching the wound back together again – unless, that is, this description referred to the marriage of Dr. Truetle and his English guide, who were united not long after their return to "civilization", or so the story goes, at least. However, as a sop to the disappointed appetites of the bloodthirsty rubes, Babb followed up all screenings of **Karamoja** with a Nazi death-camp exploitation vehicle entitled **Halfway To Hell**, with a narration by Quentin Reynolds of his own "storyline", which consisted of sections of German film captured by the Signal Corps and "smuggled" out from behind the iron curtain, and other sections shot by the Allies when the concentration camps were liberated. **Halfway To Hell** served up twenty-five long minutes of piled corpses, ovens filled with human ashes, the executions of war criminals after the Nuremberg trials and other assorted atrocities, which apparently more than made up for the dietary reticence of the Karamojans.

At one end of the anthropological spectrum, then, is the legacy left by Kroger Babb and his team in the form of the mondo film. Mondo films originally became popular in the late 1960s, when films like **Mondo Bizarro** (1966), **Mondo Balordo** (1964), **Africa Addio** (1966) and **You Are What You Eat** (1968) tried to capitalize on the original 1963 success of Gualtiero Jacopetti and Franco E. Prosperi's prototype **Mondo Cane**. The original mondo films of the 1960s included footage of so-called "cannibal" tribes chewing on allegedly "human" bones as part of their (often faked) catalogues of bizarre practises from around the world such as dog-eating in the Philippines, tribal fertility rituals, and South American cargo cults.

The mondo "shockumentaries" of the 1980s and 90s have mainly gone underground, and are now available only from independent video dealers, horror and cult film catalogues, market stalls and "under the counter" at video shops. "Shockumentaries" like **Faces Of Death I** (1978) **II** (1981), **111** (1985) and **IV** (1990); **Shocks** (1988); **Death Scenes I** (1989) and **II** (1992); and the recent **Executions** (1996), are not only more vivid and explicit than the films of the original mondo bandwagon of the 1960s, but are perhaps the nearest thing to genuine snuff movies that contemporary cinema has to offer us. These shockumentaries generally consist of unedited police and news camera footage too graphic to be shown on television, documentary out-takes, amateur or police camera-work, war footage from the African continent, stills of murder and suicide victims, mortuary scenes and close-ups of dead bodies. The footage is occasionally held together with a loose documentary-style commentary but sometimes left to speak for itself

Guinea Ama

or backed by an appropriate (or sometimes rather inappropriate) musical soundtrack. Originating in Italy, the mondo film has a massive cult following on the underground movie circuit; mondo shockumentaries are now produced in Europe, China, Japan and, of course, America, with certain "classic" clips or sequences of footage (such as the Zapruder footage of the Kennedy assassination and the Jonestown massacre) showing up again and again, from film to film. These shockumentaries are quite difficult to get hold of but highly sought-after. Their audience tends to consist of those fascinated by true crime and criminology, those with an interest in Satanism and the occult, but chiefly of that group of thrill-seeking adolescent male voyeurs that comprises the main audience for the traditional horror film. Cannibalism is suggested in a number of these videos, including the bogus Man Mau trials in Jacopetti and Prosperi's **Africa Addio** (1966), and Climati and Morrà's **Savage Man...Savage Beast** (1975). In Conan Le Cilaire's **Faces Of Death** (1978), narrator and pseudo-pathologist "Dr. Francis B. Gross" introduces us to a group of African tribesmen smacking their lips on a pile of raw ribs belonging to the decomposing skeleton of a cow. The implication is obvious: the hungry tribesmen are sometime cannibals.

Important only for its temporary appropriation of the cannibal-mondo form is **Libidomania 2** (a.k.a. **Perverted Sex, Violent World**), directed by George Smith (a.k.a. Jimmy B. Matheus, a.k.a. Bruno Mattei), and released in Italy in 1980. This otherwise unexceptional mondo movie deserves at least a brief mention for its short staged cannibal scenario. Obvious and somewhat pathetic attempts to cash in on the lasting success of Jacopetti and Prosperi's **Mondo Cane** and its less profitable imitators, **Libidomania** and **Libidomania 2** both offer up brief juxtapositions of real and faked footage of bizarre goings-on from all around the globe, from footage of the Miss Nude America contest to a woman being gang-raped while her attackers gleefully video the attack on their camcorder. The cannibal sequence in **Libidomania 2** is similarly dressed up as a piece of "home movie" footage showing how an American couple "discover" a "savage" living in the jungle, and how the American woman seduces him. We are also shown the putative results of this scenario: the woman is shown tied up in the corner of a "jungle hut", while the ungrateful savage sits in the corner feasting happily on the remains of her dead husband. And **Guinea Ama** (dir: Akira Ide, 1974), shows human bones rotting in cages as evidence of cannibal activity amongst the tribes of Papua New Guinea.

CANNIBAL TOURS

"There is nothing so strange, in a strange land,
As the stranger who comes to visit it."

So begins Dennis O'Rourke's powerful documentary **Cannibal Tours** (1988), which consists of film footage tracing three separate groups of American and European tourists visiting the tribal peoples of New Guinea and elsewhere, to observe and photograph the native "cannibals" of the secret corners of the earth.

The first group of tourists are Germans visiting a former German colony in New Guinea. Pointing to a tree stump, one of the "cannibals" explains to the tourists (via a translator) that this is the place where he and his fellow tribesmen used to "dance around the tree and cut off their heads". A heavy German tourist gets his colleague to take a photograph of himself with the "cannibal", at the place where "they" used to "eat one another". Later, the same German tourist gives the "cannibal" a bottle of cologne, for his "wife". Another of the Germans videotapes a gang of native children who paddle up in their canoes to clamber for sweets handed out to them, one by one, by a woman who acts as though she were feeding fascinating but potentially dangerous animals at the zoo.

A huge, luxury cruise boat sails grandly down a river where the natives paddle their tiny canoes. On the boat, the overfed Germans, tucking into a pair of large steaks, discuss calories and cholesterol while the undernourished natives on the riverbanks try to sell their handicrafts to make enough money in order to feed their children. On the boat a woman, smoking, flicks her cigarette ash overboard into the river. Lengthy silent footage follows of jungle animals, river birds, native idols and statues, and the tribesmen going about their businesses, working on their houses. This is a film of stark, cynical opposition.

Cannibal Tours is a fascinating film not least because it gives us the tribesmen's perspectives on the "strangers" who are the tourists. In a subtitled interview conducted in his own language, one elderly "cannibal" with filed-down teeth explains how his parents were brought up under the original German colonists, and so when the tourists began to arrive in their village, the "cannibals" were at first terrified; they believed that a crocodile spirit had brought about the return of their long-dead ancestors, clad in new skins with new faces.

Most of the "cannibals" find it very difficult to understand why the tourists come to look at them, but speculate that it must be to discover how the natives live and whether or not they are "civilized". One tribeswoman complains that the tourist trade is not a profitable one, that the tourists simply look at their handicrafts but rarely buy anything. And those who do buy things, she complains, help to destroy the local economy by encouraging dependence on cash. The "cannibal" with the pointed teeth then goes on the explain how, in the old days, his tribesmen used to fight one another, cut off each others' heads, and skin the bodies to eat them. "And when the Germans came," he claims, speaking of the early colonizers, "we fought and ate them too." But his father's way of life – "killing and eating" – is now over, and now they live "for the church and government". They allow the tourists to come and allow themselves to be photographed, claims the tribesman, because the tribe needs the cash, although he finds it hard to understand why the Europeans want to take so many pictures of them.

The second group of tourists at whom O'Rourke directs his observant lens is a party of Americans, mainly women, who are visiting New Guinea to video the natives dancing their "ritual dances" in the nude, clad only in elaborate paint and masks, to the beating of the jungle drums. One woman, after bartering over the price of a shield and sword for her art collection, comments on her enthusiasm for the "baroque" qualities of the primitive handicrafts, which remind her of Modigliani, while a second woman takes photographs of "adorable" "cannibal" children. Other American women take pictures of bushy-haired natives dressed in their traditional costumes, handing them coins after each click of the shutter. Balloons are given out to the tiny "cannibal" children. The tourists try to encourage the natives to smile for photographs and to pose in suitably aggressive modes, but they are understandably reluctant.

The third group of tourists that O'Rourke focuses on are a group of glamorous Italians – again, mainly women, but this time much younger women in short shorts – sunbathing in their canoe, bedecked with fashionable sunglasses and laden with camera equipment, sporting gold jewellery and long painted and manicured fingernails. Coming across a group of crocodiles, also sunning themselves on the river banks, the Italians discuss the issue of cannibalism, speculating on a number of possible reasons for the practise, and whether these reasons make it "necessary" or "symbolic". One of the Italian women wants a photograph taken of herself with a large group of naked "cannibal" children. She pets them like small animals and encourages them to approach her, but they are afraid to get too close. The film closes with this same group of women dressed up in native costume and face paint and dancing tribal-style, in slow-motion.

O'Rourke's film is a strange, thoughtful meditation on the fundamental issues of voyeurism, tourism, anthropology, cannibalism, and the nature of human otherness. There is no narrative voice-over, only a constant gentle backing soundtrack of classical music, which lends to the documentary a somewhat plaintive undertone. There are a large number of extended close-up shots of people's faces, both tourists and "cannibals" caught staring solemnly into the camera in sequences which are held for unnatural lengths of time. Like a curious visitor at a turn-of-the-century ethnographic showcase, O'Rourke's camera gazes in captivated fascination at the faces and bodies of its subjects as though they were a strange new species of human beings, tourists and "cannibals" together.

CANNIBAL CARNIVALS

Towards the more serious end of the "anthropological" spectrum are the carnivalesque parodies of the "cannibal-tropicalist" phase in late 1960s Brazilian cinema. These films, not quite "documentaries" in the traditional sense of the

Macunaima

term, exploit the notion of cannibalism as a metaphor, positing aboriginal matriarchy and communalism as a utopian model. The cannibal metaphor is also used as a critical instrument for exposing the exploitative social Darwinism of bourgeois society.[1]

The best known of the "cannibal" films is Joaquim Pedro de Andrade's 1969 adaptation of Mario de Andrade's novel *Macunaima*, whose cannibal theme is often associated with the work of the Brazilian literary "anthropophagical movement". The filmic version of *Macunaima* turns the theme of cannibalism into a springboard for a critique of repressive military rule and of the predatory capitalist model of the short-lived Brazilian "economic miracle". **Macunaima**, a mixture of fantasy and black comedy, is a grotesque, magical story thinly disguising the political situation in Brazil: the poor are so hungry they eat themselves; a cannibalistic ogre offers Macunaima a piece of his leg to chew on; an urban guerrilla devours the protagonist sexually; the wife of a prominent capitalist hankers after eating him alive, and a man-eating siren finally lures him to his death. **Macunaima** presents cannibalism as an exemplary mode of consumerism adopted by underdeveloped peoples: the rich devour the poor; the poor devour each other; the left devour the right; the right purifies itself by eating itself; people devour one another through social, political and economic relationships, through their consumption of products, or, more directly, through sex. Meanwhile, voraciously, nations devour their people. According to its director, **Macunaima** is the story of a Brazilian being devoured by Brazil (see Stam, 1989:143–145).

A second important film in the canon of Brazilian so-called "cannibal-tropicalist" cinema is Arthur Omar's **Triste Tropico** (1974), a kind of parodic anthropological "fictive documentary" in the style of Woody Allen's **Zelig**. **Triste Tropico**, its title inspired by Lévi-Strauss's ethnographic memoir of Brazil, becomes a distanced reflection on the whole notion of the "tropics" as Europe's exotic and disturbing "Other". The linear narrative of a doctor who arrives to practise medicine in Brazil is superimposed with a loosely connected collage of discontinuous sonorous and linguistic materials – a chaotic anthology of Brazilian, American, Argentinean and Cuban music, contemporary footage from Rio's carnival, staged scenes, and clips from other fiction films. This bricolage serves to emphasize Lévi-Strauss's notion of binary oppositions, specifically "raw" Brazil versus "cooked" Europe. This motif is supplemented by the increasingly improbable and hallucinatory narrative of the doctor, who becomes involved with Indians, compiles an almanac of herbal panaceas, becomes an indigenous messiah and finally – not unlike Kurtz in Conrad's *Heart Of Darkness* – degenerates into a practitioner of sodomy and cannibalism.

The "cannibal-tropicalist" style is picked up again in Julio Bressane's **Tabu** (1982), another "documentary"-style film celebrating the carnival-style spirit of Rio in the thirties, juxtaposing shots of festivities with footage of the daily chores of fishermen and images of natives dancing in Tahiti in an ironic hybridization of the spirit of popular culture and carnival, both early and modern. According to critic Robert Stam:

"By spreading the spirit of carnival to the South Pacific, in a kind of joyful heterotopian contamination, Bressane demonstrates, once again, the inexhaustible suggestiveness of a tradition that is rooted in anthropophagic modernism and its latter-day incarnation, tropicalism."

—Stam, 1989:153

CANNIBAL COUNTER-CULTURE

In Jean-Luc Godard's highly satiric and surrealist fantasy **Weekend** (France, 1967), a group of young French bourgeoisie, out to spend a weekend in the country, encounter an enormous traffic jam of like-minded weekenders, and are forced to abandon their car and hitch a ride from two revolutionaries driving a garbage truck. After being forced to shovel garbage, being denied sustenance and being forced to listen to the political dogma of the revolutionaries, one young couple hook up with the radicals, learn to live in the woods and go on a cannibalistic rampage of death and destruction. In the final scene of the film, a young middle-class housewife helps herself to a set of chewy ribs. On being informed that the meat stew is a mixture of pig, the leftovers of an English tourist dragged out of his Rolls, and the young woman's husband, she promises to be back for more later. Godard's film is a bizarre and sharp-edged satire at the expense of the pretentious aspirations of the French middle classes, their racism and their ignorance. It is also a barbed attack on French imperialism and the French appropriation of the political and economic resources of North Africa and the Congo.

1970 brought us Liliana Cavali's Italian countercultural epic, **I Cannibali**. This political-fiction *film fantastique*, a very liberal translation of Sophocles' *Antigone*, is the point of convergence between an enormous number of different literary and cinematic influences – classical legend, the story of the first Christians,

Weekend

the Godard of **Alphaville**, Huxley's *Brave New World*, and plenty more – all pieced together into an abstract and mosaic-like fantasy which, ironically enough, has very little to do with the literal act of cannibalism.

On a beach beside an unnamed town (actually Milan, beautifully photographed), a group of children discover a mysterious stranger (Pierre Clémanti) sleeping on a raft. The stranger, a handsome young man rolled up in a black cape and red scarf, seems to be from another world, since he speaks a mysterious language nobody understands, and cannot himself speak the language of others. Suddenly, gunshots ring out, and the children are attacked by a gang of hunters, who chase them into the streets of the town whose roads and pavements are filled with clean, nude, partially-cannibalized cadavers, but cadavers that are pale, bloodless and somehow inhuman – they are lacking in genital detail, for example.

The atmosphere changes, and the soundtrack becomes harsh and lacerating. We have been thrown into the frightening political climate of a town ruled by a generic oppressive regime dictating a reign of terror. All young people suspected of rebellion are embattled by armed police; few dare to protest the forces of order, and official notices lining the streets forbid the touching of the corpses. A small group of radical youth, led by Antigone (Britt Ekland) and the mysterious stranger, have the courage to challenge the tyranny of the state and its military laws, and the leaders of this group are tracked down and followed by the military police. During this chase, Antigone and the stranger strip off their clothes and take temporary refuge in a church, where the stranger demolishes the altar. Eventually, however, these two leaders of the resistance are finally captured

I Cannibali

and imprisoned in various military departments, torture chambers, psychiatric hospitals and prisons, all to the utmost indifference of the rest of the population, including Antigone's family, who rally round the military regime. In the end, Antigone and her strange new friend give themselves up to their oppressors, recognizing the mutual resignation in one another's eyes. However, the film's final images are of the youth of the city assembled to carry the bodies of the victims up to the mountains to be buried, with the implication that this is the beginning of general resistance to their oppressors.

The cannibalism of I **Cannibali** is clearly figurative, as well as literal, suggesting the self-consuming nature of any oppressive military or dictatorial regime. Cavali uses colour in particular to draw attention to the abstract and metaphorical level of the film, especially in the town sequences, the depictions of verdant green countryside at the edge of the sea, and the stranger's red and white costume when he is first discovered. Sometimes, this figurative aspect of the film inclines towards the hermetic and esoteric. For example, the stranger has one particular signature – the sign of a fish – which he draws on walls in chalk, and one particular word which he repeats – *"séna"* – (which might possibly be his own word for the sign he repeatedly draws). As this example shows, the system of language in I **Cannibali** is both a means of communication and a linguistic barrier, as well as a way of expressing incomprehension. The stranger, unable to penetrate or comprehend human language, tries to communicate with Antigone first by his drawings, then through sympathy, then by commonality of purpose, and finally by fraternity. In the end, Antigone is cut off from her family, her peer group and her society, and can communicate only with the stranger, through the language of rebellion. Antigone herself, in the end, has also become a stranger to the world and its laws, in her language as well as her attitude.

Claude Faraldo's **Themroc**, released in 1973, stars Michel Piccoli as the eponymous rebel/anarchist who gradually withdraws from society into a non-communicative, cannibalistic state. First he quits his day-job, then progresses to acts of incest and other sociopathic gestures, before finally barricading himself in the demolished remains of his apartment. Here he regresses to an animal level, "talking" only in nonsensical grunts and screams, and roasting on spits and devouring the cops who attempt to evict him.

Francesco Barilli's 1974 underground classic **The Perfume Of The Lady In Black** (a.k.a. **La Profuma Della Donna In Nero**) was considered far too graphic and unrelenting to secure UK or US mainstream cinema release, as was Barilli's next and only other film **Hotel Of Fear** (a.k.a. **Penzione Paura**), but both can occasionally be seen on the arthouse circuit and at private cinema clubs, and **The Perfume Of The Lady In Black** was released in a re-cut video version in 1995. From a screenplay co-authored by the director (and completely unrelated to Gaston Leroux's 1908 novel of the same name), this accomplished, unsettling psychological thriller features Mimsy Farmer as Silvia Hacherman, a young chemist who makes the acquaintance of an African couple who are conversant in the rituals of black magic. The couple put a spell on Silvia by inviting her to play tennis, then giving her a racquet with a nail sticking out of it, on which she stabs her finger and draws blood. From this point on, and in a manner similar to Polanski's **Repulsion**,[2] the film gradually slides into an elegant depiction of Silvia's trauma-ridden unconscious state, which is peopled by spectral children, serial killers, sly phantoms and a blind palm-reader named Orchidea (Niké Arrighi), who foretells disaster in Silvia's trembling hand. Day by day, Silvia is engulfed by vivid recollections of childhood traumas, including sexual abuse at the hands of her mother's lover, and the murder of her mother, who materializes in the ether before her as she descends into delirium. As Silvia's personality finally splits, her friends and neighbours begin to die in a series of violent accidents, and when she is visited by her own inner child, a demonic imp in a white dress, Silvia is goaded into making a choice: either she must come to terms with her past, or else she must continue to relive it, and the choice she makes leads to the film's climactic cannibal finalé.

Os Cannibales (a.k.a. **Les Cannibales**, **The Cannibals**), released in 1988, is Portuguese director Manoel de Oliveira's tenth feature film in a career spanning fifty-eight years, and directed when this feted Portuguese director was in his seventies. Oliveira's films, such as **O Passado E O Presente** (**The Past And The Present**, 1971), **Amor De Perdicao** (**Love Of Perdition**, 1978) and **Francisca** (1981) tend towards the operatic in style: **Os Cannibales** takes this tendency to its limits. The first half-hour of this spectacular film takes the form of an opera: an adaptation of a nineteenth century Portuguese story that effects variations on the Don Giovanni theme, with a score by Joao Paes, who ran Lisbon's opera house for seven years. The opera depicts the wedding of a beautiful young woman, Marguerite (Leonor Silveira) to the Viscount d'Aveleda (Luis Miguel Cintra) at what appears to be some time in the eighteenth century. But nothing is quite what it seems to be. The party guests arrive in limousines, the lights are all electric and the gentlemen are all dressed in top hats. The second half of the film is pure black comedy. The night of the wedding, the Viscount has to rescue his bride from the seductive advances of Don Giovanni (Diego Doria); then, in the bedroom, there are more surprises in store. In a scene reminiscent of Swift, we learn that the Viscount himself is a walking prosthesis – all his limbs and members have to be unscrewed and hung up on the bedrail at the end of the day. On learning this, Marguerite falls into a faint and topples out of the window, leaving her husband

Os Cannibales

to curse his fate and to hurl his prosthetic limbs one by one into the hearth fire. The next morning, the bridegroom – or what is left of him – has mysteriously disappeared, but there is a delicious-looking roast cooking in the fireplace, and the father of the bride (Oliveira Lopes) and his two sons (Pedro T. DaSilva and Joel Costa), hungry after the exertions of the night before, tuck in with relish. From this point onwards, the film abandons its last vestiges of realism and becomes an irreverent fantasy, with the guests turning into pigs, wolves and bears and dancing their way into infinity to the music of a playful violin.

  Os Cannibales is a film that mixes horror with the grotesque, and irony with pathos. Oliveira's satire at the expense of the idle lifestyles of the rich is tempered by a black humour that can be sometimes gentle and sometimes devastating. Despite the "accidental" incident of cannibalism, the party carries on into the following day, nothing being allowed to come between the rich and their pursuit of happiness. The only regret that the cannibals admit to is that they didn't have the opportunity to appreciate the sweet flesh of the Viscount while they were eating him, since the "identity" of the roast is not revealed until supper is over. **Os Cannibales** is completely dedicated to spectacle. The film is full of splendid and sumptuous scenes of luxury, wealth, beauty and power, all of which conspire to disguise the mundane suffering of those whose very existence provides the rich with their sustenance. But Oliveira also shows us the true nature of things in the revelations of the morning after, when, with a wave of his Cocteauesque magic wand, the director suddenly transforms the bride's father into a pig and his sons into wolves, and lets them devour him, as the laws of nature take their inevitable course.

CANNIBALISM A LA CARTE

The following year, 1989, brought us Peter Greenaway's English/Dutch collaborative venture, **The Cook, The Thief, His Wife And Her Lover**. As in all Greenaway's films the basic plot of this story is quite straightforward. Greenaway himself has described the film as "a violent and erotic love-story set in the kitchen and dining-room of a smart restaurant". Every night the gross, violent Albert Spica (Michael Gambon) goes to dine at an elegant restaurant, La Hollandaise, which he owns, and where he nightly holds court. Every night he brings along his vulnerable, browbeaten wife Georgie (Helen Mirren) and various members of his thuggish entourage such as Mitchel (Tim Roth), Cory (Cieran Hinds) and Spangler (Gary Olsen). And every night he indulges in a series of brutal and scatological monologues, berating and abusing all around him, from his wife, to the chef (Richard Bohringer), to the kitchen boy Pup (Paul Russell). As Spica enjoys his vulgar diatribe, Georgie notices a diner eating alone and reading at another table. She goes to the toilet, meets the stranger (Alan Howard) and they make love, until interrupted by the suspicious Spica coming in to look for his wife. The following evening, with the connivance of the chef, Georgie and the stranger make use of one of the restaurant's storerooms to make love again. The next night, bothered by the presence of the solitary, bookish diner, Spica drags him over to his table and he is introduced at last to Georgie as Michael, a scholar working in a book depository where he is currently cataloguing works on the French Revolution. Two days later, Spica finds out about his wife's affair from one of his henchmen, tracks Michael down in the book depository, and he and his men stuff Michael full of pages from his books until he dies. In revenge, Georgie persuades the chef to cook up Michael's corpse for a special function in the restaurant that night. When her husband arrives, Georgie wheels out Michael's roasted corpse and orders Albert to eat. As he takes his first mouthful, Georgie shoots him dead.

Like most of Greenaway's films, **The Cook, The Thief...** is a baroque fantasy whose plot takes second place to its dazzling visual imagery and aesthetic style. Each area of the restaurant, for example, has a different design and colour scheme, and the actors' extravagant Jean-Paul Gaultier costumes change colour as they move between rooms. Each section of the restaurant seems also to have a different temporal location. The kitchen, with all its constant paraphernalia of food preparation, is reminiscent of an eighteenth-century still-life; the dining room, with its lush fabrics, is nineteenth century, and the high-tech bathroom late twentieth century. This sumptuousness of imagery and the elegance of much of the film's soundtrack seem deliberately to offset the vulgarity of much of its action and dialogue, especially Spica's constant rants and physical brutalities.

Since cannibalism, albeit barely consummated cannibalism, is the central metaphor of Greenaway's film – the final image of Michael's spit-roasted body being the metaphor around which the rest of the film seems to pivot – it is important to consider what this issue comes to signify in Greenaway's text. Most evidently, **The Cook, The Thief...** is a story about appetite, about the taboo areas of sexuality and corporeality, about the fleshliness of human existence, about meat, poultry and animal and human bodies. In one scene, the wife and her lover lie naked together amongst slabs of meat and poultry; in another, on the verge of discovery, they flee naked into the cold-store and escape in a truck filled with rotting meat. The restaurant is a space in which all corporeal acts are equal:

The Cook, The Thief, His Wife And Her Lover

eating, in this film, has just the same degree of brutal intensity as does sex, violence, torture, defecation, and the last bodily function of all, death. As the title of Greenaway's film suggests, this is a story of broadly-drawn characters – archetypes, almost – who have little hesitation about committing very sensual, and often physically brutal acts. The limited space of the film's setting conveys the appetitive nature of human existence in its raw entirety. Right outside the restaurant stand two truckfuls of rotting meat that no-one ever gets around to unloading. Some ingredients are lovingly prepared and artfully cooked; others are simply allowed to rot. Food is consumed and excreted; bodies live and die. Gastronomic cannibalism is merely the final link in this unending corporeal chain.

CANNIBAL COMEDY

After receiving mixed reviews on its initial release in the US in 1982, Paul Bartel's sardonic cannibal comedy **Eating Raoul** has since become something of a cult item, attracting widespread popularity from the arthouse circuit as well as the home video audience. **Eating Raoul**, a good example of an original piece of independent but commercial film-making, tells the story of Paul (Paul Bartel) and Mary (Mary Woronov) Bland, a chaste, simple, suburban couple living in contemporary Los Angeles and disgusted by all the sex, violence and degeneracy that surrounds them in their daily life. The couple sleep in separate beds – Mary's full of stuffed animals – and consider sex to be tacky and dirty. Their dream is to move to a country house in Valencia, California and open their own restaurant, to be named "Paul and Mary's Country Kitchen", but they can't afford the down payment on the property shown to them by their estate agent friend James (Richard

Eating Raoul

Blackburn). After a series of somewhat improbable events which involve Paul being fired from his job as a liquor store clerk for ordering $500 bottles of vintage wine, and Mary being assaulted by her bank manager, the couple discover an unlikely way to make money. When a lowlife from a neighbouring apartment wanders in, throws up on the carpet then tries to assault Mary, Paul kills him by a blow to the head with a frying-pan. It turns out the drunk was a rich man, which inspires Paul and Mary to hatch up a means of both making money and cleaning up society in one fell swoop. By means of an ad in the local Hollywood contact magazine, they lure swingers looking for kinky sex back to their apartment where Paul murders them with a cast-iron frying pan just as they are about to molest the chaste Mary. Their scheme works well until they fall in with Raoul Mendoza (Robert Beltran), a passionate, macho Chicano locksmith who always returns to his clients' homes as a burglar. Breaking into the Blands' home that night, he discovers two dead bodies and proposes a deal to the Blands: he will dispose of the victims' personal effects and their bodies (which he sells to a dog food company), and split the proceeds with the couple. But the partnership works out badly and, after the Blands electrocute a hot-tub full of guests at a Beverly Hills swingers' party, and when Raoul demands the proceeds at gunpoint, the cast-iron frying pan is called upon to perform its loyal duty. With James due to arrive for dinner at any minute to close the deal on their new house, and with nothing in the refrigerator to eat, a use is soon found for Raoul's freshly-slaughtered body.

Genuinely funny in places, Bartel's tale of ridiculous extremes was made piecemeal, with money invested by family and friends, and includes a large cast playing a myriad of bit parts. Sometimes, however, the film's tone is sometimes difficult to pin down, as it swings from light character-comedy to bitter satire, and back again. "My movie touches on many things", claims Bartel: "the perversion of middle-class values, the resurgence of Nixonism, Latin machismo versus WASP fastidiousness, film noir. Finally, however, it's about how financial considerations overpower emotional ones". Not unlike Bob Balaban's **Parents** (see chapter 7), the film also makes a number of serious and mordant comments on American life and attitudes, on fifties consumerism and its dog-eat-dog spirit, and on the perversion of the American dream. The central metaphor of cannibalism, appearing not only in the final eating of Raoul but also in the metonymic device of execution by frying-pan, also has some serious social implications. Whilst condemning the way in which the dominant WASPS use and devour minority people, it also reveals how, on the decadent streets of L.A., the line between food and sex is starting to disappear.

1989 brought us a zany parody of feminist ideology entitled **Cannibal Women In The Avocado Jungle Of Death** (a.k.a **Piranha Women In The Avocado Jungle Of Death**), dir. J.D. Athens, a.k.a Jonathan Lawton (US, 1989). **Cannibal Women...** stars Shannon Tweed as Dr. Margo Hunt, an ethno-historian professor at a university's "Feminist Studies" department. The bluestocking Dr. Hunt is recruited by the government to lead an expedition into the jungles near San Bernardino to attempt to find the missing Dr. Kurtz (Adrienne Barbeau). The U.S. government suspect Dr. Kurtz has been the victim of a communist plot to destroy America's avocado crop, but it turns out the Feds are actually out to destroy an ancient tribe of militant feminists living in the jungle, preying off a neighbouring tribe of wimpy males called the Donnahews. With her airhead assistant Bunny (Karen Mistal) and bumbling guide Jim (Bill Maher), Dr. Hunt pitches a battle for supremacy against Dr. Kurtz, finally uniting the Piranha Women with their rival tribe the Barracuda Women, from whom they split long ago due to an argument over which type of dip to use when eating their male victims.

Cannibal Women... is a spoof satire on feminist ideology, on the entire genre of misogynistic Italian cannibal films (and their feminist detractors), and on Conrad's *Heart Of Darkness*, although in this case, "the horror" that Dr. Kurtz has to contemplate is that of appearing on the David Letterman show and getting insulted whilst plugging her feminist book. The theme of cannibalism in this movie is simply all part of the fun. The film was originally titled **Piranha Women In The Avocado Jungle Of Death**, and the introduction of the word "cannibal" into the title was clearly intended to give the film more of a comic punch. Most of the satire in this movie comes from the long sequences of rapid-fire dialogue, clever puns and parodic ideas, but there is not much in the way of action (possibly due to an inadequate budget), making the film most successful as a late-night video choice for cannibal completists.

Jean-Pierre Jeunet and Marc Caro's 1991 surreal comedy **Delicatessen** is set in a decrepit city within a darkly bizarre, futuristic world where food shortages have led the local butcher (Jean-Claude Dreyfus) to serve up human flesh taken from the handymen that the butcher employs. This meat is served not only to the butcher's unsuspecting customers, but also to his tenants who live in the building above the delicatessen: the Kubes (Jacques Matou and Rufus), a pair of brothers who manufacture bleating toys, the Tapioca family (Ticky Holgado and

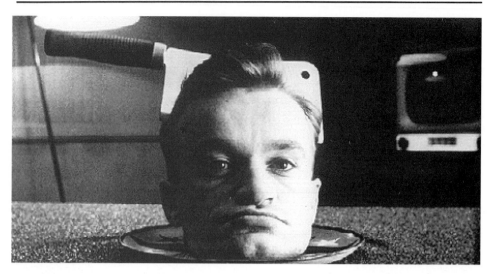

Delicatessen

Anne-Marie Pisani), the butcher's glamorous mistress Mademoiselle Plusse (Karin Viard), and the prissy Interligators (Jean-Francois Perrier and Silvie Laguna). Other strange characters who haunt the building include Monsieur Potin (Howard Vernon), who feeds himself by breeding snails and whose flat is two inches deep in water and escargot shells, and a brutish, armed postman (Chick Ortega) who holds people up when delivering the mail. The postman is in love with the butcher's short-sighted, cello-playing daughter Julie (Marie-Laure Dougnac), who is also desired by a naive comedian named Louison (Dominique Pinon), who moves into the flat above the deli after being forced to leave the circus due to his monkey partner being killed and eaten. Into this bizarre scenario bumble the Troglodins, an underground vegetarian resistance movement who live in the city's sewers and are engaged in a war on cannibal crime.

A strange and eccentric little film, **Delicatessen** gained its reputation at the Cannes film festival in 1991, where it was praised for its eerie camera techniques, including gracefully choreographed tracking shots which frame a number of memorable cinematic set-pieces, such as a sex scene between the butcher and his mistress that is shot from under the bed. The film also won praise for its dark setting in a post-apocalyptic future that has reverted to the shoddiness of wartime France. Time seems to be strangely out of kilter – characters remark that "there is nothing left outside", that "this is nowhere". Julie plays vintage songs on her record-player; Louison is seen on television doing his circus act in a decidedly retro setting. Yet at the same time, the technical style of the film, with its visual conjuring tricks, is parallel to that of French pop culture and MTV music videos.

The film opens with a close-up shot of the butcher sharpening his knives, then wielding a meat cleaver to lop a human hand off a corpse. Cannibalism is the central theme of this fascinating and morbid portrait of the darker side of human nature, which derives much of its power from the fact that the entire cast is made up of character actors, many of them quite grotesque in appearance, particularly the dwarfish Troglodins. If it can be compared to anything, the structure and style of **Delicatessen** resemble those of the circus, which plays a small but significant part in the film's subtext. Hallmarks of the circus style include

Delicatessen

distortion, exaggeration and extravagance, and it is in this tone that the expert acrobats Jeunet and Caro juggle their absurd and memorable cannibalistic motifs.

NOTES

1.   Jean-Denis Bonan's short French film **La Tristesse Des Anthropophages** (a.k.a. **The Sorrow Of The Cannibals**, 1966) also celebrates a type of carnival – the so-called "carnaval-scato" – in its depictions of a 3-star restaurant where the chefs serve up the speciality of the day hot and fresh from their bowels, and the diners perish, one by one, from dysentery. The "cannibalism" here extends only as far as eating the waste products of other people; this scatological or coprophagic cannibalism also appears in Pier Paolo Pasolini's **Salo** (1975), where girls imprisoned in a barracks are forced to eat from tureens of each others' faeces.

2.   Polanski had previously produced the original scenario for **Aimez-Vous Des Femmes?** (a.k.a. **Do You Like Women?**, 1963), a French black comedy about a society of cannibals in Paris who like to serve up tasty young girls for their dinner parties. The film was directed by Jean Léon, and the final dialogue was provided by Polanski's long-term collaborator, Gerard Brach (who also scripted **Repulsion**). Polanski has apparently had an abiding interest in the subject of cannibalism, and at one time planned to make a film based on the story of the Donner Party.

chapter two:
cannibals by nature or circumstance

"Let us eat and drink, for tomorrow we shall die."

—*Isaiah* xi. xxi. 13

DRAMATIC true adventures of human survival against all odds generally prove irresistible to film-makers, both in Hollywood and elsewhere. This following chapter provides a brief overview of films where cannibalism is indulged in because its perpetrators have either become accustomed to the consumption of human flesh as part of their daily diet, or else find themselves in circumstances where their own survival depends on their ability to overcome their natural repugnance, and feed on the bodies of their former friends.

"NATURAL" CANNIBALS

Perhaps the earliest appearance of "natural" cannibals on the cinema screen was in Walter McCutcheon's 1908 silent comedy, **King Of The Cannibal Islands** – a film notable not only for its presentation of top-hat wearing cannibals, but also for its use of D.W. Griffiths as an extra in a slapstick chase sequence. John Farrow's 1939 film **Five Came Back** (remade in 1956 as **Back From Eternity**), a jungle plane-crash adventure starring Lucille Ball and Chester Morris, was the first major fiction movie featuring "natural" cannibals in their soon-to-be familiar guise as threatening savages, although, as it turns out, they remain a threat in symbolic form only, since we never get to meet them. When we do finally meet a tribe of "natural" cannibals, in Lee Sholem's highly insipid **Cannibal Attack** (1954), it comes as something of a disappointment. **Cannibal Attack** was originally scripted as the latest of Columbia's ersatz-Tarzan "Jungle Jim" series, starring an over-the-hill Johnny Weissmuller as Jim, only Columbia had recently turned over the rights to the "Jungle Jim" sagas to its subsidiary, Screen Gems, so in **Cannibal Attack** Johnny plays Johnny, instead of Jim. The implausible narrative, fuelled with stock footage of jungle background and wild animals, begins when Johnny (Weissmuller, still adept in the water but starting to look a bit seedy), is assigned to investigate the disappearance of cargoes of cobalt from John King's mine. He eventually finds out that King's ward Luora (Judy Walsh), whose mother was the princess of a tribe of former cannibals, is implicated in a scheme to sell cobalt to a foreign power. Luora is supported by King (Stevan Darrell), who is in love with her, and by members of her ex-cannibal tribe, who carry out the cobalt thefts by donning crocodile skins, until Johnny gets involved and, after a journey down a crocodile-infested river and lots of fights with natives and crocodiles, foils the opposition with his mock-heroics, and imposes his own brand of jungle justice. The cannibals are cannibals by reputation only, and their "attack", when it comes, is somewhat less than full-hearted.

"DEATH LINE"

One of the most original and imaginative films made on the subject of circumstantial cannibalism in the last thirty years is Gary Sherman's 1972 debut film **Death Line** (a.k.a. **Raw Meat**). The original advertisements for the film prominently featured Christopher Lee, but he appears in the film only briefly, as part of a rather clumsy detective subplot. **Death Line**, a film that was mainly ignored by the critics at the time of its release, is the harrowing story of a cannibalistic race of people living in the caverns and tunnels of the London Underground. It is a film whose grim poetry lies partly in its setting. The dimly-lit, vaulted tunnels of the disused subway system combine the gothic nobility of dark, humid catacombs lit only by rays of light shining through the darkness, with the textures of the everyday – white, concrete tiles, burned ozone, and the implied stench of stale urine. The film gains much of its stark power from this contrast between the claustrophobic terror of this hideous underworld and the daylight "overworld" of tube trains, and modern civilization.

During the construction of a new London Underground station under the British Museum in 1892, a gigantic cave-in trapped a man and woman in a deserted tunnel. After all rescue efforts had been abandoned, the survivors were left to their own devices and began to breed. Over generations, plague, disease and incest have transformed their descendants, accustomed to this primitive way of life in the tunnels, into a cannibalistic clan deprived of language except for the only three words they ever hear: "Mind the doors". Eventually, the cannibals begin kidnapping people from subway platforms to feed themselves and one another.

The main body of the narrative begins with the last of the underground men (played by Hugh Armstrong), a scrofulous, drooling near-zombie covered in scars and oozing bald patches, bent in tender concern over a dying woman. He eventually loses his pregnant mate to a wasting disease after failing to revive her with the blood of a freshly-killed corpse, and is then compelled to search for a new bride from "outside" the tunnels.

After the last tube train has left Russell Square, two students from the London School of Economics, Alex (David Ladd) and Patricia (Sharon Gurney), find a well-dressed man unconscious on the platform, and learn his name from a card in his wallet. When they return with a policeman, however, the man has disappeared. The next day the two students are interviewed by Inspector Colquhoun (Donald Pleasance), who informs them that a number of people have disappeared from Underground platforms late at night, and this particular man was a high-ranking Defense Department employee. Stratton-Villiers of MI5 (Christopher Lee) tries to prevent further inquiries, but when three night workers are also murdered on the Underground, Colquhoun, an aloof and resilient loner with no apparent human ties, decides to investigate further.

The daydreaming Patricia, stranded alone on a station platform, is kidnapped by the underground man who emerges suddenly from the tunnels, grabs hold of her, steals her away into his underground world, and courts her as best he can. When she is threatened by a huge, menacing rat, the cannibal saves her by taking off its head in one huge bite and offering the twitching body to his new bride to eat. Like the fairy-tale princess, Patricia, who was always fond of books about the supernatural, is wholly transformed by this experience, her innocence tainted, her view of the world completely altered. In the closing moments of the film, she finally comes to feel compassion for the monster, whose relentless ordeal is not totally dissimilar to her own, and comes to understand that the world is far from being the clear-cut place she once thought it was. As in the story of "Beauty And The Beast", the plight of the cannibal is a sympathetic and moving one. His fragile hopelessness becomes ours, and we soon come to see him

Death Line

as an inept, plague-ridden, underground messiah with only three words to help him achieve his sacred reproductive quest, whose epic proportions are vivified by the stacks of mummified bodies of his ancestors, lining the tunnels in which he dwells. But these three words are his bible, and he pronounces them again and again, with every possible tone and nuance, as he attempts to communicate with his prospective bride, illuminating the immaculate quality of his love. The cannibal's quest, however, is ultimately in vain. He is callously killed at the end of the film when Alex, who has been searching the tunnels looking for Patricia, discovers her on the verge of being raped, and brutally crushes the cannibal's skull with the heel of his boot.

Clearly, this is a cannibal film with a conscience, and analogies between man and monster are not difficult to draw. The underground world and its denizens is an unwanted by-product of the social order – in this instance, the anonymous company responsible for the survivors' ordeal, which declared bankruptcy and abandoned the half-finished Underground station and its inhabitants, trapped in the rubble. Society is the real villain of this film – namely, the kind of capitalist society that abandons its disenfranchised children, denying them their human essence because they are the wrong colour or speak the wrong language, only to see them resurface several generations later as cannibalistic creatures – the ultimate underprivileged wretches – whose only resource is to drain the life out of the very society which created them. Much can also be made out of the implicit connections between the world above and the world below, and their unspoken dependence on one another for survival: whether literal, social or economic. The surface world of technology and social progress is inextricably linked to this terrible underground world of degraded humanity, with all the mythological overtones that it contains.

CIRCUMSTANTIAL CANNIBALS

A group of explorers are trapped in a cave for days, without provisions or hope of rescue. Finally, they decide to draw straws in a lottery to decide who will sacrifice a part of his body so the others may live. One man pulls the short straw; his arm is cut off and eaten. Rescue suddenly comes, just hours after the event; the man bitterly swears revenge. The survivors go their separate ways.

Years later, they begin to die, one by one, in mysterious and violent circumstances... Such is the premise for Thomas S. Alderman's **The Severed Arm** (1973), a bizarre low-budget entry in which enforced cannibalism leads to psychosis not – as usual – in the cannibals, but in their victim.

1973 also saw the release (briefly, since Warner Brothers withdrew it and disowned it shortly afterwards) of **Welcome To Arrow Beach** (a.k.a. **Tender Flesh**), directed by and starring Laurence Harvey. A teenager escapes from a car-crash and finds herself on Arrow Beach, where she encounters a photographer (Harvey) and his sister. They offer her a room for the night, but she finds herself being stalked by the man, who is seeking to prey on her flesh. It turns out he was marooned on a deserted island during the Korean War, and was forced to eat the bodies of his co-pilots to survive. He thus acquired the taste for human meat which he has had to indulge ever since. All in all, a bizarre movie and an even more bizarre final appearance by Laurence Harvey.

The year is 2002. New York City is an over-populated, smog-insulated police state governed by impersonal authorities in strange foreign uniforms. Food has become a luxury item; most of it is made synthetically, from the sea. When the people begin to riot over shrinking food supplies, huge, power-operated scoops neatly lift the demonstrators off the streets and dump them in handy garbage receptacles. So begins Richard Fleischer's 1973 sci-fi cult movie, **Soylent Green**, developed from a script by Stanley R. Greenberg of the story by Harry Harrison.

Detective Thorn (Charlton Heston), a man who genuinely believes in the social system but has been imbued by his job with a tendency towards bullying and abuse, is assigned to the assassination of the well-known industrialist Joseph Cotten whose company, the Soylent Corporation, is no longer able to make synthetic food and has begun to reconstitute the bodies of the dead: a plausible answer to overpopulation and the gradual diminution of the planet's food supply. Thorn's superiors, Hatcher (Brock Peters) and Santini (Whit Bissell) want the assassination covered up; his aide Sol Roth (Edward G. Robinson) reminisces about the old days of green fields, flowers, and natural foods. Complications arise when Thorn falls for Shirl (Leigh Tyler-Young), Cotten's mistress, abandoning his own piece of "furniture" – the word used in this world for wives and mistresses – Martha (Paula Kelly).

Ironically for a role that turned out to be Edward G. Robinson's valedictory performance, Sol Roth elects to end his life with the facility of the suicide "pleasuredome", wherein a huge, cinerama-type presentation of flowers, animals and fresh water ushers the willing victim into the bowels of the Soylent factory so that his body may be reconstituted into food to the strains of his own choice. This episode is one of many similar restrained and understated depictions

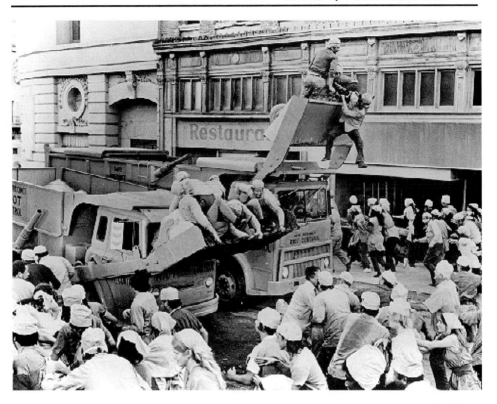

Soylent Green

of very proximate and credible future anxieties, whose plausibility to a contemporary audience helped Fleischer's film achieve its high cult status.

One of the most civilized and redemptive incidents of cannibalism in the recent history of cinema occurs in Jon Avnet's heartwarming trip to the old south, **Fried Green Tomatoes At The Whistle Stop Café** (1991). The story is told in nostalgic flashback by Idgie Threadgood (Jessica Tandy), now an old lady but once a feisty tomboy (Mary Stuart Masterson). In her youth, the gambling, trouser-wearing Idgie was best friends with the God-fearing Ruth (Mary Louise Parker), who subsequently married a brutish and abusive husband Frank Bennet (Nick Searcy), who takes her away with him to Georgia. On learning of her friend's abuse, Idgie, helped by the son of the family's seamstress, rescues Ruth from the clutches of her husband and brings her back to Whistle Stop, where the two of them open up a café popular with both blacks and whites. When Frank comes to town with his fellow Klansmen, he is prevented by the townsfolk from taking Ruth's new baby. When he tries again, he is hit on the head with a frying pan, and Idgie ominously tells Ruth that he will not be returning. Later on, at the end of the film, the aged Idgie reveals the truth about Frank's disappearance for the first time. After the fatal blow with the frying pan, a barbecue for the townsfolk disposed of the evidence.

The well-known story of the Donner party catastrophe, which saw snowbound pioneers reduced to cannibalism in the Sierra Nevada during the bitter winter of 1846, provided the inspiration for two films: the Classics Illustrated telepic of 1978, and Ric Burns's polite, elegiac PBS documentary **The Donner Party** (1992). This later film is impeccably researched, and relies for its impact on an array of photographs, documents, maps, letters, writings and original footage of western landscapes, all of which help to vivify and personalize a distant time. Burns assembles a range of well-known actors to read letters and diary entries, and historical commentary is used to back up footage of the plains, mountains and snowstorms of the Sierra Nevada. Apparently, Roman Polanski had been considering a movie based on the story of the Donner Party since long before the Sharon Tate murders. Polanski's version, had he made one, might have been less thoroughly researched and less historically accurate than the PBS version, but perhaps would have been more vivid and dramatic in expressing the raw, shocking realities of the events. Whilst Burns's **The Donner Party** is a compelling historical documentary, its genteel style is somewhat inadequate for evoking the destructive elemental forces that doomed the party, and the extremes of behaviour to which they were reduced. In the end, Burns's film is closer to the lame Classics Illustrated telepic than the true horror of what actually happened in the mountains.

"Their soul abhorred all manner of meat: and they were even hard at death's door."

—*Psalms* cvii. 18

The Andes plane crash of 1972, during which a plane chartered by an amateur rugby team crashed in the Andes, led to a number of made-for-TV movies and a few decent films, among them **Survive!** (a.k.a. **Supervivientes De Los Andes**), directed in Mexico by René Cardona in 1976, and Frank Marshall's **Alive!** (US 1993, with John Malkovich and Ethan Hawke). Based on Piers Paul Read's best-selling book of the same name, **Alive!** is rather less graphic and vivid than Read's version of the events, but equally well-researched nonetheless. The movie begins with a brief introduction to the distinguishing characteristics of each personality as the boys play in the small aircraft, laughing, taking photographs of one another and throwing rugby balls around. Hitting a pocket of cloudy weather above the *cordillera*, the plane begins to shake, but most of the boys are unconcerned, climbing around on the seats and joking with each other about the bad weather. These very first scenes establish the film's central issue: conventional behaviour and its counterpart – the transgression of social and moral prohibitions.

The film's technical achievements are considerable, particularly the jaw-dropping air crash sequence, courtesy of Industrial Light and Magic, in which the plane literally comes apart before our eyes, sucking out several passengers. But the accident itself, whilst replicated down to the most terrifying detail, still seems to be attributed somehow to the unforeseen weather conditions rather than pilot error, which – as Read makes clear – was actually the case. Similar diversions from Read's account of the catastrophe include, as might be expected, the fact that Parrada, Canessa, Vizintin and the other boys are, without exception, handsome, athletic and clean-looking, even after seventy days in the mountains. The filthy, bedraggled scavengers of Read's account are virtually unrecognizable in the blond, clean cut, Nordic-looking Ethan Hawke (as Parrada) and Josh Hamilton (as Canessa). It is also rather unfortunate that a strong physical resemblance amongst some of the actors coupled with indistinct personalities make it sometimes difficult to keep track of the narrative.

Some incidents are recreated just as Read describes them, including the removal of a steel pipe from one boy's intestines, the allocation to each survivor of a capful of wine and a piece of chocolate each per day, the way in which order very quickly begins to disintegrate and people's self-control quickly starts to

Alive!

collapse, and especially the resentment fostered by Antonio Perez as self-appointed leader. Marshall is also honest and accurate in his depiction of the burial of the dead bodies in a blizzard, the meagreness of the food rations, the boys' gradual physical weakening, and the airplanes which occasionally pass by overhead, constantly raising and frustrating the team's rescue hopes. Other scenes which reproduce the accuracy of Read's account include Perez's disgust and anger at discovering the boys pilfering from the food supply, incidents of mutinous outrage and fighting amongst the survivors, the eight deaths during the avalanche, Liliana Methol's decision that she wants another baby (ironically, only a day before her death), the splitting up of the survivors into cliques, the agonized cries of the injured keeping the boys awake at night, and the importance to the whole group of their Catholic faith, manifested in the form of prayer and the recitation of the rosary. These heroic elements, however, as the survivors' ranks dwindle, aren't always uplifting enough to make it worthwhile. But the film poignantly evokes the boys' dashed expectations, tragic misjudgments, bad timing and misguided faith with a raw and emotive power.

At the same time, Read's compelling version of events is made less stark and traumatic by Peter James's romantic cinematography. Shots of the mountains in a hazy blue light are backed up by gentle South American pipe music or, at more optimistic moments, the cumulative strains of a full orchestra. Pipe music also accompanies the mass said by the survivors at the graveside of their dead companions, and Christmas carols are sung in the plane at night. Marshall also enlivens and romanticizes Read's version of events with the addition of new or embellished incidents and images. A guitar somehow survives the crash, and its strings are plucked romantically by various members of the team from time to time. Canessa collapses through the snow and is saved by the skin of his teeth from falling down an enormous precipice. Later, the boys shoot gleefully down the sides of the mountains on makeshift sledges, and, in fun, use paper money to light their cigarettes.

The film does its best to evoke the individual personality of each character and to give an accurate impression of the changing dynamics of the group. Marshall makes much of the way Nando gradually comes to replace the autocratic Perez as group leader, and the way he persuades the weakening Javier Methol to finally take a portion of meat. As Read suggests, tensions become extremely torn and ragged during the various expeditions, and Roy, who virtually cracks up under the pressure of the miserably slow progress, eventually becomes something of a scapegoat for the other boys. Perez too, in the end, breaks down in tears, professing that he no longer has the strength to attempt to save his companions. In general, however, the survivors are portrayed as being far more upbeat, united and organized than Read seems to suggest they were. Marshall also feels it necessary to adapt the character of Ramirez, the steward, into that of a loopy and belligerent mechanic.

It is Nando, in the film, who first addresses the subject of consuming human flesh, suggesting light-heartedly that they should begin by eating the pilots, since they were responsible for crashing the plane in the first place. After Perez hears the news on the radio that the search has been finally called off, Nando, believing the survivors to be on the verge of death from starvation, brings up the subject again, and this time more seriously. At first, as Read relates, most of the survivors found the notion of cannibalism quite disgusting until they managed to rationalize it theologically, in terms of the relationship between body and soul. Still, the remaining survivors stay up all night discussing the step, praying, debating and considering, and finally pledging that if they themselves should die, they will allow the others to use their bodies as food. Only after rationalizing human cannibalism as a kind of ceremony of initiation, or magical ritual akin to the Catholic communion, do the remaining survivors manage to overcome their initial reluctance and set about cutting up the dead bodies for food.

This descent through various levels of human desperation into the extremes of cannibalism is what makes the story of the Andes survivors so shocking and compelling. For understandable reasons, perhaps, Marshall's film makes the process appear far more wholesome and natural than it is described in Read's book. In Marshall's **Alive!**, the uncooked flesh looks uncannily like chicken drumsticks. Cooked flesh bears more of a resemblance to streaky bacon, and looks even rather appetizing. According to Read, however, after only two weeks of starting to eat the bodies of their companions, the survivors' crash site became strewn with pieces of flesh and fat, odd bits of gristle, brain, and human bones. The film shows us nothing of the survivors' scavenging pieces of skin, tendons or blood clots, or bones to gnaw on, nor the human hands and feet taken into the body of the plane to assuage midnight hunger pangs. Indeed, whilst cannibalism is still transgressive enough a subject to make the story of the Andes survivors especially shocking and exciting, the subject is treated extremely tactfully. Director Marshall and screenwriter John Patrick Shenley take pains to play down this theme, and turn the thrust of the picture to religion, including plenty of redundant and clichéd dialogue about God being all around in the mountains. Nor are we shown the socks full of human flesh packaged for the expeditions, nor the survivors' quest for new gastronomic tastes:

"[T]hey... sought to make what food they had last longer by eating parts of the human body which previously they had left aside. The hands and feet, for

example, had flesh beneath the skin which could be scraped off the bone. They tried, too, to eat the tongue off one corpse but could not swallow it, and one of them once ate the testicles... They also ate the blood clots which they found around the hearts of almost all the bodies... the entrails... the small intestine... the liver... muscle, fat, heart and kidneys, either cooked or uncooked, were cut up into little pieces and mixed with the brains."

—Read: 1992:162–3

In the end, whilst it is sometimes a compelling film, Marshall's **Alive!** never completely succeeds in evoking the fraught, stark agony of the ten-week ordeal. There is too much romantically-lit photography, beautiful mountain scenery and tender scenes of togetherness and camaraderie, particularly between husband and wife Javier and Liliana Methol, who spend most of the film gently singing lullabies to one another and reminiscing nostalgically about their home and children. The early phases of the film are too full of big, emotional flourishes. The infected wounds and physical injuries, described so vividly by Read in his book, are made little of, and the two principal protagonists are all in all too clean-shaven, athletic and healthy-looking to be on the verge of death by starvation. The avalanche, when it comes, is less devastating and destructive than Read describes it in his book, and the proceeding scenes of the burial of bodies and the clearing of snow are set to lively, uplifting music accompanied by much talk of God and mystical experiences. Finally, Parrada and Canessa's final expedition – an exhausting and lengthy trek over monotonous terrain, according to Read – is made highly dramatic, and full of gripping incidents and near death escapes amidst dramatic natural scenery: gigantic waterfalls, huge precipices and lofty, snowcapped mountains. Peter James' cinematography romanticizes the sweeping mountain vistas, in stark contrast to the cramped surroundings of the plane's cabin, where the survivors huddle seeking refuge from the blistering cold. In the end, the uneven, bitter, anti-climactic ending to Read's depressing narration is transformed by Marshall into a joyful carnival of celebration and reunion backed by a solo rendition of Bach's *Ave Maria*.

Perhaps understandably, there is no attempt made in Marshall's film to come to terms with the final chapter in Read's fascinating account, which details some of the confusing aftermath of the tragedy. This involved an ugly struggle amongst the survivors for media attention, widely-publicized photographs of the limbs and bones of the cannibalized victims, angry claims and counterclaims about the group dynamics during the accident, and the fact that at least one of the survivors currently suffers from mordant obesity, amongst other severe eating disorders related to their ordeal.

1995 saw the video release of a production by Cannibal Films Ltd. called **Alferd Packer – The Musical** (a.k.a. **Cannibal – The Musical**), purporting to be recovered footage from a 1954 musical of the Alferd Packer case (see chapter 1) which was, at the time, upstaged by the success of *Oklahoma!* and is now being presented in its own right for the first time. The gimmick is, of course, a hoax, introducing us to the blackly comic tone of a musical written, produced and directed by Trey Parker, a film student at Columbia University, who also plays the leading role in the film (under the pseudonym Juan Schwarz). Parker also wrote many of the songs, and collaborated on the score. After raising $75,000 from friends, family, and private investors, Parker, together with fellow film school students Matt Stone, Jason McHugh and Ian Hardin (average age twenty-three), formed the Avenging Conscience Production Company and employed fellow

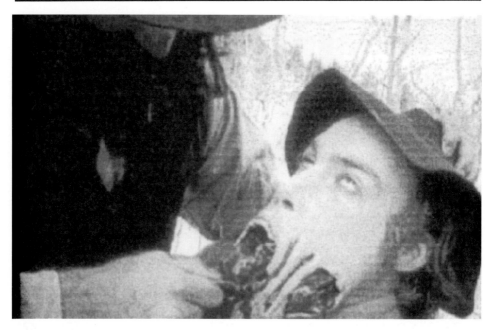

Alferd Packer

students as cast members, stepping into one another's shoes behind the camera when necessary. From conception to completion the film took twelve months, and received a warm reception at screenings and film festivals, drawing comparisons to Mel Brooks, Monty Python and George A. Romero.

Described elsewhere as "Cannibal Apocalypse meets Oklahoma", **Alferd Packer** claims to be "a singalong story of gold, cannibalism, and a simple man's love for his horse" boasting "seven wonderful songs, magnificent mountain vistas and a flesh-eating madman". The musical opens with a gloriously sickening reconstruction of Packer's alleged crime, including Packer pulling off and eating the arms of one of his still-healthy companions, chewing out another's neck tendons, and finally – Herschell Gordon Lewis-style – pulling out the enormous tongue of another by the root, and dangling it, still twitching, above his drooling mouth. The film then cuts, disappointingly, to Packer in a court – found guilty and sentenced to execution – asserting that "that's not the way it happened". The rest of the film presents Packer's version of events as flashback, as told from his prison cell to Polly Pry (Toddy Walters), a local reporter.

In 1873, a group of four gold prospectors and a butcher, Wilson Shannon Bell (Ian Hardin), guided by Packer, leave Brigham Mine in Utah for the town of Breckenridge in Colorado Territory. An honest simpleton in love with his horse, Leanne, Packer leads the cheery Mormon miners through all manner of adventures and distractions, including a confrontation with a weird prophet who tells them they're all doomed to die, a death-defying encounter with a bear trap, a dangerous river crossing, a meeting with a vicious set of trappers and some terrible jokes (including one involving the introduction of some fudge simply because of its resonances with the guide's surname). The miners have Jesus on their side, and plenty of rousing, cheery songs to help them on their journey east, but when after three weeks they are only just outside Provo, and Packer's horse has vanished, a note of anxiety creeps into their collective mood.

A few weeks later, they cross over into Colorado Territory and meet a group of Chinese Samurai dressed as Red Indians who take them to their encampment in Delta, Colorado. At the Indian camp, a re-encounter with the vicious trappers and the discovery of Leanne's food bag leads to a lengthy argument about whether trappers are better than miners, and the trappers burst into a memorable song-and-dance routine including the chorus "I love the sound of metal/snapping on an animal's head;/sometimes they struggle, sometimes they whimper,/but they always end up dead". When the trappers leave the reservation with Leanne, Packer and his men attempt to follow them, but Packer turns out to be not much use as a guide and gets lost on the way to Breckenridge, deep in the Rocky Mountains. The men lose all hope when they run out of food; one goes mad and the others shoot him; the rest are forced to barbecue their boots. A discussion of the Donner Party leads them to form the idea of eating one another as they die off, one by one. They begin with the body of their mad companion, all tucking into his severed limbs with relish – all, that is, except Packer, who tries just a small bite then throws up demonstratively. The next day, the men make a camp and Packer goes on ahead to check the route. When he returns, all the remaining member of the party are dead except for Shannon Bell, the butcher, who seems to have gone over the edge into a state of crazed delirium and seems on the verge of killing Packer as well. In self-defense, Packer does what he has to do and sinks a cleaver into the mad butcher's face, a barbecue skewer in his eye, and a pick axe in his chest.

chapter three:

cannibal families

"Bone of my bones, and flesh of my flesh"

—*Genesis* I. 23

A CCORDING to anthropology, a culture is compelled to repeat, through its own narratives, the symbolic tale of its origins. In early societies, myths were used to deal with the particular series of semiotic and iconographic elements that represent a culture's value systems, rituals, ethical conflicts and moral inconsistencies. In today's society, it has been argued that the modern version of myth is the film genre, which involves a ritualized and systematic exploration of a culture's founding values by way of an institutionalized, mass-mediated popular culture. The western, for example, has much in common with the epic, while the horror movie relies for its innate symbolic resonance on the structure of the fairy tale.

The many different functions of the fairy tale within modern society have been explored in depth, by Freud, Bettelheim, and others. It is generally agreed that fairy tales, whether early or modern, have much to teach their young readers or audiences about the conditions of human consciousness, about the inner problems of human beings, and about finding the right solutions to their physical and psychological predicaments. More specifically, according to Bettelheim, the fairy tale helps its young reader to master the psychological problems of growing up, problems which involve such difficulties as "overcoming narcissistic disappointments, Oedipal dilemmas, sibling rivalries, becoming able to relinquish childhood dependencies, gaining a feeling of self-worth, and a sense of moral obligation" (Bettelheim 1976:6). Through its unambivalent plots and archetypal polarization of human characteristics, the fairy tale entertains the child, enlightens him about himself, and fosters his personality in development. In its narrative and allegorical capacities, the fairy tale, it has been claimed, enriches the child's existence in a multitude of diverse ways.

In Freudian terms, the importance of the fairy tale relates to the fact that such stories unfold within an animistic universe, governed by the belief that spirits, good and bad, inhabit all things, and that thoughts and wishes are all-powerful over physical reality. Animism is the force that forges the mind of the child, and also the mind of the neurotic, and represents the primitive incarnations of all cultures. Freud argues that none of us has passed through this animistic stage of development without unconsciously retaining certain residues and traces of it which are still capable of manifesting themselves in those feelings of fear and terror Freud refers to as the uncanny: "everything that now strikes us as uncanny fulfils the condition of touching those residues of animistic mental activity within us and bringing them to expression" (Freud 1923:240–1). This is the symbolic structure linking the fairy tale with the horror film. The fairy tale takes place in a primitive, animistic universe ruled by spirits and magic: the horror film also gives us glimpses of this animistic state of mind, but in a repressed, unconscious form, and thus recognizable only as terrifying, bewildering, and often malefic.

Most traditional horror films share the functions of the fairy tale in that they serve to teach their mainly teenage audiences of the dangerous consequences of inappropriate sexual (and other) behaviour, thereby serving as a ritual process of acculturation for the modern adolescent, just as the fairy tale helps the child to come to terms with many of the psychological problems of growing up. Most horror films, by affording their audience uncanny glimpses of the fairy tale's animistic universe, lead them through the dangers of the adolescent sexual predicament, reinforcing the culture's taboos in a ritual display of rule-breaking. Occasionally, and often accidentally, certain films are made which transgress the structures and traditions of a genre, sometimes with notorious consequences. This chapter will be examining a brief selection of some such films.

Perhaps the most infamous of these inverted fairy tales is Tobe Hooper's **The Texas Chain Saw Massacre** (1974), in which a sustained inversion of the symbolic rituals and motifs of the fairy tale creates an apocalyptic narrative of negativity and destruction, wholly unredeemed by any single element of plot, mood or characterization. Through its systematic inversion of the fairy tale structure, **The Texas Chain Saw Massacre** functions not, as most horror films, to acculturate its adolescent audience into the difficulties of adulthood and the inconsistencies of human consciousness, but serves instead to mislead, misdirect and confuse its audience in a bewildering nightmare of violence and bloodshed.

The film begins with a fairy tale warning:

"The film which you are about to see is an account of the tragedy which befell a group of five youths, in particular Sally Hardesty and her invalid brother Franklin. It is all the more tragic in that they were young. But had they lived very, very long lives, they could not have expected, nor would they have wished to see as much of the mad and macabre as they were to see that day. For them, an idyllic summer afternoon drive became a nightmare. The events of that day were to lead to the discovery of one of the most bizarre crimes in the annals of American history. The Texas Chain Saw Massacre."

A group of teenage friends are enjoying a day out in their camper van: Sally Hardesty (Marilyn Burns), her wheelchair-bound brother Franklin (Paul A. Partain), her boyfriend Jerry (Allen Danziger), and their friends Kirk (William Vail) and Pam (Teri McMinn). During the trip, the radio reports a series of bizarre grave robbings in local cemeteries. The friends, worried about Sally's grandfather, stop at one of the cemeteries but Sally is unable to locate her grandfather's grave. Moving on, the friends pick up a "weird looking" hitchhiker (Edwin Neal) with a huge birthmark and twisted face, who proceeds to disgust them with tales of the local slaughterhouse (where Sally and Franklin's uncle also works), then takes Franklin's pen-knife, slits open the palm of his hand and proceeds to turn the knife on Franklin. Thrown out into the road, he smears the van with blood, laughing and cursing.

Pulling into an isolated garage, Kirk discovers that they are short on fuel and there will be no gas delivery until the next morning. The friends drive a short distance to a dilapidated house by a creek, owned by Sally and Franklin's grandfather. Sally and Jerry explore the old house, leaving Franklin downstairs, while Pam and Kirk set off for a swim. Discovering the creek has dried up, however, they decide instead to investigate a neighbouring house they believe may have a gas pump. Pam remains in the garden while Kirk goes inside. Here, he is attacked and killed with a sledge hammer wielded by Leatherface, a huge

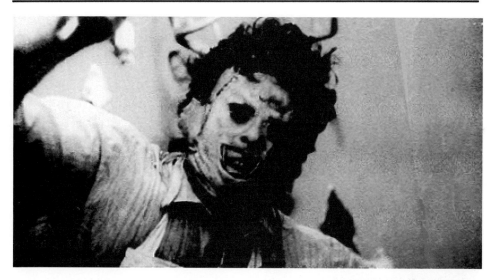

The Texas Chain Saw Massacre

masked figure in a leather apron (Gunnar Hansen). Pam, looking in the house for Kirk, discovers a room full of bizarre artifacts and human remains. She too is attacked by the masked man, dragged into a back room and impaled on a meat hook. Pam is followed by Jerry who, exploring the house, discovers Pam's dead body in a meat freezer, then is killed himself by a hammer-blow to the head.

Meanwhile, back at the van, the sun has set and Sally and Franklin decide to go in search of the others together. Sally pushes Franklin up the hill in his wheelchair, but on the way the pair are attacked by Leatherface, wielding a buzzing chain saw, and Franklin is killed. Sally, chased into the house, runs into the attic where she discovers what appear to be the decomposing bodies of two people and a dog. She escapes by hurling herself through the window and runs to the garage for help. Here, however, instead of helping her, the garage owner (Jim Siedow) attacks her with a broomstick, puts her in a sack and drives her back to the house where she is tied to a chair at the dinner-table and tortured and tormented by a whole family of slaughterers, including the hitch-hiker, until she once again manages to escape, again through the window. In the light of early dawn, she limps, blood-splattered, to the highway, pursued by Leatherface with his buzzing chain saw, where she flags down a truck (which runs over the deranged hitch-hiker on the way) whose driver, in a vain attempt to rescue her, is killed by Leatherface, but not before a brief fight during which Leatherface is injured by his own chain saw. Moments later, Sally flags down a second truck and manages to climb in the back, leaving Leatherface swinging his chain saw through the air with rage and frustration.

Chain Saw has spawned three sequels, none of which contain anything like the violent impact of the original. **Texas Chain Saw Massacre 2** (Tobe Hooper, 1984) stars Dennis Hopper as a saw-wielding preacher on the trail of his nephew's murderers in a disused funhouse. Jeff Burr's **Leatherface – Texas Chain Saw Massacre 3** (1989) is set in the deepest swamplands of the south, and camps up the cannibal theme of the original, while Kim Henkel's **Return Of The Texas Chain Saw Massacre** (1994) is a re-make of the first movie with additional characters and sub-plots. Although Henkel was co-writer of the original **Chain Saw**, his version pales beside it.

The Texas Chain Saw Massacre 2

Made four years later, Wes Craven's **Chain Saw**-influenced **The Hills Have Eyes** tells a similar story, introducing a number of new angles to the original "cannibal family" motif. En route to California in their mobile home, the Carters, from Cleveland, take a detour into the deserted mountains to check out a diamond mine left to them by relatives in a will. When Father is swerving to avoid a rabbit, the van's axle snaps and the family are stranded. Father (Russ Grieve), known as Big Bob, decides to walk back to a gas station they passed a few miles back. Son-in-law Doug (Martin Speer) ventures out in the opposite direction, to see if he can find any material for fixing the axle. The two dogs, Beauty and Beast, run off into the mountains. The youngest son Bobby (Robert Houston), searching for them, discovers the mangled body of Beauty, her intestines lying on the rocks beside her.

Night falls. Back at the camper van, the family are getting nervous. Doug returns, empty-handed. Just as the family (minus Big Bob) are retiring for the night, screams are heard in the hills. Big Bob, on his way back from the gas station, has been attacked by a savage family of cave-dwelling cannibals and his body set alight. Doug, Bobby and mother Ethel (Virginia Vincent) run to his rescue, but it is too late – his body is virtually unrecognizable. Meanwhile, the cannibal family have launched their assault on the trailer. Pluto (Michael Berryman), a monstrous, bald-headed giant, breaks into the family's kitchen, steals meat and milk from the fridge, strangles the family's pet canary, and drinks its blood. He then begins to rape the youngest daughter Brenda (Susan Lanier), until interrupted by his brother Jupiter (James Whitworth). Instead, Pluto steals the oldest daughter's baby (Katy), kills the daughter (Lynne, played by Dee Wallace-Stone), shoots Brenda, then shoots Mother on her return to the trailer. The cannibals then escape into the night with the baby, leaving only Bobby, Doug and the injured Brenda left alive.

The cannibal family then return to their den in the hills, exhibiting the wailing baby to their savage father (John Steadman), wild mother (Cordy Clark)

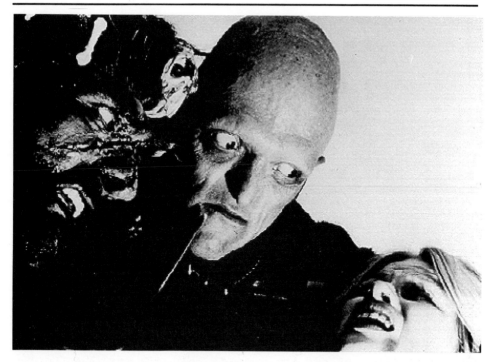

The Hills Have Eyes

and tearaway sister Ruby (Janus Blythe). However, the remaining members of the "civilized" family are about to launch their counter-attack. Doug locates the cannibals' den, while Bobby and Brenda use their mother's corpse to trick Pluto and booby-trap the trailer with explosives to kill his father. Finally, with the help of his dog Beast and the cannibal daughter Ruby (who is unable to bring herself to destroy the crying baby), Doug finally confronts Jupiter in the hills, tricks him into being bitten by a rattlesnake, then finally finishes him off with his pocket knife.

1985 brought us **The Hills Have Eyes Part 2**, which, although directed by Wes Craven, retains very little of the life and verve of the original. Funded by British home-video companies and shot in California in the fall of 1983, **Part 2** retains only four members of the cast of the original: Michael Berryman (Pluto), Janus Blythe (Ruby), James Whitworth (Jupiter) and Robert Houston (Bobby). Bobby Carter, now grown up, is plagued by nightmares of the desert massacre he survived in the original movie. Bobby has invented a new petrol formula which his local motor-cross club is testing in an upcoming race. Ruby, who has escaped her cannibal family and hooked up with the survivors, is taking the bikers to the race in a red school bus when they foolishly try to take a shortcut across the desert to make up for lost time.

From this point on, the original version is replayed, this time with one attractive teenager after another being slaughtered in a vengeful attack by Pluto and Jupiter, the two surviving cannibals.

Part 2 is really little more than a pointless cash-in, with numerous flashbacks by characters replaying the events of the original film, and when Craven runs out of human survivors, even the surviving dog, Beast, is given a flashback of its very own.

Parents

Bob Balaban's 1989 cannibal movie **Parents** begins in 1950s suburbia, when little Michael Laemmle (Bryan Madorsky) moves, with his parents, to his new home in a small Indiana town. The world of his parents seems increasingly bizarre to Michael, who spends most of his time with another new kid in town, Sheila (Juno Mills-Cockell), a little girl who claims to be an alien. Michael is terrified of his bullying father Nick (Randy Quaid), and his mother Lily (Mary Beth Hurt) seems to spend most of her time keeping up a fashionable appearance. Michael's parents seem to share an unusually secretive private life which Michael finds rather difficult to understand; they also seem strangely fascinated by food, and copious quantities of red meat are always available at home. Michael's mother describes them as "leftovers", but never lets us know precisely what they are left over from.

Michael begins to suffer from recurring nightmares around the theme of red meat, and, at school, paints a picture of family life so disturbing and so heavily crayoned in red that his teacher Miss Baxter (Kathryn Grody), who already finds him eccentric, brings Michael's picture to the attention of the school psychiatrist, Millie Dew (Sandy Dennis). Miss Dew, on the wrong track, suspects that Michael's growing sexual awareness is responsible for his bloody nightmares and strange picture.

Determined to find the roots of his parents' unusual passion, Michael secretly follows his father to work one morning. Mr. Laemmle is employed by a laboratory where the effects of new chemicals are tested on recently deceased (and sometimes still living) human bodies. Michael is almost caught and escapes discovery only by hiding under a dissecting trolley while his father works on cutting up a corpse. That night, exploring the cellar, Michael comes across a human leg hanging from a meat hook. Next day he tells Miss Dew what he has seen, and she accompanies him home and discovers a corpse, but before she can leave she is attacked and killed by Michael's father.

That evening, at dinner, when confronted by a pile of juicy steaks, Michael refuses to eat, and demands an explanation. His father reassures him that he'll soon get a taste for human flesh, just like his mother did. Michael tries to stab his father with a steak knife but, protecting her son, Mother is accidentally killed, and Father, chasing down his son, sets off a gas explosion that destroys the house – but not before Michael manages to escape. Sent to live with his loving grand-parents, Michael is settled down in bed with a midnight snack: a glass of milk and a sandwich, stuffed full of raw, red meat...

In Wes Craven's 1989 film **The People Under The Stairs**, the cannibal family is more traditional, and thereby somehow more frightening. In the deprived ghetto of an unnamed city live a poor black family, consisting of a young son, Poindexter (Brandon Quintin Adams), his older sister Ruby (Kelly Jo Minter), and their mother (Conni Marie Brazelton), who is dying of cancer. The family are the last in their building to resist eviction at the hands of the local slum landlord, and when news of their eviction finally comes, the family are desperate. A local hood, Leroy (Ving Rhames), suggests to Poindexter (known to his friends as 'Fool') a way in which he could both avoid eviction and pay for his mother's operation at the same time. According to Leroy, the slum landlord – a ghoulish figure living in the rich part of town – has a valuable collection of gold coins that Fool could easily steal.

The landlord (Everett McGill) and his wife (Wendy Robie) live in a beautiful but bizarre large wooden house with padlocks on all the windows. Their only daughter, Alice (A.J. Langer), is kept dressed like a little girl and locked in her bedroom in the attic. Taking advantage of the landlord and his wife's temporary absence, Leroy and Fool manage to sneak into the house and fend off the guard dog, Prince. Fool finds his way into the cellar where he is horrified to discover a group of pale, groaning near-zombies feeding off a dead body and moaning for more. Fool is rescued by Alice and the pair of them try to save Leroy, but he is shot and killed by Father, who has meanwhile returned home. Escaping back behind the walls of the house with her new friend, Alice tells Fool the story of her terrifying family.

Her mother and father, claims Alice, always longed for the perfect boychild, but all the boys they had "ended up bad", in one way or another, so her parents "cut out the bad bits" and put what remained of the boys in the cage in the cellar, where they are fed from time to time by Father tossing them hunks of human flesh to gnaw on. One son, Roach, who had his tongue cut out by Father, escaped from the cage and now lives in the walls of the house, where Father is

The People Under The Stairs

constantly hunting him down, shotgun in hand.

After discovering some of the pieces of gold, Fool and Alice climb to an attic window and shout for help. When no-one hears them, Fool jumps off the roof, lands in the pond and escapes into the ghetto, where he uses the stolen gold to pay his rent, and to pay for his mother's operation. At the same time, he learns from his grandfather that the landlord and his wife are not even married, but are in fact a brother and sister whose house was originally a funeral parlour. Over time, the siblings grew crazier and crazier, and began to abduct young children from the ghettos and conceal them in the cellar of their house. Alice herself, like Roach and all the boys in the cage, was one of those children. Learning this, Fool sends around both the police and the child welfare officers, but when they are all fobbed off by the cannibalistic "parents", Fool takes matters into his own hands, makes his way into the house and, as the blacks from the ghetto congregate outside, sets about rescuing Alice and getting rid of the murderers. In the final battle, the lost children emerge from all over the house – under the stairs, inside cupboards and chimneys, to escape outside. Finally. moments before he and Alice escape, Fool blows up the whole house with dynamite, destroying its evil inhabitants, and their hidden stash of stolen money floats down over the impoverished streets of the ghetto.

SATURN IN RETROGRADE

Like many horror films, the basic narrative structure of these four movies has elements in common with a number of popular fairy tales. Like "Jack And The Beanstalk", **The Texas Chain Saw Massacre, The Hills Have Eyes** and **The People Under The Stairs** all share the ascent into a secret world, ruled by an ogre, and the descent back into the "real" world at daybreak, given chase by the axe-wielding giant. The films also share structural parallels with "Beauty And The Beast" in the notion of the beautiful daughter being "stolen" by the ugly beast and dragged off into his own world (and note the fairy tale names of the pet dogs in **The Hills Have Eyes** and **The People Under The Stairs**: "Beauty", "Beast" and "Prince"), and "Little Red Riding Hood" in the notion of the girl being lured into the house by a monster in disguise. Like "Bluebeard", **The Texas Chain Saw Massacre**, **The People Under The Stairs** and **Parents** all revolve around the "dreadful room" with its terrible secret, and, like "Goldilocks", these three films all present us with an innocent child encountering a bestial family sitting round their table at dinner. "Young lady, we'll fetch you some supper", says Father to Sally in **Chain Saw**, in a macabre parody of Daddy Bear, and when she later regains consciousness, still tied to her chair, a plate with a knife and fork beside it have been placed on the table in front of her. "Mama Bear Carter calling", says Mother in **The Hills Have Eyes** into the CB radio in the trailer. And the monstrous family in **The People Under The Stairs** not only address each other as "Mommy" and "Daddy" (when they are, in fact, brother and sister), but dress their "little girl" in an old-fashioned pinafore dress, and sit her in a baby's high chair to take her meals. And, of course, both **Chain Saw**, **The People Under The Stairs** and **The Hills Have Eyes** share important structural parallels with "Hansel And Gretel", especially the notion of children lost in the woods or the mountains, stumbling across an attractive house owned by a cannibalistic fiend who kidnaps them and attempts to use them for food.

Other elements of these films' structures incorporate a number of random fairy tale symbols and motifs: the forest, the mountains, the broomstick, the woodcutter's axe, the mousetrap, lost children, the child in a sack, cage or oven, the bucket, gold coins, the dinner table, food preparation, the cellar, the fire and fireplace, the poker, the cave, the farm, cows, chickens and pigs, the giant, mice and rats, grandparents, the disguise, and the 'escape' back into the 'real' world at sunrise. Moreover, all four films revolve around the pivotal theme of the family. In **Parents**, the obliteration of the nuclear family group leaves Michael alone with his doting grandparents. In **Chain Saw**, just as the lost children comprise one family group – two young couples and a brother and sister – the fairy tale family is paralleled by the wizened and macabre family of men: Grandpa (virtually a corpse), Grandma (actually a corpse), their dog (mummified), Father (the garage owner), Leatherface (the eldest son), and the younger brother, Hitchhiker. **The Hills Have Eyes** also presents us with a fairy tale family: Mother (Ethel), Father (Big Bob), son (Bobby), two daughters (Brenda and Lynne), son-in-law (Doug), baby granddaughter (Katy), two pet dogs (Beauty and Beast) and a canary. This union finds its counterpart in the savage and terrifying anti-family of savages: Mama, Papa, three sons (Mercury, Jupiter and Pluto), a daughter (Ruby) and her pet piglet, a frightening anti-baby. And, most clearly of all perhaps, **The People Under The Stairs** pits its romanticized dysfunctional ghetto family (mother, daughter and son) against the barbaric cannibal siblings in the guise of Mother, Father, Daughter and their underground cage full of demented and mutilated sons.

The clan construction of the **Chain Saw** family reminds us, as Christopher Sharrett points out, that the story takes place in Texas, "a State brimming with folklore and key signifiers of frontier experience: the Alamo, Davy Crockett, cattle drives, frontier justice, Indian wars..." (Sharrett 1984:270), but due to the pathological inversions of this perverse folktale, Leatherface's mask is made not out of buckskin, but human flesh. **The Hills Have Eyes** takes place in the dark mountains of Death Valley, the home of ghost towns deserted in the gold rush, abandoned mining villages, streets given over to balls of floating tumbleweed, empty ranches like the Spahn movie ranch, home of the eerie Manson "family". In stark contrast, Balaban's **Parents** is set in a suburban Indiana town in 1958 and evokes the earnest respectability of family life, the importance of domestic gadgets, soap powders, television-commercial furniture and fashionable domesticity concealing a growing cultural turbulence. And **The People Under The Stairs**, as an allegory of the American economic situation, shows us the archetypal junk-riddled ghetto in stark juxtaposition with the genteel abundance of the suburbs, their bourgeois inhabitants living off the physical and emotional well-being of the poor. "You can't get out", says Alice of her parents' decadent household. "No-one ever has. People have tried." "It's as if we're the prisoners," says Mommy to Daddy later, "and the criminals roam free."

From the very opening of Hooper's **The Texas Chain Saw Massacre**, there are intimations of anarchy and disorder. Sally tries to restore a sense of stability, but she cannot even locate her grandfather's grave. By the time of her capture, the narrative has descended into a dark carnival of chaos and hysteria. Order and control have been abandoned; the potential violence of the dinner party recurrently lapses into absurdity as Grandpa, too weak to grasp the hammer, is unable to deliver his famous killing blow. All dialogue is drowned out by Sally's uncontrolled screaming, which does not abate as the film ends but transforms itself into hysterical laughter. Narrative stability evaporates right from the film's outset, when the radio report about grave robbings diverts Sally and her friends from whatever trip they were planning to take on that "idyllic summer afternoon", and leads them instead into the Other film: the unconscious of the traditional horror film narrative.

Similarly, the family in **The Hills Have Eyes** take a detour to find an abandoned diamond mine that doesn't even seem to be on the map. Mother has very little sense of direction, and despite being warned, like Little Red Riding Hood, to "stay on the main road", the family are soon lost in the darkness of the hills. After witnessing the violent death of his dog Beauty, Bobby becomes virtually catatonic, and when faced with the charred, twitching corpse of her husband, Mother collapses into a fit of hysterical, laughing denial ("That's not my Bob! That's not my husband!"), echoed by the gibbering of her son ("That's not my father!"). In **Parents** the reverse scenario is witnessed: Mother's obsession with domestic cleanliness and order, indicated by the spotless kitchen with its pristine array of domestic gadgets, disguises the parents' savage and chaotic dietary disorder, which turns their home into a gruesome slaughterhouse. Familial denial is also a theme here: Michael's violent attack on his father with a steak knife ends up with him murdering his mother in what is possibly an unconscious enactment of repressed desires. And in **The People Under The Stairs**, any semblance of racial or economic stability disintegrated long ago, leaving the pitiful grandeur of the suburbs under constant assault from the apocalyptic disarray of the ghetto. The surviving family, in this case, is the dysfunctional one. The decadent traditional family, descended into incestuous lunacy, have turned into cannibalistic child abusers who keep their "children" in a cage under the stairs. A funeral parlour becomes a family home; the face of a snarling Rottweiler is framed in pride of place on the mantelpiece; children live behind the walls, or are chained up in the chimney. In Alice's sick, topsy-turvy wonderland, as she tells the wise young Fool, "sometimes in *is* out".

The fairy tale is controlled by a mythic order and a ritual narrative script. The story of Hansel and Gretel, for example, gives body to the child's anxieties about abandonment, separation anxiety, being deserted or devoured, suffering from starvation or being punished for oral greediness. But the children are victorious in the end, when Gretel achieves freedom and independence for both, and the witch is utterly defeated. By bodying forth the child's anxieties, fairy tales help him to understand and overcome these difficulties, as well as come to terms with Oedipal tensions within the family by separating and projecting various aspects of his own personality and those of, for example, his parents, into different characters in the story. Since fairy tales begin from an animistic standpoint, they lack the aspect of involuntary repetition characteristic of adult manifestations of the animistic – in the uncanny images of the horror film, for example. Most horror films share the positive, pragmatic functions of the fairy tale in that – when they do allow unconscious material to come to awareness and work itself through in our imaginations – its potential for causing harm is greatly reduced. As with the fairy tale, the traditional horror film generally works to serve positive acculturating purposes (see Bettelheim 1976:7).

Hooper's **The Texas Chain Saw Massacre** inverts this mythic order and upsets the ritual narrative script – and on a cosmic level. The inverted fairy tale narrative is not simply a tale of personal tragedy, but – like all fairy tales – works to universal dimensions. This apocalyptic sentiment is suggested first by the film's "documentary" aspect. On one level at least, the film is meant to be approached as a "true story", and has many stylistics of the documentary, such as the opening "explanation" and the specification of an exact date printed on the screen ("August 18, 1973"). In fact, the story is based very loosely on the bloodthirsty exploits of Eddie Gein, the mild-mannered and retiring grave-robber from Plainfield, Wisconsin who also provided some of the inspiration for the character of Norman Bates in Robert Bloch's original story *Psycho* (see chapter 2). **The Texas Chain Saw Massacre** is compelled to repeat a fixation on a non-regenerative apocalypse, an end to history, a cosmic destruction ultimately denied by the film's ending. Sally's escape, however, is not a forestalling of the apocalypse, but simply a postponement of the end of the ritual violence. Her escape signifies a return to the cycle of horror, never to be redeemed by any sense of an ending. As Christopher Sharrett points out:

"The denial of causality and emphasis on ritual structures suggest an atmosphere that is both primitive and modernist in spirit. The 'primitive' aspect refers to the ritual atmosphere surrounding the film's horrors and the way characters interact in a situation of chaos; the "modernist" aspect denies the primitive belief in a cyclical view of history and asserts instead an absolute dead end without possibility of renewal or even resolution."

—Sharrett 1984:262

The mythic dimensions of Hooper's film are constituted by four separate groups of images. Firstly, elemental images of solar fire during the opening credits are counterbalanced by visions of a huge moon, then again, at dawn, images of a gigantic, blazing sun. These elemental images are compounded by the lunar-style symbol smeared in blood on the side of the van by Hitchhiker, which starts to make Franklin nervous. Secondly, the use of totemism as an iconographic emblem brings a cosmic element to the narrative in the opening shots of exhumed corpses propped into bizarre tableaux, Leatherface's mask of human skin, and the symbolic resonance provided by the recurrence of bones, teeth, skulls and other human offal. Thirdly, a prescient chorus to the drama takes the form of an old

The Texas Chainsaw Massacre

laughing drunk in the cemetery. "Things happen hereabouts," he tells the teenagers. "I see things. You think it's just an old man talking. Them that laughs at an old man knows better." This choric warning is echoed by a macabre series of images: a dead armadillo lies on its back in the road; a huge hornets' nest has been built in the corner of the room in the old house where Sally used to stay, before her grandmother died. An apocalyptic series of disasters is reported on the radio news – which includes, apart from exhumations and grave-robbery, references to an "18-month old daughter kept chained up in the attic". Finally, Pam spends the journey reading horoscopes aloud from an astrological magazine – and the forecast, as she warns her friends, is far from auspicious. Saturn is in retrograde, its powers of malefluence increased. Franklin's horoscope forecasts "a disturbing and unpredictable day". Sally's is even worse: "there are moments when you can's believe what's happening to you is really true. Pinch yourself, and you might find out that it is".

　　The Hills Have Eyes also deals in a series of cosmic images of ritualized violence. The film is full of elemental imagery, particularly of blood, and shadows across fire. The first victim in the film is Beauty (the dog), immediately inverting any overtones of the fairy tale narrative, just as in **The People Under The Stairs** an early casualty is a dog named Prince. **The Hills Have Eyes** also includes a cautionary tale about an inauspicious birth. Fred, the monstrous father of the cannibal clan, "came out sideways" covered in hair, weighing almost twenty lbs. By the time he was ten he was bigger than his father. It was at this point, Fred's father tells Big Bob, that strange things started to happen around the farm. Dogs were found at the bottom of wells; chickens were discovered with their heads cut off. One day, Father returned from town to find his farm burned to the ground

The Hills Have Eyes

and his favourite oldest son dead. Beside himself with rage, he attacked Fred with an iron, split his face wide open, and left him in the mountains to die. But Fred "stole a whore no-one missed", and had kids, and the "devil kids grew up to be devil men".

These 'devil children' bear elemental names. Pluto is a bald-headed freak, Jupiter and Mercury half-crazed savages, and the youngest son Mars a gibbering half-wit in a Red Indian-style feathered headdress. When picked up by this lunatic family, the simplest messages get misconstrued. The cannibals' muttering into the CB radio is mistaken for static, Jupiter's snarls are thought to be the growls of Beast, and Bobby thinks he is talking to the police when he is actually communicating with the family of snickering savages. And whilst the "good family" are victorious in the end, it is only after they have left their mother's corpse out in the desert sun to be used as bait, and indulged in torture and murder on their own behalf, relying wholly on the violent animal instincts of their remaining dog, Beast.

Balaban's **Parents**, in striking contrast, poses its characters amid the glossy surface of small town America, and to a soundtrack of Perry Como, Perez Prado, and the Big Bopper. But the images of elemental chaos which recur amidst the cosy domesticity reveal a mockingly subversive tale of unreliable adulthood, with its masks, its secret desires, and its sudden, uncontrollable hungers. Visions of juicy, blood-red steaks are juxtaposed with images of corpses on the dissecting trolley. The same steak knife is used for both meat and murder. Michael's drawing of his home life is heavily crayoned in red. In his nightmare, he hurls himself on to his bed and promptly sinks into a huge tide of blood. Ironically, **Parents** also ends with a bang. After Mother is accidentally knifed to death, Father, staggering through the house after his son, unintentionally sets off a gas explosion that burns the house down as Michael gets away. Yet the escape, such as it is, seems hardly a progressive one. Michael's removal to the home of his grandparents suggests that it will be less than easy to escape the time-honoured family tradition of feeding off the flesh of others.

The People Under The Stairs opens with the turning over of a tarot deck, but if Poindexter is far from being the archetypal Fool, other characters are unquestionably elemental, from the cannibalistic ogre to his barefoot Cinderella of a "daughter", Alice. The terrible house is full of inauspicious images. Rats run wild in the kitchen whilst a blood-soaked rag doll is caught in the mousetrap. Shadows and whispers haunt the dark staircase, and the cellar is littered with human skulls. Despite the film's nightmarish imagery, however, the ending of Craven's film is by no means regressive. Of the four films, this alone finishes on a note of high optimism, and with yet another sudden explosion. After the captive children have escaped from their prison and Alice has stabbed her "mother" to death with a carving knife, Fool sets off a deliberate explosion to aid his own escape, which causes Father to be blown into a pit filled with half-eaten corpses, and money to rain down in the streets of the ghetto.

CANNIBAL CHARACTERS

The traditional fairy tale is based on a narrative structure composed of symbolic and iconographic elements which are, according to Jung (amongst others), fundamentally universal, since the basic elements of human consciousness are held in common by all mankind. Every child is born of a mother, has to grow up, attain independence, and win a mate, and yet details of such a progress will vary from culture to culture. In a similar way, variations will be found in the manifestation within each culture, and even within each genre, of archetypal elements: elements which all four films discussed in this chapter ritually invert, one by one. Perhaps the best known and most important fairy tale archetype is the Wise Old Man, the benevolent Father in "Hansel And Gretel" and "Beauty And The Beast", who in other fairy tales takes the form of the good Grandfather, the Wizard or the Wise King, giver of judgment and knowledge, sharer of wisdom. According to Jung, the Wise Old Man represents the factor of intelligence and knowledge, or superior insight.

The counterpart to this pillar of wisdom in **The Texas Chain Saw Massacre** is the mute, hammer-wielding Leatherface, the Wise Old Man's devilish shadow. With his huge, bloated body, his tangled curly hair, his leather apron and his mask made from pieces of human skin, Leatherface communicates through a series of grunts. After the murder of Jerry, he runs off swinging his kill-hammer and squealing like a pig. In **The Hills Have Eyes**, the evil anti-Father is Fred, the child born sideways and covered in hair, who grows up to breed his own pack of savage children living in the darkness of the hills. After stabbing to death his own father, he then mocks and teases the father of the "good" family ("daddy, daddy, come and get me... daddy, daddy, don't fall down") before burning his body alive before the eyes of the horrified Carter family. Nick Laemmle, the devilish father in **Parents**, seems initially to be the model dad of the fifties – he's tall, brawny, likes a round of golf, and is a big eater of red meat and offal, the building blocks of every macho American father – except that he replenishes the larder from the morgue. For a living, he develops pollutant chemicals for a company called Toxico. His real nature, however, is concealed from us until we see him through Michael's eyes, leaning over him (and us) in distorted close-up, his bland reassurances emerging from his huge mouth like pronouncements of dire warning. Most terrible of all, though, is the father in **The People Under The Stairs**, who sits in his armchair before a blazing fairy tale fire, chewing on human flesh and spitting out bullets into a side dish as though they were olive pits ("damn buckshot!"). This father not only whips and beats his "daughter", but mutilates his "sons" before feeding off their dismembered bodies, feeding his remaining "children" with the flesh and blood of their own friends and siblings.

In the history of cultures, these devilish anti-Fathers bear a number of similarities to a set of abject Hindu ascetics known as the Aghori. Polluted and contaminating Wise Old Men, the Aghori are filthy mystics who dress sometimes in the skins of beasts, sometimes in human flesh, and many of whom are simply insane, in the medical sense. The Aghori perform austerities at, and live on, the cremation ground or cemetery, sometimes in a mud shack, into the walls of which are set human skulls. They may go naked or clothe themselves in shrouds or skin taken from a corpse, wear necklaces of bones around their necks and their hair in matted locks. Their eyes are conventionally described as "burning red", and, like these terrifying cannibalistic anti-Fathers, their demeanour is awesome. Another "inverse" Wise Old Man, the true Aghori is entirely indifferent to what he consumes, drinks not only liquor but urine, and eats not only meat but excrement, vomit, and – like all four of these anti-Fathers – the putrid flesh of corpses. According to early anthropological sources, the Aghori

"...roams about in dreadful cemeteries, attended by hosts of goblins and spirits, like a mad man, naked, with dishevelled hair, laughing, weeping, bathed in ashes of funeral piles, wearing a garland of skulls and ornaments of human bones, insane, beloved of the insane, the lord of beings whose nature is essentially darkness...."

—Briggs 1938:153

THE CANNIBAL COTTAGE

A second recurrent archetypal element of the fairy tale is the house, the rooms inside the house, and their internal decorations. Houses – either the family house or an isolated house discovered in the middle of a forest – play a significant part in many of the best-known fairy tales, including "Little Red Riding Hood", "Jack And The Beanstalk", "Beauty And The Beast", "Goldilocks", "Bluebeard", "The Three Little Pigs" and "Hansel And Gretel", where the house is made of gingerbread. Rooms within the house figure prominently in "Little Red Riding Hood", "Goldilocks", "Beauty And The Beast", "Hansel And Gretel" and "Bluebeard", where the virgin entrusts the girl with the keys to thirteen rooms, twelve of which she may open, but not the thirteenth. The internal decoration of rooms plays a significant part in "Hansel And Gretel", "Goldilocks" and – again – "Beauty And The Beast", where inanimate objects, including items of furniture, turn out to have human properties, and comfort Beauty in her loneliness.

Two houses are featured in **The Texas Chain Saw Massacre** – the dilapidated cottage owned by Sally and Franklin's grandparents, and the house of horrors inhabited by the family of slaughterers. The latter, like most fairy tale houses, is attractive and welcoming from the outside, with a brightly-lit porch, swing chair, and the possibility of a gas supply. Inside, however, things are a different matter. The house is almost totally in shadow. Downstairs, it has been divided into two sections. A thick steel door separates the front room and hallway from the slaughterhouse at the back. The front room is decorated with a gruesome selection of human offal. The floor is scattered with bones. Skulls and more bones hang suspended from the ceiling. Feathers and human teeth lie on the floor, bizarre sculptures made from skulls and jawbones are mounted at the windows, the corners of the room are covered in cobwebs and, hanging from the middle of the ceiling, a huge chicken is stuffed into a tiny cage. Outside in the yard, tin cans, cups and pieces of metal are strung from the bushes and trees. Elsewhere, a pig squeals faintly.

Upstairs in the attic (which is also used as the dining room), the main decoration consists of the mummified corpses of Grandma and Grandpa (who revives upon tasting fresh blood sucked from Sally's slit finger in a grotesque parody of Hitchhiker's gleeful self-mutilation in the van), and the stuffed corpse of their dog. This is the room in which the armchairs, quite literally, have human arms. During the dinner party sequence, the dinner table is festooned with bones, skulls, scalps and other graveyard detritus, around which buzz a number of thick black flies. During this parody of the fairy tale feast – the film's most protracted and frightening sequence – the food about to be consumed is Sally herself. Leatherface is smartened up for the occasion in evening dress and black tie, and keeps leaning over to peer at Sally through his mask. The rest of the family all sit round in their allotted, neatly-laid places and whoop, cry and gibber in a bizarre parody of Sally's terrified screams. Eventually Grandpa, "the best" killer, is brought out to deal the blow: Sally is undone from her chair and led to kneel at his feet with her head over a bucket.

In **The Hills Have Eyes**, the home under assault is the family's small trailer. The violent attack on domesticity in this film is symbolized by the savage Jupiter rummaging through the family's personal possessions – stealing an axe, knives, forks and other utensils, taking handfuls of milk and meat from the fridge, and – most grotesquely of all – strangling the family's pet canary and drinking its

The Texas Chain Saw Massacre

still-warm blood, and all beneath an embroidered sampler wishing "Good Cheer" to all. A few moments later, Pluto, interrupted in his rape attempt, goes crazy in the kitchen smashing up domestic appliances such as icecube trays, pots, pans, crockery, tables, and chairs. The familiarity of the trailer has its counterpart in the savage family's hilltop cave, where the cannibals sit around chewing on chunks of raw human flesh.

Michael Laemmle's home in **Parents** looks itself like something out of a fairy tale, with its colourful, suburban American facade conveniently disguising the turbulence beneath. The glossy surface of the Laemmle's home derives from its bold, emblematic colours, modern domestic gadgets and show furniture, and is kept sparkling clean by mother Lily, slightly daffy but a slave to her kitchen. But it is this American dream-home that hosts the gradual revelation of difference between things as they appear to be, and things as they really are. The shiny cutlery is used for cannibalism and the steak knives for murder. Michael knows how to peel the skin off a cat and cook it in the broiler, and Michael's school psychiatrist is murdered with a golf club, status symbol of the rising professional class. As the club swings towards the camera, Balaban fades out rapidly and then fades in on a juicy rump steak sizzling on the barbecue in the Laemmle's back yard.

In **The People Under The Stairs**, the terrible house may look prosperous from the outside, but there are rats in the kitchen and flies buzzing around the fridge. There's a bad smell in the hallway, and all the cabinets have strange locks on them. The stairs creak; a clock chimes; bizarre statues line the walls. All the doors close and lock automatically; all the windows are bolted shut; half-eaten corpses lie inside the walls. Candles, statuettes and crucifixes deck the hallways. The strange series of tunnels inside the walls connects with the kitchen cupboards,

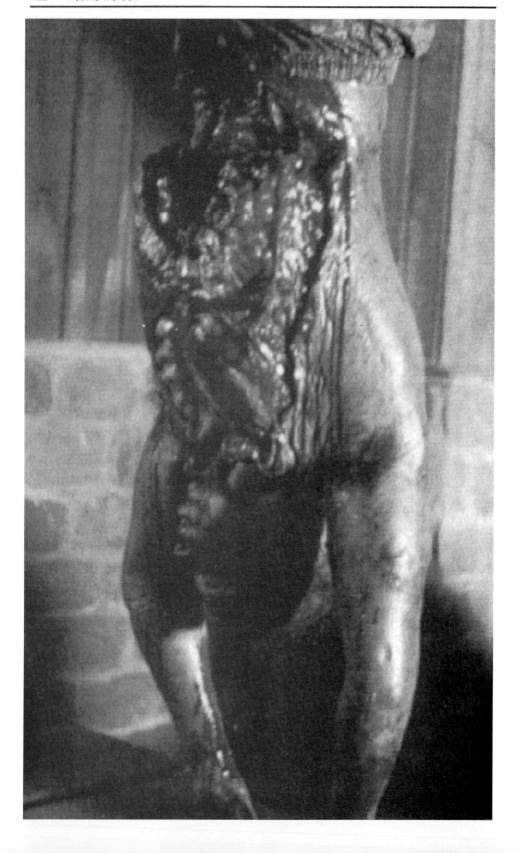

the chimney, the fireplace, Alice's bedroom and the disused oven in the cellar. When we come across a room labelled "Embalming", the uncanny nature of this terrible house becomes clear. The cannibals have continued to use the old funeral parlour as their family home – a perfect site for their monstrous and unfamiliar activities.

According to Jung, the motif of the house in fairy tales stands for the unavoidable entrapment of our minds in archetypal relationships and modes of thought. Sometimes the house is replaced by the symbol of the maze hiding its secret – the minotaur, symbol of man's duality and mortality, the half-man, half-beast to whom young people are sacrificed. As Bettelheim notes, the house is the central image of the "residues and traces" of a previous animistic world-view, with the motif of the forbidden room connoting sexual knowledge. The mysterious house in **The Texas Chain Saw Massacre** is not a house of life and knowledge but a house of death whose counterpart may be found – again – in anthropological sources. Its division into living space and slaughterhouse recalls the Tikopian house in Polynesia, one half of which is not actually lived in because underneath the mats which cover the floor are buried the former occupants of the house (Strathern 1982:17)[1].

Human remains are also frequently used decoratively within such cultures, but generally with some regenerative symbolic significance. In the Melpa of the West New Guinea Highlands, for example, the jawbones of pigs are hung up on fences in commemoration of sacrifice, and at death – prior to the influence of the Christian missions, at least – the skull of an important man and some of his limb-bones might also be taken as relics and established in a *peng manga*, or "head house" (Bloch and Parry 1982:28). And for the Doubains of Melanesia, all creation is the metamorphosis of one thing into another. Yams, for example, are metamorphosed people, and they still retain many of their human characteristics. They have ears and hear, are susceptible to magic charms, walk about at night and give birth to children. In such societies, as in the fairy tale, human relics are associated with the regenerative properties of the corpse, and other inanimate objects are give life by spirits and magic, as is usual in the animate universe. Bettelheim points out that the fairy tale hero proceeds for a time in isolation, just as the child often feels isolated. He is helped by being in touch with primitive things – a tree, an animal, nature – just as the child feels more in touch with these things than most adults do (Bettelheim 1976:11). In "Beauty And The Beast", for example, the human element attributed to inanimate objects allows Beauty to befriend them, and they comfort her while she is away from her sisters and her father.

In these four films, however, this symbolic process is again inverted. Here, rather than inanimate objects having special, magical powers of life, even living things are reduced to mere objects or superficies, such as the armchair in **The Texas Chain Saw Massacre** made out of human arms, and the table ornaments composed of human remains. Instead of imagining a world animated by spiritual magic as in childhood and primitive cultures, each of these four films presents a world not only antipathetic to "normality", but forged out of an aversion finally to life itself, showing existence drained of all value: an ultimate, apocalyptic threat to the vital principle (see Telotte 1984:25).

GENERATION AND DEGENERATION

Most fairy tales deal in one way or another with family relationships and the transition of power and authority through generations. For example, many fairy stories centre around a family where one of the parents is either an "evil" substitute, or else missing completely (as in "Snow White", "Hansel And Gretel" and "Jack And The Beanstalk"). Others, such as "Beauty And The Beast", begin with the death of a mother or father which creates a number of ongoing problems, just as it does in real life. Yet other fairy stories, as Bettelheim notes, tell about an aging parent who decides that the time has come to let the new generation take over. But before this can happen, the successor has to prove himself capable and worthy (Bettelheim 1976:8). Fairy tales which deal with orphaned children or animals (such as "The Ugly Duckling") represent, according to Freud, a displacement of the child's fantasy in which both his parents are replaced by others of better birth. Freud claims that this exaltation of the parents is a reminder of the time when the child believed his parents to be supreme, noble and strong (Freud 1923:3).

The Texas Chain Saw Massacre presents us with two separate families: the "good" family of children, and their evil counterparts. The children are closely interlinked: Kirk and Pam are a couple, Sally and Jerry are a couple, and Franklin is Sally's brother. There are also references to Sally and Franklin's father, their grandfather – the owner of the old house by the creek – and their uncle. It is not clear quite to what extent the family of slaughterers are related to one another, since there are no female members of the family (with the exception of Grandma, now a well-preserved corpse). Basically, the males of the family are all retired (but still practising) slaughterhouse workers, made redundant by the mechanization of the local slaughterhouse, who have decided to use their talents on human prey ("a whole family of Draculas!", exclaims Franklin in the van). Hitchhiker, the youth of the family, seems to be the grave robber, responsible for the macabre series of exhumations reported on the local radio. Leatherface, his older brother, follows in the steps of his grandfather as the family butcher of carcasses, and Father, the garage owner, is "nothing but the cook", who sells human barbecue at his roadside store. "I can't get no pleasure in killing", he complains to Hitchhiker during the dinner party. "It's just something you gotta do. Don't mean you gotta like it".

Similarly, the extended family in The Hills Have Eyes are pitted against the savage family of cannibals: father, mother, daughter, and four macabre sons, each one more degenerate than the next – "a goddamn bunch of cut-throats", as their grandfather calls them, just seconds before his own throat is cut by his second son. Mother, like her son Mars, dresses in a Red Indian headdress. Father, in a sick parody of Daniel Boone, sports a coonskin cap and knocks back whisky from the bottle. Daughter Ruby spends much of the film chained up to a rock by her bare ankles. In one morbid scene, as Doug and Lynne are making love in their car at night, Pluto creeps up on them and sucks petrol out of the tank of their car, an image of the cannibal family draining and sapping the bodily fluids that the generate couple are busy producing. But even this family of degenerates has its own hierarchy and order, however vestigial. Pluto's attempted rape of Brenda is interrupted by his older brother Jupiter ("you just wait till you get to be a man"), who proceeds to rape her himself, instead. The prize stolen by this degenerate family from their generative counterparts is the baby, Katy, concrete evidence of

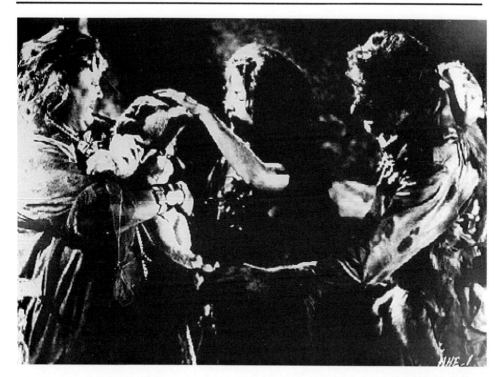

The Hills Have Eyes

the family's vitality and health. When Brenda and Ethel try to save the baby, they are both shot by Jupiter, and Ethel is killed. And yet this evil family, bedecked with ornaments of bone, has its own kind of pride in its murderous lineage. After "fixin' Grandpa good", Father returns to his family's cave with the corpse of Big Bob, his generate counterpart, against whose family he directs a fulsome tirade of proud and violent abuse:

"Your dog made sport of my blood, you pagan. I'm gonna kill your kids for that. You come out here, you stick your fingers in my pie... I thought you were smart and tough – you're stupid – you're nothing... I'll see the wind blow your dried up seeds away! I'll eat the heart of your stinking memory! I'll eat the brains of your kids' kids! I'm in! You're out!"

In **The People Under The Stairs**, Alice suffers from constant parental abuse, from having her hair pulled by her "mother", to being whipped by her "father". This is another family whose female principle is dysfunctional. Alice, although a teenager, is treated like a little girl and dressed in little girls' clothes. Her "parents" address one another as "Daddy" and "Mommy" even though they are in fact brother and sister. In one scene, Alice's "father" comes on to her sexually, and in another, Mother tells Father to "go straight to your room!" and "don't forget to say your prayers" (which include the lines "...if I should kill before I wake, I pray the Lord my soul to take"). Mothers and sisters are strangers; fathers and brothers are lovers; daughters are women and children; sons are for dinner. This is one very mixed-up family indeed. As Fool says to Alice, "your father's one sick mother. Actually, your mother's one sick mother too". In fact, the lives of

The People Under The Stairs

Alice and the other "stolen children" are saved only by the bonding together of Fool's dysfunctional family, and the other families in the ghetto. Fool's wise old grandfather tells him the history of the cannibal landlord and his so-called "family", and his older sister arrives at the house in a brave – albeit misguided – attempt to save her little brother, who is eventually saved by the uniting of all the poor black families in the ghetto neighbourhood.

Anthropologists have drawn attention to some of the ways in which those who bear the responsibility of disposing of corpses serve an important and practical function as cultural scapegoats. Lowest in the hierarchy of Cantonese society, for example, are those menial labourers employed to handle the corpse and dispose of clothing, bedding, and other materials most directly associated with death. The corpse-handlers, apparently, are considered "so contaminated by their work that villagers will not even speak to them; their very glance is thought to bring misfortune" (Watson 1982:157). The same pragmatic scapegoating is seen in the Hindu attitude towards the Aghori, whose fascination with decomposition is sometimes regarded as a spasmodic reaction against the excessive sensuality of their culture, particularly its younger generation (Huizinga 1974:65). By systematically embracing death and pollution in life, the Aghori aims to suspend time, to enter an eternal state of *samadhi* in which death has no menace (see Briggs 1938).

Similarly, the death of the parent or the displacement of their power in the fairy tale not only helps the child to come to terms with death, especially the anticipated future death of the parent, but also dramatizes the natural transition of power and authority from generation to generation, thereby exploring the eventual takeover of the New Age. In **The Texas Chain Saw Massacre**, this transition is blocked and inverted – traditional values are refuted and negated by monstrous parent figures who destroy children. Robin Wood has noted how the "terrible house" of the chainsaw family signifies "the dead weight of the past crushing the light of the younger generation" (Wood 1984:188), an obliteration that has no redeeming or regenerative qualities whatsoever. There is a Hindu expression *alp mitru* (meaning "death in life") which is used as a synonym to mean an "untimely death" such a death being always *ipso facto* degenerative, in any narrative or culture (Parry 1982:83).

Whilst on the one hand the monstrousness of these four anti-families suggests a parallel with the stultifying bonds and tensions of the "normal" family life that most of these films' adolescent viewers are currently dealing with, on the other hand there are plenty of scenes of breakdown and alienation within the "normal" families themselves. In **The Texas Chain Saw Massacre** there are two scenes of crisis. The first occurs when Franklin, unable to climb the stairs to join the others in his father's old house, is left outside, spitting, crying and imitating his sister's laughter. The second comes when Sally's frustration with Franklin leads to a violent scuffle over the possession of the flashlight. In **The Hills Have Eyes**, Brenda and Bobby are often squabbling, and Ethel has one or two brief spats with her husband as they begin to lose their way in the mountains. Little Michael in **Parents** is so traumatized and terrified by his overbearing father that he says virtually nothing at all, creating a cipher at the film's centre. And in **The People Under The Stairs**, Fool argues with his big sister over everything from drugs to payment of the rent. Writing about **The Texas Chain Saw Massacre**, D.N. Rodowick has argued that in scenes such as these, the bourgeois family "manifests a degree of violence which equals or exceeds that of its monstrous aggressors, effectively implicating the family in the monstrosity it is trying to combat".

SACRED AND GRATUITOUS CANNIBALISM

The final fairy tale motif mocked and inverted by the apocalyptic economy of these four films is the very theme that connects them: that of cannibalism. Like many forms of death and violence in the fairy tale, cannibalism seems to be generally associated with regenerative functions. In this form, the threat of cannibalism helps the child to come to terms with his fears of punishment for oral greediness and – correspondingly – his own fear of being devoured or "swallowed up" by the parent. The same is true of cannibalism in its anthropological manifestations. On a symbolic level at least, the consumption of sacred flesh during the Eucharist involves "replenishing the spiritual aspect of a culture and reminding society of its sense of communion" (Sharrett 1984:265). This regenerative notion is also the basis of scalping and tribal head-hunting, where the killer takes the substance of his enemies in order to recharge his own strength and power.

In **The Texas Chain Saw Massacre**, however, the cannibalism is gratuitous and functionless. Hitchhiker's graphic description in the teenagers' van of the making of head cheese (boiling the cows' heads, scraping out their flesh, muscles, eyes, ligaments and so on) leads to a violent act of self-mutilation that parodies this family's means of sustaining and nourishing itself by slaughtering people and robbing graves, then either consuming the bodies themselves or selling them off as barbecue. Pam's body is strung up on a meat-hook then transferred to the deep freeze. Jerry and Kirk are both killed with a sledge-hammer. The sacrifice of these children inverts the regenerative ritual of cannibalism – it is empty of any kind of cultural or pragmatic signification in the sense unusually associated with collective violence and other acts of ritual aggression (Sharrett 1984:266).

In **The Hills Have Eyes**, food consumption is associated directly with violence and aggression. The film opens with a series of jokes on the subject. The family, baking in their hot trailer, joke about being made into "human French fries". Doug jokes about Beast eating a poodle, and Big Bob being responsible for the vet's bills for the dead animal. Not long after that, the jokes are at the family's expense. The murder of the garage owner, stabbed in the head and neck by his psychotic son, is abruptly and deliberately juxtaposed with Brenda and Bobby making barbecue ("you want some cheese on this? There's plenty left", cries Brenda's voice immediately after the murder). The "good" and "evil" families are both shown to be taking their meals at the same time, except, whereas the "good" family eat wholesome American barbecue, the "evil' family feed on Beauty, the pet dog whose brains were bashed out by Mercury and whose meat Ruby spits out, and Father crams in his mouth. During the assault on the family's trailer, Pluto spots an even more tempting morsel – the family's baby, Katy. "Baby's fat... fat and juicy", he slavers, wide-eyed, and – deciding the baby will make a perfect Thanksgiving treat – he steals it from beneath a gaping **Jaws** poster in the bedroom. Back at the cave, Father, chewing huge chunks of dog meat, warns Jupiter to "keep an eye on that young tenderloin baby", worried that its daddy's "going to come a-lookin' for it". "I'll rip his lungs out!", vows Jupiter. "You do that, son", says Father, proudly.

The cannibalism in Balaban's **Parents** seems equally gratuitous. Michael's venture into the cellar, where a human leg hangs suspended from a butcher's hook, is a deliberate echo – as Balaban acknowledges – of **The Texas Chain Saw Massacre**. The Laemmle family's cannibalistic tendencies embody the festering underside of the American way. And whilst Balaban is hardly suggesting that American parents of the 1950s were literally cannibals, he is certainly suggesting that there was a lot more going on that anybody let on. Similarly, in **The People Under The Stairs**, the family literally live off one another's flesh, although additions to the "family" are abducted on a regular basis from the streets of the ghetto. Fool first tries to get into the landlord's house by selling cookies to his "wife", but she turns him away brusquely – hers is a more substantial diet. The half-starved idiot-boys in the cellar, produce of their crazed parents' incestuous

Parents

union, are killed periodically to feed one another, as well as their parents. No sooner has Leroy been killed than one of the children starts chewing on his dead body. Half-eaten corpses strew the house's passageways; the family's dog, Prince, is reared and fed "by hand" (quite literally – he is fed on human hands), and children are born or stolen whenever the food supply is getting a little bit low.

CANNIBAL APOCALYPSE

In fairy tales, this kind of terrible punishment is not a deterrent to crime so much as a means of persuading the child that crime does not pay. Morality is promoted not through the fact that virtue always wins out at the end of the story, but because the bad person always loses, and, as Bettelheim has noted, because the hero is most attractive to the child, who identifies with the hero in all his struggles (Bettelheim 1976:26). In these four upside-down fairy tales, however, humanity is completely powerless, and the annihilation is complete. There are no heroes nor heroines, only victims and villains. Sally Hardesty, Lynne and Bobby Carter, Michael Laemmle and Fool Poindexter would all be heroes or heroines if there were anything rational or calculated they could do to escape their situations, but there is nothing, and, when they do escape, it is by pure accident. In these fairy tales there are no clues, no magic passwords, no treasures to rescue or battles to fight because this is not a narrative governed by any logical order. Neither victims nor slaughterers have any kind of control over themselves or each other, and this lack of control is cosmic and universal. Malevolent predictions come true. Not one of these young victims – with the possible exception of Fool – has any control over their destiny, suggesting that our defense against horror is finally subject to the forces of an arbitrary fate. Robin Wood has described **The**

Texas Chain Saw Massacre as a "collective nightmare" which "brings to focus a spirit of negativity, an undifferentiated lust for destruction that seems to lie not far below the surface of modern collective consciousness" (Wood 1979:191). Christopher Sharrett agrees:

"The idea of 'redemption' that occidental man has assigned to the spirit of art, underlined by the 'great works' continuing the concepts of sacrifice and the revivification of society, is parodied here, even if the parodic process is itself unconscious... Tobe Hooper's film is one of cinema's strongest statements of the general paucity of myth and communal belief in the contemporary world."
—Sharrett 1984:272–3

These kinds of inverted fairy tales are perhaps some of the only stories of true horror that our culture can allow. These films' narrative disorder, illogical sequences of action and apocalyptic sense of destruction are ritualistic, but without the regenerative or collective functions usually associated with ritualized violence. In the fairy tale, virtue is as omnipresent as evil; good and evil are both given body in the form of some figure and their actions. But in these fairy tales there is only evil. The good that once existed is either defeated, annihilated or driven away. The morality of the fairy tale is inherent in its potential for assurance of success. Most fairy tales teach us about the possibility of mastering life's difficulties. Fairy tales which mislead, bewilder, confuse, and ultimately deliver the expectation of defeat, are dangerous stories indeed.

NOTES

1.   According to the Melpa, bone comes from the father and flesh from the mother. Similarly, for the Bara tribe of Madagascar, it has been observed that life is a precarious balance between the sterile forces of 'order' associated with bone derived from the father, and the chaotic forces of 'vitality' associated with flesh derived from the mother. In death, the balance is upset: the corpse is reduced to bone, order and sterility (see Huntingdon 1973:65–84). Such traditions may help to explain the connection between the preponderance of bone imagery in **The Texas Chain Saw Massacre** and the sterile, wizened family of men, lacking a female principle.

chapter four:
eating italian

ALTHOUGH a number of memorable cannibal moments have emerged from films made in European countries other than Italy, such as the Spanish contingent of Eloy de la Iglesia's **Cannibal Man** (1972), Jesús Franco's **Mondo Cannibale** (1979) and **The Devil Hunter** (1980), and Jacinto Molina's **El Carnaval De Las Bestias** (1980) (see chapter 8), it is the Italians who are really the most serious connoisseurs of the underground and "fringe" horror genre. As every gore-conscious film-fan knows, the Italians do an excellent line in cannibal films, both supernatural and natural; the best-known Italian cannibal/zombie productions (such as Lucio Fulci's seminal **Zombie Flesh-Eaters**, Marino Girolami's **Zombi Holocaust**, Bruno Mattei's **Zombie Creeping Flesh** and Antonio Margheriti's **Cannibal Apocalypse**) are studied in more detail in chapter 6, but this chapter is devoted to narratives set within the precincts of the possible – mainly themed around white intruders being killed and devoured by jungle "savages".

Significantly, a number of the films discussed in this chapter have been released in a variety of versions for a wide range of different markets, and consequently bear a number of different titles, as well as alternative video titles, although any versions found circulating on the British market will be almost undoubtedly heavily cut. The Italian horror movie "Mafia" – Deodato, Fulci, Cozzi, Lenzi, Martino, Margheriti – are generally lumped together as a like-minded bunch of brutish, second-rate Argento imitators, but the cognoscenti of cannibal films can discern a fertile ground of difference between their various narrative and cinematic styles.

CANNIBALIZED CADAVERS

After a series of exploitation movies in various genres, director Umberto Lenzi unwittingly prefigured the cannibal movie craze with **Deep River Savages** (a.k.a. **El Paese Del Sesso Selvaggio** a.k.a. **Mondo Cannibale**) in 1972. **Deep River Savages** is a tale of natives in the jungles of Thailand and Burma. A European photographer (Ivan Rassimov) is witness to their savage rites of sex, torture and cannibalism, before being forced to marry the chief's daughter (Me Me Lai); he then becomes chief himself. Lenzi lingers on the graphic scenes of violence, paving the way for bloody cannibalism to become a key motif for the next decade of Italian exploitation cinema.

Ruggero Deodato's 1976 jungle expedition drama **Last Cannibal World** (a.k.a. **Ultimo Mondo Cannibale**, a.k.a. **Cannibal**) properly set the ball rolling for a series of "cannibal rescue" sagas with feeble claims to verisimilitude. The opening title, something of a hallmark of the genre, declares that everything depicted in the forthcoming narrative is completely true, and the experiences of the hero led to the discovery on the island of Mindanao of a hitherto unknown tribe living in "stone age conditions". This bold claim, not unlike Kroger Babb's outlandish advertising for his 1946 production of **Karamoja**, traditionally stands

Last Cannibal World

Last Cannibal World

as a showman's stamp promising plenty of scenes of sex, torture, and savage brutality.

In **Last Cannibal World**, it is two prospectors working for an oil company who have gone missing in the Philippine jungle and need to be tracked down by a light aircraft carrying Robert Harper (Massimo Foschi), pilot Charlie (Suleiman Shamsi), Rolf (Ivan Rassimov) and Swan (Judy Rosly). The party are forced to crash-land on a deserted jungle airstrip, and while Charlie is making repairs, Harper and Rolf find evidence that the missing prospectors have been murdered by the "savage natives". When Swan is abducted by the cannibals, the others go in search of her. Charlie is killed by a lethal man-trap (another staple of the genre), and Harper and Rolf come across a tribe of cannibals eating Swan's remains. The two men escape and try to get back to the plane on a raft, but are overturned in the rapids and Rolf is presumed drowned. The sudden swelling of bird cries confirms that Harper is now left to face the deadly jungle alone. What follows is a protracted but effective sequence where the camera prowls through the undergrowth confirming the hostile presences that lurk in every corner of the jungle, and when Harper collapses from fatigue, he is kidnapped by the cannibals who drag him to their cave, strip him, try to make him fly, and finally cage him as a curiosity.

Harper is befriended by a woman of the tribe (played by former TV hostess Me Me Lai, who spent the latter half of her career playing half-tamed jungle women in Italian cannibal movies), and takes her with him when he escapes. During their trek through the jungle, the native girl brings Harper gifts of food and they indulge in some atavistic, stone-age-style sex (the man mounting the woman from behind, as is often the case in cannibal films). During a thunderstorm they take shelter in a cave and discover Rolf, injured but still alive, who joins in their trek. The group fail to attract the attention of a helicopter and they are within sight of the airstrip when they suffer a final, terrifying attack by the cannibals. The native woman is killed and eaten, and Rolf is further wounded. In a desperate attempt to prove his strength and supremacy, Harper kills one of the cannibals, disembowels him violently and sets about eating the steaming entrails, revelling in his savage new appetite. The intimidated cannibals continue to follow Harper and the now moribund Rolf, but allow the plane to take off. As soon as it is airborne, however, Rolf dies, and only Harper is left to return alive to civilization.

Emmanuelle And The Last Cannibals, a film made in 1977 by Joe d'Amato (a pseudonym of Aristide Massaccesi), was an attempt to cash in on the mixed-race-combo sex scenes popular in seventies B-movies after the success of Russ Meyer's **Mandingo**. This is yet another sex-&-cannibalism "Black Emmanuelle" feature, of which there are at least twelve in circulation in theatrical, home video and pay-cable distribution, most of which star Laura Gemser as Emmanuelle. In 1984 this film, dubbed with various different accents, was re-released on video in the U.S. under the uninspired title **Trap Them And Kill Them** and is, according to the film's introductory credit sequence, "a true story as reported by Jennifer O'Sullivan".

The story opens with an extraneous segment in which Emmanuelle is working undercover in a Manhattan lunatic asylum, giving lesbian attention to a young woman who has savagely bitten the breast of a nurse in a cannibalistic fashion. Location photography in Manhattan reveals that Emmanuelle is, in reality, an undercover reporter for the *New York Evening Post*, and, inspired by the incident in the asylum, she organizes an expedition, led by Professor Mark Lester (Gabriele Tinti, Gemser's real-life husband), to seek out a tribe of cannibal Indians living on the Amazon river.

After some underlit South American jungle footage, involving countless adventures and many phoney-looking special gore effects, most of Lester's party

are sacrificed by the cannibal tribe until Emmanuelle, who has studied the ancient secrets of the race, paints her belly with a sacred symbol, masquerades as the Goddess of the Waters, foxes the cannibals, escapes back home to Manhattan, and lives to tell the media her dramatic tale.

Sergio Martino's seminal medium-budget 1978 film **Prisoner Of The Cannibal God** (a.k.a. **Mountain Of The Cannibal God**, a.k.a. **Montagna Del Dio**

Prisoner Of The Cannibal God

Cannibale) picks up on Deodato's narrative footsteps in another jungle expedition saga involving another group of westerners setting out to investigate the savage goings-on of another dangerous primitive tribe. In this case, ethnologist Harry Stevenson has gone missing in New Guinea while investigating the cannibalistic Puka tribe dwelling beneath Ra-Ra-Mi, "the Mountain of the Cannibal God". Harry's wife Susan (Ursula Andress) and her brother Arthur (Claudio Cassinelli) persuade Dr. Edward Foster (Stacy Keach) to lead a "secret" expedition to the haunted island of Rocca to discover what has happened to Harry. On the way to the island, the native guides sacrifice an iguana and when Arthur interferes and objects to their cruelty, three of the guides abandon the expedition. Arriving at the island, the appearance of a mysterious and frightening masked man leads to the disappearance of the lead native guide, Asaro. Three natives remain, all of whom are subsequently dispatched in horrible ways: one eaten by an alarmingly violent crocodile during a river-crossing, the second caught in the ubiquitous lethal man-trap, and the third decapitated by another of the mysterious masked men.

The search party takes refuge in a friendly village, where Arthur makes friends with Shura (Luigina Rocchi), a native girl, but while the two are indulging in some characteristic stone-age sex, Shura is speared to death, her elderly husband Pancho is found hanged, and Dr. Foster is fatally wounded in the leg – but not before he is able to kill his murderer, who turns out to be the native guide Asaro. The search party learns with alarm that the mysterious masked men are in fact the cannibalistic Puka tribe. They are joined in their quest by Manolo (Antonio Marsina), a white doctor from the village. As they press on to the Mountain of the Cannibal God, their canoe is lost in the rapids and Foster plunges to his death over a waterfall. Reaching the mountain, Susan and Arthur prove to have an ulterior motive for their expedition, appearing suspiciously interested in the mountain's uranium deposits. Before they can return, however, they are punished for their imperialistic attitude in a blood-curdling cannibal finale at the hands of the Puka tribe. Arthur is killed and eaten; Susan is forced to sample the decomposing remains of her late husband Harry, whom the cannibals worship as a god, and Manolo is tormented by a cannibal dwarf. That night, however, Manolo slips his bonds, brains his tormentor, rescues Susan and effects their escape from the island.

CANNIBAL HOLOCAUST

In 1979, a film was released which solidified the merging and fusion of two fascinating cycles in the history of Italian cinema. Ruggero Deodato's **Cannibal Holocaust** represents the first "cannibal mondo" movie, standing at the crossroads between the cannibal cycle of the late 70s and early 80s, and that other celebrated Italian cinematic tradition, the mondo film. Critics of **Cannibal Holocaust** were not slow to pick up on the way in which Deodato appropriates the Italian mondo tradition and whilst pretending to denounce it, makes a film that is, in its way, even more gruesome, even more exploitative, and even more scandalous.

Others complained about the film's structural incoherencies, its naiveties of *mis en scène*, improbable scenarios, audacious schemata of identification, and factual complacencies. *Variety* condemned the "patently phoney tale of cannibalism and the white man's mistreatment of native tribes" (*Cannibal Holocaust* 1985:74). *Cahiers du Cinéma* complained about the "abysmal construction" of a film which allows its director to simulate moral condemnation of the footage which he has created expressly for our entertainment and credulity, making daring implications (though never fully affirming them) of the "authenticity" of certain sequences (Gere 1981:63). Only a few of its reviewers – and only very fleetingly, even then – were able to acknowledge the violent, excessive, fascinating intelligence behind a film that progressively but deliberately breaks down the boundaries between spectator and camera, between spectacle and violence, between shock and freedom, thereby questioning the nature of cinema, of voyeurism, and of the rights of the filmmaker to fictionalize reality and to realize fiction. As one reviewer put it, "the title alone is enough to stop one in one's tracks" (Cros 1981:39).

Four young television reporters have disappeared during the filming of a documentary about a stretch of South American jungle – known as the "Green Inferno" – peopled by primitive cannibals. The television team – Alan Yates, his girlfriend Faye Daniels, Jack Anders and Mark Tomazzo – are well known for their grim, shocking and realistic documentaries. Two months later, a search party sponsored jointly by New York University and the Pan Am Broadcasting Corporation is sent out to find them. The search party is led by the somewhat implausible Professor Harold Monroe (played by porno veteran Roberto Bolla, a.k.a. Salvatore Basile), "NYU's noted anthropologist" and specialist on primitive cultures. Accompanied by a native guide and Chako (Ricardo Fuentes), a mercenary soldier of ambiguous nationality, Monroe sets out into the Green Inferno to experience a series of embattling adventures, including a close escape from a jaguar attack, the witnessing of a savage rape, and the discovery of the partially decomposed body of Fillippe, the documentary team's guide. Finally, Monroe and his colleagues make tentative contact with the Tree People or the "Yanomomo", the tribe that killed the documentary team. As proof of this, they find the bodies themselves, propped into a fetishistic tableau of decomposing corpses crawling with worms, huge spiders and swollen beetles. Miraculously however, their boxes of film are still intact, and it is these which Monroe and his team bring back with them to New York.

The television executives at Pan American want to begin screening the initial part of this "lost footage" right away, but Monroe first insists on revealing a little more about the ethics of Yates and his crew. Through brief interviews with family and clips from previous documentaries, we learn that Yates is a highly immoral and unethical egotist who, in the past, paid African troops to stage executions for his camera. On the African trip, we learn, he killed tribesmen and staged massacres for his documentary team, apparently unstoppable in his quest for the violent and excessive scoop. Knowing something of their illicit methods, the television executives then sit down to analyze the subsequent jungle expedition footage scheduled to be broadcast the following Wednesday night on BDC-TV as **The Green Inferno**.

From this point, the filmmakers Alan Yates (Robert Kerman), Faye Daniels (Francesa Ciardi), Jack Anders (Perry Perkamen) and Mark Tomazzo (Luca Giorgio Barbareschi) are the real focus of **Cannibal Holocaust** as we are shown the newly-discovered footage – shaky, scratched and unfocused though it is. This documentary, which takes up the second half of the film, is a cinematic coup. We are first shown footage of the four colleagues fooling around at their camp in a clip which establishes not only the amateur character of an expedition involving no special equipment in a terribly inhospitable environment, but also – and more subtly – that the team are using a pair of separate, hand-held cameras. Developed and projected, film from these cameras has captured the horrible truth – that Yates and his team did not hesitate to "organize" the scenes of violence and cruelty that they filmed, and made themselves victims of their own egotistical pattern for exploitative sensation.

The camera crew spend six days walking through the jungle in search of the Tree People. Their guide Fillippe catches a huge turtle which he and Jack skin

and mutilate with a pocket knife while Faye vomits over a tree stump. When Fillippe is bitten in the toe by a poisonous snake, the team gleefully set about hacking off his leg on-camera, then burying his fatally mutilated body in the leaves. Eventually, the rest of the team come across a single member of the Yanomomo tribe, whom Yates shoots in the leg so he can lead them slowly to the rest of his people. On arriving at the village, Yates tortures and shoots a wild pig then rounds up the Yanomomo into grass huts and torches the whole village. Other atrocities witnessed are the forced aborting of a human fetus and the clubbing to death of its mother, the expiration of tribal elders, the rape of a Yanomomo virgin by Anders, Tomazzo and Yates, and the later discovery of the same woman impaled to death on a stake which enters through the vagina and emerges through the mouth. In the battle that finally ensues, Jack is captured, castrated and tortured by the Yanomomo before being eaten alive. A similar fate awaits Mark and Faye while Yates, professional to the end, carries on filming right until the moment his own head is bashed in.

Back in the BDC-TV studios, the producers decide that the material must be destroyed and Professor Monroe, wandering out into the New York Streets, wonders to himself just who the real cannibals are. One final coda: the end credit suggests that the television station's projectionist illegally smuggled out the footage we have just been shown after it had been ordered to be destroyed on Professor Monroe's recommendation, for which he was allegedly fined the sum of $10,000.

The controversy surrounding the release of Deodato's cinematic coup centred, predictably, around its use of "authentic" footage, most notably in the killing and mutilation of animals – with all its associated implications of a vicious and abhorrent attitude towards living human beings, and the possibility that some

of the on-camera "atrocities" are in fact, as the filmmakers claim, authentic. These intimations of authenticity are enhanced by the poor quality of the film-within-a-film: shaky hand-held camerawork, numbers flashing up on the screen, flickering lights, and the constant physical and verbal references to the camera by the documentary team, although – as Kerekes and Slater point out – "it doesn't seem to matter that a wavering tree branch or the ever-reliable pop, start or film hiccup should occur always at the most technologically advantageous moment – that is, when Faye's head is about to be lifted from her shoulders or Jack is about to have his chest split asunder by the savages" (Kerekes and Slater 1994:70). The final nail in the coffin of the film's success – in the U.K., at least – was provided by a series of scandals associated with its distribution. Firstly, a French magazine, *Photo*, published an article entitled "Grand Guignol Cannibale", suggesting that **Cannibal Holocaust** was, in fact, a "genuine" snuff movie, in which men were really dismembered, beheaded, castrated and *"mangiati vivi"* (see Kerekes and Slater 1994:69). In Italy, four weeks after it opened on the 8th February 1980, **Cannibal Holocaust** was confiscated and declared obscene by the High Court, and later banned outright under an old law forbidding the torture of animals, although Deodato fought the decision and in 1983 the film was released back into Italian cinemas in its entirety. In Britain, however, the film was banned under the long-lamented "Video Nasties" Act and a copy of **Cannibal Holocaust** confiscated in Birmingham in April 1993 prompted predictable outcries about "snuff movies" (see Kerekes and Slater 1994:69). As a result of these calumnies, **Cannibal Holocaust** was a huge *succès de scandale* in Italy and elsewhere in Europe, and in Japan – allegedly – **Cannibal Holocaust** is second only to **E.T.** as the "most successful" production of all time.

Deodato's film, then, consists of two separate narratives: the story of Yates and his team disappearing in the jungle, and the story of Monroe and his team on their quest to discover the lost film footage. The protagonists of these two narratives are set in opposition to one another. Yates represents the worst extremes of mercenary capitalism – a man who, in the quest for monetary rewards, has no hesitation about involving himself in the most ignoble excesses, including the torture and mutilation of his fellow human beings. Monroe, on the other hand, stands for decency and humanitarianism – his brave genius incarnates the values of an idealized American democracy. Yates's story is one of chaos, anarchy, violence and the apocalyptic collapse of moral boundaries; Monroe's is one of wary restoration and resolution. The structural system that both these narratives deal with is one as old as cannibalism itself, as old as mankind: the system of give and take. What the "lost footage" documents is the collapse of the exchange system, that most basic and primitive ritual of civilization. Monroe's narrative then begins, albeit tentatively, to restructure these social codes by warily initiating a very simple but fundamental structure of exchange. In other words, **Cannibal Holocaust** presents us with two short narratives: the "improper" film (which, to confuse matters somewhat, comes second chronologically) – a story of taking and taking back – and the "proper" film, a restorative narrative of give and take.

The film footage taken by Yates and his crew, given the title **The Green Inferno** by BDC-TV, is a terrible warning of what happens when the most primitive structures of human civilization collapse. It is a tale of flesh debts, cannibal vendettas, morally unsanctioned gifts, collapsed boundaries and the violation of all rites of exchange.

Appropriately enough, from what we can gather about the documentary crew, they are all the product of failed parenting, or broken homes. Alan Yates, as we know, is an unscrupulous double-dealer, capable of staging massacres and executions for the camera, obsessive in his quest for the ultimate scoop. From brief clips of the team clowning around theatrically, we learn that he has persistently refused to marry his long-term girlfriend Faye Daniels, and a crew member who dropped out of the documentary team at the last moment describes Alan as "pushing his people to the limits, demanding every thing, including

blood... God have mercy on his soul, he was one ruthless son of a bitch". Faye's sister, a nun, informs us that not only was Faye adopted as a child but that she changed her Christian name from the one her adoptive parents had given her, and Jack's abandoned hippie wife, living on welfare with her fatherless child, is interested only in asking her interviewer whether "you guys think I could get any bread out of this?" Finally Mark's father, Mr. Tomazzo, a hardened and cynical blue-collar worker, reveals simply that he has disowned his son long ago ("my son was no good... that son of a bitch, my son is dead"). These brief interview clips are enough to establish what we have already surmised: that Yates and his team represent the most decadent extreme of the Age of Aquarius – adrift from their homes and families and without any moral ties to speak of, they are united only in their obsessive quest for the scoop, and the financial rewards it might bring them.

In the same way, we learn, this is a group of people who have no respect for public and private boundaries, nor for the dignity of the individual human body. Their expedition knows no notion of privacy, and there is no personal act that does not find its way into the film. We first see Faye emerging nude from a shower, filmed by Mark, while Jack wrestles with her, steals her panties and throws them across the room ("a crew of clowns – they had a great sense of the theatrical", comments Monroe in the BDC-TV viewing room. "Like I said, they were real professionals"). Later, when the gruesome mutilation of the turtle prompts Faye to seek a private corner in which to vomit, the camera follows her, filming the act with relish. She is even filmed defecating in the forest, something she accepts with equanimity ("I had to wait in line, with the rest of the animals", she laughs). Later, Alan is filmed urinating, and Mark having a shave. When his massacre of the Yanomomo has excited Yates erotically, he is filmed pulling off Faye's jeans and making love to her violently – a precedent for the eventual gang-rape of a young Yanomomo girl, a "little monkey", who is raped by Jack, Mark and then Alan, each taking it in turns to hold the camera. And then, of

course, there are the private moments of bodily death, made public by the ever-present camera. When Fillippe is bitten by a snake, Alan gleefully films the fatal mutilation of his leg and the cauterization of the bloody stump. Other private acts made gruesomely public include the induced abortion and execution of a native woman, the Yanomomo girl's impalement on a stake, the death, castration and mutilation of Jack, the decapitation of Faye and Mark, and finally Alan – achieving the ultimate scoop – manages to catch even his own death on-camera. Historians and anthropologists have often pointed out that this collapse of public and private boundaries, allowing the public to impinge on the private and vice versa, is one of the most notable hallmarks of a decadent civilization.

Another characteristic of the team's degeneracy is their unflinching indulgence in animal mutilation – the chief reason for the banning of **Cannibal Holocaust** in Britain. Snakes and spiders are killed as a matter of routine, but the turtle mutilation is another matter. Still alive as Fillippe dismembers it and prizes the shell off its back, its feet continue to flap and twitch and its head, lying some distance away, continues to gasp and croak. Later, on arriving at the Yanomomo village, Alan kicks a wild piglet around to make it squeal helplessly before shooting it in the side.

Thus we are introduced to the documentary crew – a team who have set about shooting this footage for reasons no more altruistic than the desire to win awards ("keep rolling – we're gonna get an Oscar for this!", cries Mark at one point) – and all the financial benefits that such success can bring ("this's gonna make us rich and famous!", yells Alan, "this's gonna make us lots of money!"). For Yates and his team, crossing the border between Brazil and Peru seems to represent the breakdown of those moral boundaries that protect human dignity, self-respect and privacy: the Green Inferno is a zone of transgression and taboo. Here, even the primitive human ritual of give and take is reduced to a cruel farce.

Yates and his team all take from the jungle – carving up the turtle, shooting the pig, pinning rare butterflies to a board – but have nothing to give in return. They take the service of Fillippe, their loyal guide, and repay him with a cruel and violent death. They take a monkey from the trees, kill it and throw its head into the jungle. When a brave Yanomomo tries to take the head for food, they pepper him with bullets, forcing him to move slowly enough for them to be able to follow him to his native village. Taking burning brands to the villagers' huts, they herd up the natives like cattle and burn down their homes. They take film footage of a private ceremony of execution, take the virginity of the Yanomomo girl in a particularly violent gang rape, then take more footage of her bizarre ritual impalement. For the sake of the microphones, Alan comments hypocritically on the grotesque tableau before him ("it's unbelievable, it's horrible, I can't understand the reason for such cruelty... it must have something to do with some bizarre sexual rite, or with the profound respect these primitives have for virginity"). Finally, of course, the Yanomomo wreak their fatal and legitimate revenge on their persecutors by taking part in the ancient and symbolic practise of ritual cannibalism, thereby taking their enemies' lives.

As anthropology has often testified, there is nothing bizarre, taboo or forbidden about cannibalism – particularly exophagy – so long as it takes place for a morally sanctioned reason (see chapter 1). What happens in **Cannibal Holocaust**, however, is something rather different. The Yanomomo's mutilation, decapitation and consumption of the four reporters takes place for reasons neither of protein lack, nor as the result of extreme necessity, nor for morally sanctioned magico-religious reasons. What happens in Deodato's film is a different kind of cannibalism altogether: the extreme and terrifying reaction of a society whose moral boundaries have been forced to collapse, whose foundations have been forcibly shaken and whose basic system of exchange has been exploited and abused. This is the kind of cannibalism whose morally unsanctioned nature would have led it to be seen in the same category as witchcraft, as the exhumation of decaying flesh to eat from graveyards, or – latterly – as psychosis. This is the repayment of flesh debts, transmuted into a violent quest for total vengeance, an ultimate demonstration of hatred or scorn. The cannibalism of the Yanomomo in **The Green Inferno** functions as payback homicide: exophagy intended to shame and insult the anarchic foreigners. It is cannibalism that takes place as a hysterical reaction to moral and social collapse.

The Green Inferno is an "improper" film because it is a film of chaos and warning. It warns of the consequences of social breakdown, of moral collapse and the failure of the system of exchange, of what happens when the system of giving and taking is replaced by a selfish and aggressive one of taking and taking back. The system of exchange has become a system of vendetta, of morally unsanctioned thefts, of the payment and repayment of flesh debts. In an ironic twist, the BDC-TV projectionist, joining in the chaos, steals the footage and smuggles it out of the projection booth instead of destroying it, as Monroe tells him to, thereby preserving this moral tale of near-apocalypse for our gleeful entertainment and horror. Little surprise, then, that the film ends with Monroe gazing round the streets of New York City, wondering just "who the real cannibals are".

In the first section of **Cannibal Holocaust** – the narrative of Monroe's search party – we are told that the apocalyptic transgression of Yates and his team have cast an "evil spell" over the Green Inferno. Upon capturing a Yanomomo warrior whom Chako recognizes from his symbolic body markings to

be "the son of a shaman who has been consecrated to the spirit of a jaguar", we are informed that "the Yanomomo are not really cannibals", and their anthropophagic assault on Yates and his team was, in fact, part of "a religious ceremony to chase the spirits of the white men out of the jungle" – a ceremony which, apparently, is still in process. It is the task of Monroe and his search party to disperse this evil spell by enacting a narrative of propriety and ordered exchange, thereby re-establishing the solid boundaries between public and private, the "proper" system of giving and taking which Yates and his team did so much to destroy.

Firstly, unlike the crack team of scoop-hunters, Monroe is – however implausibly – carefully characterized as an "official", and his search party is formed with altruism, rather than exploitation, as its motivating force. The trip is sponsored jointly by New York University and "Pam Am Broadcasting Corporation". Monroe is described as "NYU's noted anthropologist, specialist on primitive cultures", and first seen walking across the lawns of an appropriately collegiate-looking institution. His status as the brave and humanitarian representative of an idealized American democracy is ratified by the mercenary Chako, who comments, on first being introduced to Monroe, that "you anthropologists and missionaries are made out of special stuff... I would give anything to be somewhere else".

Secondly, Monroe's narrative begins tentatively to re-establish the "civilized" social boundaries between public and private worlds. Although the camera lingers in voyeuristic close-up over Chako's picking fat slugs off Fillippe's corpse and Monroe vomiting at the sight, the Yanomomo's private ceremonies are never interfered with. When the search party encounter a Yanomomo warrior enacting "a ritualistic punishment for adultery" – the rape and murder of a native woman with a nail-encrusted gourd – Monroe tries to intervene but Chako holds him back, reminding him that this kind of punishment is considered a divine commandment, and "if he had not killed her, the tribe would have killed him". At the Tree People's village, Monroe and his team observe the rites of the warriors from an unobtrusive hiding place, anxious that the Yanomomo still behave towards them "with a mixture of fear and distrust" and observing the rituals of the tribe from an appropriate distance, never intervening. "We were permitted to observe the execution of one of their warriors – death by mutilation", whispers Monroe into his tape recorder. "From the way the criminal was destroyed, he must have done something horrible to incur the wrath of his own people. It's not clear if this was to pay a debt of honour to us, or only to demonstrate how they dispense justice". Monroe, Chako and their guide Miguel mix with the Tree People only at certain times, when invited to join in particular ceremonies. Otherwise, they keep to their own tent. But perhaps the most solid indication that Monroe's narrative is one of social order and the re-establishment of boundaries is his attitude towards the developed rolls of film. The executives at BDC-TV attempt to persuade Monroe, as an "eye witness", to host the screening of **The Green Inferno**, to "let the public know the truth" and "let the public judge". But Monroe, knowing this to be a voyeuristic invasion of what is essentially a private apocalypse, orders the material to be destroyed.

Thirdly, everything that is taken from the jungle or its inhabitants is either shared, restored, or replaced with gifts of equal value. This civilized process of giving and taking is established right from the outset by a series of communal exchanges between Chako and Monroe. At the camp, when Monroe asks Chako to switch off his tinny radio, he does so without question, offering to share his beer supply with the professor, which Monroe politely declines (and not without reason: "a skunk must have pissed in it", gags Chako, spitting the beer out into the jungle). This symbolic exchange is later repeated at their encampment in the

Yanomomo village, when Chako offers to roll Monroe a cigarette but the professor, again amicably, declines.

These private rituals of exchange are symbolically acted out on a public level between Monroe's team and the Yanomomo. In this part of the narrative, the system of exchange takes place in the context of public drama – with nothing secret about it – and is directly associated with public esteem, the distribution of honour, the sanctions of religion and respect for the dignity of the human body. When Miguel catches a muskrat with his bare hands, although he slits its throat with almost as much relish as Fillippe skins the turtle, he shares out the pickings equably, tossing the muskrat stomach to their Yanomomo guide who scoffs it raw, snickering to himself greedily. His dessert is a line of white powder – presumably cocaine – shared with him by Chako, albeit with the intention of stopping him from escaping that night, since they are by now very close to the Yanomomo encampment and their guide can "already smell his own". Early the next day the search party arrives at the village, in range of the tribal drums. So as not to alarm the Indians, Chako and Miguel conceal themselves behind a log, sending Miguel (who takes off his trousers and remains naked) and the Yanomomo guide as their welcome party. The villagers then shoot a series of arrows at Miguel's feet – a symbolic gesture which is, according to Chako, supposed to "demonstrate their good intentions", although Monroe remains dubious ("I don't know about this", he remarks anxiously, "I think they want us for dinner tonight"). His concern is not groundless. Although Miguel and the guide are welcomed into the village with a chattering celebration, as soon as the Indians catch sight of the white men, chaos ensues. The natives begin screaming and wailing, tearing at the ground, gesticulating wildly towards a pile of skulls and the muddied corpses of two native women – their lives taken from them by Yates and the anarchic path of destruction he brought in his wake. Fortunately Miguel, familiar with the laws of the jungle, relieves the tense situation by simulating a series of magical gestures with his flick-knife, which he finally gives to the Yanomomo chief as a token of friendship and goodwill: a gift. "It's alright now, professor", says Chako to Monroe, and he is right. That evening, the search party are welcomed with a ritualized meal where a cauldron containing a thick, pasty white liquid is passed around from the villagers to their guests. The next day, the liaison is reinforced when Monroe, "naked and unfettered", decided to join a group of young native women chasing and frolicking in the river.

Upon discovering the existence of the cans of film footage, however, Monroe is faced with an enormous problem. To the Yanomomo, Yates's film cans are a totemic fetish commemorating the tribal massacre, and they are not willing to give them up. Although "they hadn't an inkling of what was really in those cans", as Monroe explains later to a BDC-TV executive, "they just knew that they were a threat. The Yanomomo understood how important these film cans were to Alan Yates and his crew... They thought this silver box contained their power – a power which, I must say again, caused much damage and violence". Knowing how valuable the silver tins are to the Yanomomo, Chako is ready to give up and return to the border, but Monroe can't bring himself to turn back empty-handed. First he tries offering firearms in exchange, but the Indians are unimpressed. Finally he decides to try an experiment, playing them a tape-recording he made the night before of the Yanomomo chief's magic wailing, backed by the beat of tribal drums. Slowly but gradually, the natives begin to emerge from their treetop hideaway, grunting and chanting excitedly. A dead body is lowered from the treetop, covered in blood: the evening menu. "You did it, goddammit", cries

Chako, "they just invited us to dinner!". The exchange has been accepted: film can for tape recorder. The deal is ratified that evening when Chako and Monroe, to the accompaniment of the tape-recorded wailing, are invited to participate in a cannibalistic feast – this time a celebration, a ceremony of chanting and dancing, of jubilant mutilation where the Yanomomo pluck handfuls of raw, dripping entrails from the fresh corpse and hand them to the pale dinner guests to bite into. Monroe – like Yates, professional till the end – manages to join in the spirit of things and partakes, with Chako, of the magic feast. The curse is lifted. "They thought that since I was capable of capturing the human voice I was also capable of capturing their spirits", he explains later, in the television studio. "This convinced them that I was the only one capable of breaking the evil spell that had been cast over the tribe by the murder of the whites".

Since **Cannibal Holocaust** is so clearly conservative in its narrative impact, so obviously the depiction of structural systems collapsed and restored, so straightforwardly an illustration of the morally sanctioned gift cycle upholding the social cycle, it is difficult to understand why reviewers considered it to be such a destructive and disturbing film. Clearly, this is a film with much to be desired in terms of formal qualities, acting talent, narrative plausibility, character development and so on, but to condemn **Cannibal Holocaust** for its moral and ethical implications seems to be somehow rather beside the point.

A major objection of the film's critics seemed to be the voyeuristic nature of its scenes of explicit violence and cruelty. *Image Et Son* declared itself shocked by a film in which humans are "rounded up, forced to flee, mutilated, decapitated, flayed, degraded..." (Lelande 1981:39). Zimmer, also in *Image Et Son*, describes the film as beating all the records of ignominy: "rapes, feasts of raw flesh, gross shots of decomposing corpses, interminable flayings and diverse mutilations are depicted with a great luxuriance in sordid details to culminate in an apotheosis of voyeurism in which the team cameraman films the atrocious agonies of his companions" (Zimmer 1981:50). *Variety* condemned "Deodato's inclusion of much extraneous gore effects and nudity, as well as the genre's usual (and disgusting) killing of animals on camera" (*Cannibal Holocaust* 1985:72). Alain Garsault in *Positif* commented that Yates and his team "appear well-placed amidst the source of horror, which is so atrocious to the sensibilities of the television executives that one of them orders it to be burnt – after we have seen it, of course" (Garsault 1981:35), and *Cahiers du Cinéma* claimed that "the sole but not negligible effort of the spectator consists partly in overcoming his repulsion at this defiling of phobic objects and traumatizing scenes, partly in not abandoning himself to the only desire that this film excites: that of censorship" (Gere 1981:63).

Other critics had more of a difficulty with the ethical problems created by the film, particularly its alleged racism. Jean Roy in *Cinéma 81* described **Cannibal Holocaust** as "a racist and fascist film which was made in this way to shock us by the inclusion of everything we find degrading", and had just one question to ask: "how much did they pay the unfortunate Indians to make us believe that they are nothing but vulgar beasts?" (Roy 1981:125). *Positif* mentioned the film's "aggressive misogyny and... old racist clichés" (Garsault 1981:35). Lelande ridiculed the "generic guise" of the "wild Yanomomos" (Lelande 1981:39)[1], and Gere in *Cahiers du Cinéma* was primarily offended by "an explicit racism which, I must say, I haven't seen the like of for some time" (Gere 1981:63).

Above all, however, the film's critics were united in outright disgust at what they considered to be studied hypocrisy in the way the film purports to condemn that which it clearly takes a voyeuristic delight in displaying. "The anthropologist declares that it would be odious to show such films to the public", comments Jean Roy in *Cinéma 81*, "[but] what do you think the spectator is shown for the next hour and a half? The famous ignominious footage, with occasional breaks to tell us how disgusting it all is. And yes, it certainly is" (Roy 1981:125). *Variety* ridiculed the film's "liberal" message of civilized man's cruelty to primitive peoples as "ludicrous" and "old hat" (*Cannibal Holocaust* 1985:72), a criticism with which Garsault agreed in *Positif*:

"A product of overkill in the domain of horror, Cannibal Holocaust would merit no more than an accusatory silence, were it not for the enormous hypocrisy of its director, Ruggero Deodato, and producer Gianfranco Clerici.... The last phrase of the dialogue – 'I wonder who the real cannibals are' – carries with it an assertion that is not only clichéd, but rarely employed with such total and evident bad faith. The discredit it places on these filmmakers is worse even than that inspired by the lengths they have gone to to find out how they can excite the most repulsion in the contemporary spectator."

—Garsault 1981:35

And Gere, who begins his review by suggesting that – were it not for the accompaniment of so much hypocrisy – one might be able to find something likable and amusing in "this mixture of formal carelessness and intellectual naivety" becomes more and more scathing and critical in his vitriolic indignation at the film until concluding with the most vicious attack of all: "of Ruggero Deodato one can only say, as the English said of Mussolini in 1940, 'if you see this man, cross over the street'" (Gere 1981:63).

If part of the "improper" film involves explicit and voyeuristic pleasure in cruelty and barbarism, it is only in order for the "proper" film more fully to clear the rubble in preparation for new social relations to be restored. The "proper" film illustrates that the best way of maintaining the virility of the indigenous social structure is by allowing the periodic redistribution of structural forces.

Contemporary critics and reviewers of the film did not seem to realize that Deodato's cannibal saga is, in fact, a film of restoration and redistribution rather than a film of chaos and destruction. Most seem to have been distracted by Deodato's alleged voyeurism from attending to the film's restorative implications, preferring instead to condemn it as a tale of racist hypocrisy. Or perhaps the film's narrative structure detracts from its restorative impact. In other words, the reversed chronological order – showing Monroe's "proper" narrative before Yates's "improper" film – perhaps leaves the spectators with a final taste of chaos and destruction, rather than order and repair. Or perhaps there is a third reason.

In fact, **Cannibal Holocaust** consists not of two films, but of three. At BDC-TV in New York City, Monroe studies one of Yates's earlier documentaries, **The Last Road To Hell**, to get a little more background information about the team of ill-fated film-makers. **The Last Road To Hell**, it is claimed, was made by Yates and his team a year and a half ago, in Africa. This flickering black-and-white footage, with a haunting and romantic soundtrack, consists of images of blacks being slaughtered at the hands of a Third World dictatorship. A firing squad cuts down a line of men; piles of corpses lie abandoned in the road; men and women are tied to posts and executed; trussed-up cadavers are tossed casually into the back of a truck; the mutilated and the dead are laid out in a public square. For this section of the film, Deodato utilizes actual news footage: "the atrocities

meted out in this archive material are undeniably real" (Kerekes and Slater 1994:68).

"Pretty powerful stuff, huh?", asks the BDC-TV executive. "Well, just to give you an idea how Alan and the others worked, everything you just saw was put on... That was no enemy army approaching. Alan paid those soldiers to do a bit of 'acting' for him", implying, of course, that the whole massacre and series of executions had been "set up" and paid for by the film-makers. In the fiction of **Cannibal Holocaust**, **The Last Road To Hell** is intended, like **The Green Inferno**, to be a "genuine" snuff movie. In fact, it is a series of news-footage out-takes of "real-life" deaths.

The Last Road To Hell serves a number of highly significant narrative functions. Principally, through its irrefutable realism, the sheer numbers of bodies mown down, the understated tone and unsensational, undramatic depiction of fast, simple executions, this footage throws into perspective the only too patent phoneyness of what one reviewer referred to as "*l'enfer vert déodato-amazonien*" (Lelande 1981:39), with its flickering, scratched, elaborately unfocused, dramatically "amateurish" cinematic style. In other words, **The Last Road To Hell** is a testament of the actual transgression of all those rules that **The Green Inferno** merely pretends to break, particularly those of voyeurism and the public appropriation of what is essentially a private moment – the moment of death. The real "genuine" footage slips by quickly, briefly, undramatically and with little attention drawn to it; the fake "genuine" footage, on the other hand, is announced elaborately, exotically and melodramatically, and – in return – attracted elaborate, exotic indignation from the film's critics. The staged voyeurism of **The Green Inferno** plays at breaking the rules of boundary-breaking cinematic intrusion which **The Last Road To Hell** breaks for real, thereby explaining why this pseudo-voyeurism is necessary. **The Last Road To Hell** is the secret token hidden inside **Cannibal Holocaust** which categorically endorses, consolidates and sanctions the film's narrative consequence. **The Last Road To Hell** is a fleeting and crucial glimpse of the unimaginable reality which **Cannibal Holocaust** (falsely) disguises itself as. When the very rules we unconsciously desire to break are actually broken without our knowledge, it slips by unnoticed, but leaves a highly unpleasant taste in the mouth: a taste which we then indignantly attribute – and quite wrongly so – to the central narrative of **Cannibal Holocaust**. No wonder so many critics made such a meal of it.

In trying to account for the large numbers of uninfected skeletons discovered in the leper graveyards of western Christendom and the Latin kingdom of Jerusalem in the east, cultural anthropologist Mary Douglas maintains that the people of the period may have been trying to cure a real social blight by isolating an imaginary disease (Douglas 1992:97). Other, such as Bryan Turner, argue that it is more likely that they were confusing a real disease with imaginary sins. It is highly possible that a similar process is in place with regard to **Cannibal Holocaust**. Indignantly condemned for hypocrisy and voyeurism, Deodato has committed none but imaginary sins. In fact, by telling a story about a collapsed system of exchange, of public and private boundaries falling in on one another, about theft, blame and libel, **Cannibal Holocaust** is the kind of story which, by causing its audience to reconsider the signification of moral and social forces, is the safest way to maintain the strength and vitality of our shared process of social exchange: the simple system of give and take.

CANNIBAL CARRION

1980 brought a whole feast of cannibal films to Italian cinema and video screens. Most significantly, from Umberto Lenzi came **Eaten Alive** (a.k.a. **Doomed To Die**, a.k.a **Mangiati Vivi!**, a.k.a. **Eaten Alive By The Cannibals**, a.k.a. **The Emerald Jungle**, a.k.a. **Mangiati Vivi Dai Cannibali**), filmed in November and December 1979 in location in Sri Lanka, New York, and the Niagara Falls. In the tradition of **Cannibal Holocaust** and like so many other similar productions, the film was condemned for its explicit footage of (genuine) animal butchery and (inexpertly faked) human mutilation, which led to the film's cult popularity amongst fringe horror video audiences. Nevertheless, **Eaten Alive** is an above-average Italian cannibal feature, greatly benefiting from some atmospheric photography, a fine musical score and a thoughtfully scripted plotline.

The film opens with an assassination at the Niagara Falls, where a man is killed by a mystery assassin using cobra venom-tipped blow-darts. When the assassin is crushed under the wheels of a truck on a New York street, his death leaves a vital clue to the whereabouts of the enigmatic Reverend Melvyn Jonas (played by cannibal regular Ivan Rassimov), leader of a Jim Jones-style doomsday cult which opposes civilization and is attempting to reunite man with nature by means of various ancient purification rituals of dubious authenticity. This clue is a small piece of 8mm film, which Professor Carter (guest "star" Mel Ferrer) matches up with a similar piece of film belonging to Diana Morris (Paola Senatore), a wealthy woman who has recently gone missing under suspicious circumstances. Learning the news, Diana's younger sister Sheila (Scandinavian porn actress Janet Agren) puts out $100,000 to hire the services of Vietnam deserter and all-round soldier of fortune Mark Butler (porno regular Roberto Bolla,

working here under the alias of Robert Kerman), who agrees to accompany her
to the jungles of New Guinea (although these sequences were actually filmed in

Anthropophagus, The Beast

Sri Lanka) to search for her missing sister.

At this point, the action really gets going. Highlights include battles with the ubiquitous local cannibals, footage of animals devouring one another and a man-eating crocodile. The fact that much of this human-and-animal-mutilation footage was culled from other Italian jungle films (including Deodato's **Last Cannibal World** and Lenzi's own **Deep River Savages**) does little to detract from the exhilarating brutality of the second half of the film. After encountering the Reverend Jonas and getting caught up in the bizarre purification cult, Sheila and Butler escape, aided by a sympathetic native girl (the ubiquitous Me Me Lai in her regular role), and Jonas flees after having his followers commit mass suicide in the style of the Guyana Jonestown massacre. As cult Italian cannibal films go, Lenzi's **Eaten Alive** is one of the best, crammed full of classic set-pieces of human and animal savagery.

In the same year, from the lens of Joe D'Amato (a.k.a. Aristide Massaccesi) came the unforgettable **Anthropophagus, The Beast** (a.k.a. **The Savage Island, The Grim Reaper, Man Beast, Anthropophagous**). If it is remembered for nothing else, **Anthropophagus** will go down in cinema history as the only film to climax with the villain dementedly chewing on his own intestines. The narrative presents us with a group of tourists, including Julie (Tisa Farrow), Alan (Saverio Vallone), Daniel (Mark Bodin), Arnie (Bob Larson) and Ariette (Rubina Rey), visiting the scenic locations of a beautiful Greek island (the cue for some superb island vistas), including its historic catacombs. When they come across a disfigured cannibalistic psycho (played by scriptwriter Luigi Montefiori, cast due to his imposing physical stature and the fact that – if the script is anything to go by – he obviously didn't

Anthropophagus, The Beast

have much work to do), the result is a barrage of murder, violence, death, pain, gore and slaughter. One memorably frightening moment occurs when the Beast is first introduced, lurking in the darkened corner of a room, his presence suddenly revealed by an atmospheric flash of lightening. So reviled was the film by journalists and other media commentators that, following raids upon the homes of British video collectors, a clip from **Anthropophagus** was broadcast on British television with the claim that it was actually a scene from a "genuine" snuff movie, a claim that seriously affronted the film's director, Joe D'Amato, who

Cannibal Ferox

considered it "ridiculous... it's just a movie, that's a terrible claim". According to D'Amato, "these [movies] exist because people want to see such violence. It's not a fact that I like these things. ...these movies are just jobs I do".[2]

1981 brought us the memorable anthropophagic saga **Cannibal Ferox** (a.k.a. **Make Them Die Slowly**, a.k.a **Cannibal Ferrox**, dir. Umberto Lenzi, Italy 1981). This cannibal classic, from one of Italy's most infamous hack directors, benefits enormously from a higher budget than many similar cannibal productions, enabling Lenzi to afford to shoot on location in South America and in New York City, and to afford a fine cast of cannibal stalwarts including John Morghen (a.k.a. Giovanni Lombardo Radice) and the ubiquitous Roberto Bolla (a.k.a. R. Bolla, Salvatore Basile, Robert Kerman). It also boasts a perfunctory voyeuristic brutality, some powerful special effects and a rare tone of gleeful nihilism pitched at an undiscriminating, violence-seeking audience, which is spoiled only by some sloppy post-synch dubbing and a retro seventies soundtrack.

In New York City, drug pusher Mike Logan (John Morghen) falls out of favour with a group of fellow gangsters and wants to make a quick exit out of town. He needs a place to hide, and heads for the cannibal-infested jungles of Colombia in South America in search of cocaine and emeralds. Here, he runs into a team of anthropologists, consisting of Gloria Davis (Lorainne de Selle), her brother Rudy (Brian Redford), and their friend Patricia (Zora Kerowa). Gloria is in the process of researching her doctoral thesis for New York University[3], attempting to prove that cannibalism does not exist, that it is a myth created by white oppressors to justify their own oppression (possibly after spending too much time reading William Arens's book *The Man Eating Myth* – see chapter 1). "Cannibalism", explains Gloria, "was an invention of racism and colonialism, which

had a vested interest in creating the myth of the ferocious, sub-human savage fit only for extermination. The myth of cannibal ferox was only an alibi to justify the greed and cruelty of the Conquistadors". As we might have expected, it isn't long before humble pie isn't the only thing on the menu.

One night in the jungle, Logan and Joe, strung out on cocaine, apparently butcher a handful of natives. Their retaliation, when it comes, is brutal, monstrous, and grotesque. Amongst the usual scenes of genuine animal mutilation and abuse, a small monkey is eaten alive by a leopard, Logan unnecessarily stabs a baby piglet to death, the cannibals gut a small crocodile and devour its intestines, and – of course, in a scene without which no self-respecting cannibal film would be complete – another turtle's shell is prized off, the turtle cut up and eaten alive (barely). While the cannibals prepare to torture the intrepid women, Gloria and Patricia sing a heroic round of "Red River Valley" to keep their spirits up, but in this film, the stoicism doesn't last for long. Patricia is forced to suffer a double indignity: not long after being plied with cocaine and seduced by Mike, her breasts are skewered by large hooks and she is strung aloft to die in agony while Gloria is forced to watch. After a spate of maggot-eating, Joe dies from fever, and the cannibals slice open his body and eat his intestines raw. Rudy manages to escape, but while hiding from the cannibals by the river's edge, he is bitten by pirhanas and leeches and is recaptured.

Logan, after spitting in the eye of the cannibal chief, is vividly castrated on-camera: the cannibal chief slices off his penis and eats it. Logan then escapes, is recaptured, and has one of his hands lopped off. A police plane lands, but the natives make up a story that the white people died, having being eaten by crocodiles when their dinghy capsized. Soon satisfied there are no survivors, the police leave. Failing to learn his lesson, Logan escapes again and is again recaptured before having the top of his skull sliced off and, in a vivid and realistic

little vignette, is placed under a large table with a hole in the centre and transformed into a living cannibal fondue. The top of his head is sliced off, and his brains are eaten fresh out of the top of his skull.

As in many similar films, the usual assumptions about the superiority of strong, white, blonde-haired Westerners and the inferiority of the "savages" are simplistically countered by the presence of monstrous, brutal whites (especially the sadistic, cocaine-crazed Logan), re-acquainting us with some old clichés about "who the real cannibals are". The film closes back in New York, as Gloria presents her findings to the university panel. She is awarded a Ph.D. for her dissertation "Cannibalism: The End Of A Myth". All traces of brutalism and savagery are hushed up, and the assembled learned audience are informed that "cannibalism does not exist". Gloria smiles gratefully as she is presented with her doctorate, obviously in a state of heightened denial.[4]

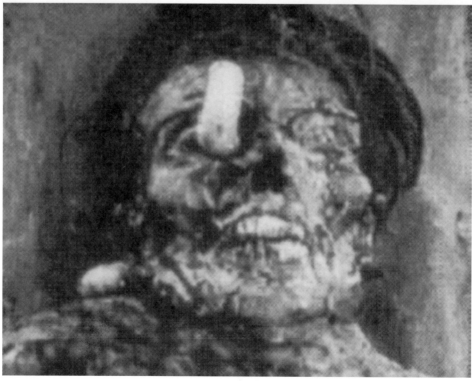

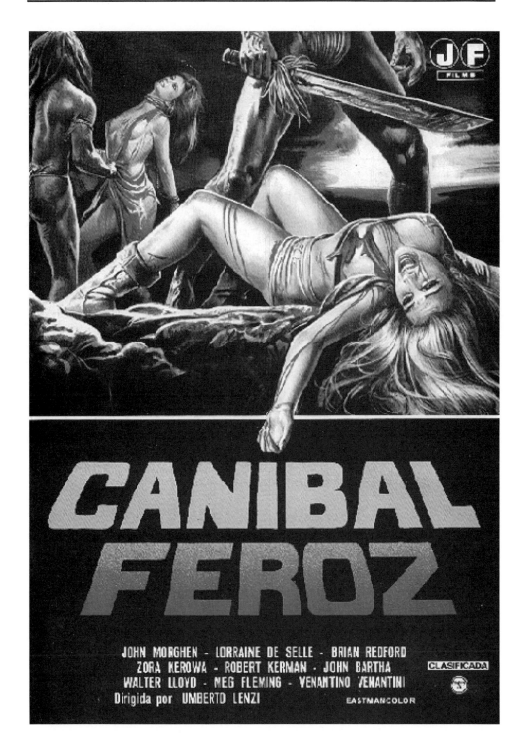

NOTES

1.　　　Lelande also condemned the film's hauntingly beautiful soundtrack – composed by Riz Ortolani, who won an Academy Award for his "Theme From Mondo Cane" – as "syrupy preparatory music".

2.　　　D'Amato had already touched on the cannibal theme in 1979 with **Buio Omega** (a.k.a. **Blue Holocaust**). In this gruesome epic, a mad taxidermist exhumes his dead lover and eats her heart while disembowelling and stuffing her; he then bites out the throat of a female intruder, who "comes alive" in the oven. D'Amato also directed Laura Gemser in **Papaya: Love Goddess Of The Cannibals**.

3.　　　(Which, if Italian cannibal films are anything to go by, seems to be a hotbed of "specialists" in the rituals of "primitive tribes".)

4.　　　A belated entry, Mario Gariazzo's **Amazonia** (a.k.a. **White Slave**, 1984) tells the tale of a blonde English woman who is adopted by an Amazon tribe after her parents have been decapitated and eaten by cannibals. She falls in love with one of the tribesmen. Scripted by Franco Prosperi (creator of **Mondo Cane**), the film is little more than an afterthought to the hardcore carnage of previous years.

chapter five:
cannibals by psychosis

WHILST some cannibals are born into their particular eating habits, and some are cannibalistic by accident or circumstance, perhaps the most frightening kind of cannibalism is that of the cannibal criminal. Whilst psychotic cannibalism in reality is perhaps less rare than many of us would like to believe (see chapter 2 for a varied selection of recent examples), in cinema, this kind of cannibalism has proven a staple motif of the horror genre from the early 1930s, and is still going strong today. Sagas of "natural" cannibals may provide the film-maker with an exciting jungle setting and some thrilling stone-age behaviour, but narratives of cannibalism by psychosis combine madness and mayhem with the exhilarating frisson of the broken taboo – and all in an otherwise "civilized" setting. Not surprisingly, then, the recent history of cinema provides us with a wide variety of cannibal crazies, from Fuad Ramses and his "Exotic Catering Shop" in the classic **Blood Feast**, to Hannibal Lecter, the psychotic gastronome in **Silence Of The Lambs**.

CANNIBAL CRAZIES

The dark and curious film **Dr. X** (dir. Michael Curtiz, U.S. 1932), based on a play by Howard W. Comstock and Allen W. Miller, stars Lionel Atwill as the mysterious Dr. Xavier, principal of a medical academy whose professors are virtually all, in one way or another, connected to the practise of cannibalism. Professor Wells (Preston Foster), the first academic we meet, is a one-armed student of cannibalism, and the author of a book on the subject. Two of the other professors employed at the academy, Professor Haines (John Griffith Wray) and the one-eyed Professor Rowitz (Arthur Edmund Carewe), were both shipwrecked a year ago in Tahiti, along with a third scientist, for twenty-four days. When they were finally rescued, Haines and Rowitz were both delirious, and the other man was missing – presumed drowned, though some more closely connected with the expedition had reason to suspect skulduggery afoot. The last professor we meet in Dr. Xavier's academy is Professor Duke (Harry Beresford), an ill-tempered old man in a wheelchair.

The story begins with the latest in a series of horrific murders by a mystery fiend known only as the "Full Moon Killer". Examining the victim's body in the morgue, police discover the trademarks of the killer – an incision made at the base of the brain, and parts of the body torn right out with the teeth ("gentlemen... this was cannibalism!"). Discovering that all the murders have taken place within the vicinity of Dr. X's academy, and that all were committed with a scalpel from Dr. X's institution, the police decide to interview everyone in the medical academy – followed at a distance by Lee Taylor, a newspaper reporter played by Lee Tracy who has a soft spot for Dr. X's glamorous daughter Joanne (Fay Wray). Terrified of possible publicity, Dr. X manages to persuade the police to let him conduct his own investigation into the murders.

Dr. X

To this end, Xavier takes his team of research scientists to a lonely, deserted house on Long Island, along with his daughter, a maid, and the butler, and tailed by the reporter, Lee. Gathering his staff together, Xavier explains the purposes of his experiment. "One of us in the room", he declares, "may be a cannibal". He believes that one of them, "at some point in the past, was driven to cannibalism", and "the memory of that act was driven like a nail into that man". By wiring each professor up to an electrical generator which amplifies the heartbeat four thousand times (and demonstrates their pulse reactions in coloured mercury in test tubes right before their eyes), and by re-enacting the circumstances of each murder, Xavier is convinced that the true cannibal will reveal himself. Professor Wells, because he only has one hand (and cannot, Xavier assumes, have committed the murders), operates the machinery, while Xavier ensures that he himself is included in the experiment. The first attempt backfires when the electric current short-circuits and there is a blackout, during which Rowitz is murdered, and his body partially devoured. The second experiment reveals the truth behind the "Full Moon Killer". We are shown Professor Wells putting on a facial mask and a fabricated hand both constructed from "synthetic flesh", a substance he has created from "the flesh of real people, the flesh that Africans eat", in order to indulge his clandestine appetites. But before he can get his hands on his chosen victim, Joanne, he is attacked by Lee and thrown through a glass window into the sea below.

What makes **Dr. X** such an interesting film is not only its morbid fascination with the cannibal theme, but the unusual level of symbolism which the narrative – sometimes unconsciously – employs. The full moon, for example, becomes something of a fetish in the film. Xavier has a theory that "locked in the human mind is a little world all of its own", that "a knot, a kink" may be "tied in the brain by some past experience", and the "reactions of the heart can make phobias surface and manifest themselves". Unbeknownst to Dr. X, this is exactly what the full moon represents to Professor Wells, whose desperate act of cannibalism some time in the past obviously took place during the light of the full moon. Or perhaps Xavier is somehow aware of this fact, since – for reasons unexplained – he cannot bear the sight of the moon himself. Ironically, Professor Duke's work at the medical academy involves the diagnosis of what Duke refers to as "moonstroke" – that is, the disorienting effect of the full moon "which powerfully affects certain neurotic types". "The moon", claims Duke, "drinks up water like some old scrubwoman". The victim of that night's murder was herself "an old scrubwoman murdered in very peculiar circumstances", and the constant gloomy notes of foghorns sounding through the night remind us that there is a full moon outside, tonight. In a further irony, Lee wangles his way into Xavier's private residence by flirting with the Xaviers' scrubwoman, who showers him angrily with a basin of dirty water from an upstairs balcony as he leaves.

Dr. X is also a film full of the symbolism of unconscious repression, from the half-eaten bodies examined under their sheets in the morgue, to the secret cupboards, back stairs and back passageways of Xavier's Long Island mansion. In order to understand precisely what is being repressed in this narrative, however, it is necessary to look at some of the film's many references to hands, and their use. Despite the success of his experiment with electricity which has kept alive a human heart for three years, Dr. Wells is crippled by his lack of a right arm (and, we learn, "the murderer is horribly disfigured"); he sometimes wears a false arm, but this "troubles him", as he confesses to Xavier. The first thing he does upon sight of the full moon is to pull off his false arm; the purpose of his experiments with synthetic flesh is, he claims, "to make a crippled world whole again". And should there be any doubt about the phallic symbolism of the missing arm, its sexual significance is vividly illustrated by a scene involving Professor Haines who, despite his claims that he is working on some delicate brain-grafting, is discovered to be concealing a girlie magazine in his lab.

And if Professor Wells's missing hand is a symbolic indicator of his impotence, his counterpart is to be found in the active, daredevil reporter Taylor, who scales walls and climbs through windows, slyly handles Joanne's photograph, and whose line in practical jokes runs to exploding cigars and a ubiquitous handshake buzzer. This latter item shows up in almost every scene in which Taylor is present. Policemen get buzzed in the morgue, Otto the butler gets buzzed in the closet, and when describing to Joanne how he got the "upper hand" in the battle against the monstrous Professor Wells, Taylor blames his victory solely on the handshake buzzer, before goosing her with it and making her squeal. Taylor's handshake buzzer is the symbolic equivalent of the phallic power that Professor Wells lacks, and Taylor proves the point by finally winning the hand of the doctor's daughter.

In 1936, the British director George King produced a highly successful film version of George Dibdin-Pitt's stage melodrama *Sweeney Todd, The Demon Barber Of Fleet Street*. The original play was turned into a film script by Frederick Hayward and H.F. Maltby, and filmed at Shepperton Studios. Although the script includes several inconsistencies in plot development, and although the film now seems very stagey in both its direction and its acting, the narrative was gruesome and absorbing enough to ensure the film's popularity with contemporary cannibal fans.

The film version is told as a flashback, with the present proprietor of

Sweeney Todd's barber's shop telling the story of his infamous predecessor to one of his customers. In his heyday, Todd (Tod Slaughter) would meet sailors and merchants at the docks, returning from the far East with their money and other treasures. Todd would encourage them to come to his barber's shop for a shave and a "polish up", where he would proceed to murder and rob them before turning the bodies over to his female accomplice Mrs. Lovatt (Stella Rho), owner of the neighbouring baker's shop, to turn into her well-loved meat pies. One day, one particular sailor, Mark Ingestre (Bruce Seton) is robbed but saved from murder by a sudden argument that breaks out between Sweeney Todd and Mrs. Lovatt. However, without his fortune, Mark is unable to marry his sweetheart Johanna Oakley (Eve Lister), the daughter of shipowner Stephen Oakley (D.J. Williams) who has also been robbed by Todd, partly because Todd himself is also hoping to marry Johanna. In disguise and followed secretly by Johanna, who fears for his safety, Mark returns to Sweeney Todd's shop to attempt to recover his treasure. Here, due to a couple of well-timed accidents, Todd is caught in his own trap, allowing Mark to win back both his treasure and his sweetheart, and both live happily ever after.[1]

BLOOD FEAST

One of the cinema's most reviled renditions of cannibalism was made for a mere $24,000 in 1963. Herschell Gordon Lewis's infamous **Blood Feast** is regarded – when it is regarded at all – as the absolute nadir of exploitation cinema. Original publicity posters, declaring the film "more grisly than ever, in blood color", promised its audience they would "Recoil and Shudder" when witnessing "the Slaughter and Mutilation of Nubile Young Girls – in a weird and horrendous Ancient Rite!". The extravagant advertising worked. The film was shot in four days of principal photography without a single rehearsal using crew left over from Lewis and Friedman's soft-core girlie film, **Bell, Bare And Beautiful** (1963); the script was written on a few sheets of paper and some napkins; the pyramid and sphinx which appear during the film's credits was the logo of the Suez motel in north Miami where Lewis just happened to be staying at the time. Despite all this, **Blood Feast** was Lewis's biggest and most profitable hit in a twelve-year film-making career devoted to the making of almost forty money-spinning exploitation films.

Academic and critical film theory erects a number of barriers to protect and defend itself from the threat of films like **Blood Feast**, including laughter, ridicule, contemptuous dismissal, the phenomenon of the late-night horror show on television, terms like "schlock" and "splatter", and the treatment of the horror movie as camp. Whilst it is true that audiences respond to **Blood Feast** with laughter and disdain because it is, by classical Hollywood standards, a wretchedly made movie – even Herschell Gordon Lewis has talked about the limitations of the actors' abilities and the fact that the script stresses gore at the expense of plausibility and coherence – there is something to be said for the film's transgression of classical cinema's barriers and limitations. Both Robin Wood and Carol J. Clover make the point that exploitation cinema displays quite openly and spectacularly before us images and meanings that most other kinds of films merely suggest or imply (Wood 1979; Clover 1992:236), and whilst there is a place in cinema for suggestion and implication, there is equally a place for transparency and display.

By operating at the "bottom line", argues Clover, "low" or exploitation horror reminds us that every movie has a bottom line, no matter how covert, disguised or sublimated it might be. Although clumsily produced and low in budget, films in the tradition of **Blood Feast** are deeply frank and energetic and repress nothing, speaking to unconscious fears and anxieties in the flattest of terms. According to its director, **Blood Feast** is a film that works in the tradition of "the crude power of a play by Aeschylus, as opposed to a polished play by Sophocles" (Vale & Juno 1986:20). Lewis, an exploitation filmmaker who would do anything to promote his films, clearly enjoyed these games of extravagant self-promotion. But this is not to say he is wrong: **Blood Feast** is an integrally primal and powerful movie, both in its role as the *ur*-text for the slasher genre's treatment of violence and spectacle, and its confrontation with the ancient taboo of cannibalism.

The narrative of **Blood Feast** centres around the character of Fuad Ramses (memorably played by Mal Arnold), a mysterious lame Egyptian chef with "wild eyes" and a dragging left (and sometimes right) leg. Ramses is the proprietor of a catering company which specializes in "exotic feasts", a cover-up for his worship of the blood goddess Ishtar, whose altar is hidden in the back room of his shop. The arrival of spring heralds Ramses' preparations for the Blood Feast, an ancient Egyptian ritual whose observance requires the traditional consumption of a bloody stew made of certain organs and limbs removed from the bodies of beautiful young virgins. On the seventh day of the feast, if all goes according to plan, the goddess Ishtar will rise from the tomb and show herself in flesh and blood, a part of the people.

In order to gather together the ingredients for the sacred feast, Ramses commits a series of grisly ritualistic murders. The film opens with an attack on a young girl in the bath. Ramses pokes out her eye with a sword then hacks off her legs and wraps them in newspaper. His second victim, Marcie (Ashlyn Martin, *Playboy* playmate of April 1964) is making love to her boyfriend on the beach when she is attacked, murdered and her brain removed, still quivering. A third girl (Astrid Olsen[2]) is stalked to a motel where Ramses pulls her tongue out of her mouth with his bare hands. A fourth victim, whose murder we do not witness, has "the whole side of her face hacked away" but survives long enough to inform the police that her assailant was a "horrible old man" with "wild eyes" who said "it was for *Eetar*...."

Meanwhile, Mrs. Dorothy Fremont (Lyn Bolton) is planning a surprise birthday party for her daughter, Suzette (Connie Mason, *Playboy* Playmate of June 1963). When Mrs. Fremont visits Fuad Ramses' Exotic Catering Shop on the recommendation of a friend, she is hypnotized by Ramses into agreeing to host an authentic Egyptian feast for Suzette, a devotee of Egyptian history and culture. The day before the feast, one of Suzette's friends is stalked and captured by Ramses and taken to the altar of Ishtar where she is tied up and flayed to death, her blood gathered in a silver goblet. In the meantime Suzette's boyfriend Pete Thornton (Thomas Wood), a detective on the case, has pieced together the word *Eetar* with the cult of Ishtar, something that he has recently learned about by attending a lecture on Egyptian history with Suzette. Pete and his men raid the catering shop, where they discover the body of the latest victim and the preparations for the Blood Feast spread out on the altar of Ishtar. The police speed to the Fremont residence where Ramses, having lured Suzette into the kitchen, is on the verge of sacrificing her on the kitchen counter with a machete. The murder is averted, Ramses is chased out of town by the detectives and takes

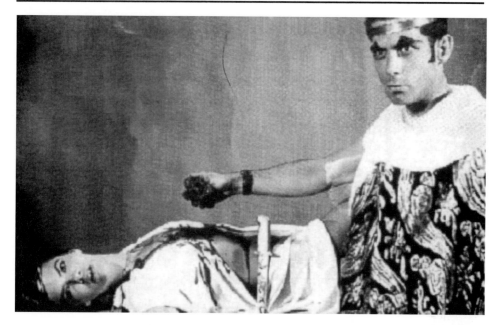

Blood Feast

refuge by hiding in the back of a garbage truck where he is accidentally crushed to death, "like the garbage he was".

At the time of its first release, **Blood Feast** was reviewed extensively in *Time*, *Newsweek* and *Variety*, to almost universal distaste. Ever since, it has attained the status of a cult classic as "the infamous first gore film" (Weldon 1983:70) and "the original splatter film" (O'Neill 1994:68). Critic Danny Peary describes the film as "one of the most inept pictures of all time. The acting is ghastly, casting abominable, scoring (by Lewis) miserable, camerawork clumsy" (Peary 1983:25-27). James O'Neill comments that although the film is "technically inept" and features "ludicrous acting", the "slash-happy bloodbath" is "sick fun, thanks to its ludicrously over-the-top gore effects" (O'Neill 1994:68). Lewis went on to direct a whole string of similar exploitation films through the mid-sixties and early seventies, including **Two Thousand Maniacs** (1964), **Color Me Blood Red** (1965), **The Gruesome Twosome** (1967) and **The Gore-Gore Girls** (1972). None of these luridly-titled B-movies were ever quite as successful as **Blood Feast**, but they were all financially lucrative[3].

As its title clearly suggests, **Blood Feast** is a film all about cannibalism[4]. Fuad Ramses is a modern-day cannibal who murders his victims so that he can eat their bodies – or, at least, parts of their bodies – in the worship of Ishtar. Ishtar herself, we learn, is a cannibalistic goddess, worshipped like Venus and Aphrodite of the Greek and Roman civilizations, except that "hers was an evil love that thrived on violence". Had the Blood Feast been successful, Mrs. Fremont, along with her guests, would have been dining on the flesh of her daughter. Instead of the birthday feast being held in honour of Suzette, Suzette would have become a part of the feast itself – along with the first victim's eye and legs, the second victim's brain, the third victim's tongue, the fourth victim's skin and face and the last victim's heart. And in the end, of course, Ramses himself is symbolically ingested, ground up into a bloody pulp and swallowed by the crushing metal jaws of the garbage truck. But what is crucial to the narrative of the film is that the

Blood Feast itself never actually takes place. The meat is cooked, the stew prepared, the flavour added and the table laid, but the sacrament never occurs. Fuad Ramses is caught (quite literally) red-handed at the very last moment, and chased from the kitchen by police. The Blood Feast is prepared but uneaten. In fact, although this is a film all about cannibalism and cannibalistic rituals, no actual cannibalism ever takes place, as Mrs. Fremont's final line makes clear:

Pete: Mrs. Fremont, I'm afraid this "feast" is evidence of murder.
Mrs. Fremont: Oh dear. The guests will have to eat hamburger tonight.

Blood Feast is a curious film with a substantial role in the subsequent history of exploitation cinema, slasher movies and cannibal films. The film is particularly curious because – like a number of archetypal folk tales and mythological narratives – it is governed by the central metaphor of cannibalism averted. Although the entire film revolves around the murderous preparations for the Blood Feast of Ishtar, the only actual instance of human consumption in **Blood Feast** is Ramses' "filthy death" in the form of a symbolic disappearance into the grinding metal jaws of a garbage truck. Moreover, the historical standing of the film is also consequential, as it is regularly cited as the definitive *ur*-text of the slasher movie genre. Both points deserve further explanation.

Understanding the narrative of **Blood Feast** as a metaphor can help us to come to terms with the way in which psychoanalytic evaluation of the patient needs to pay utmost attention to what is repressed in that patient's thoughts, words, writings and dream-narratives, since the manifest content of such narratives can be regarded as a symbolic manifestation of what is not told: the story that is lost. The governing narrative of **Blood Feast** is a metaphor for the psychoanalytic paradigm, where nothing is more significant than that which does *not* happen. For it is only by directing our attention to that which does *not* happen that we can start to pick up the clues to solving the puzzle of what *did* happen, once upon a time.

William Friedkin has suggested that an audience's emotional engagement with a horror movie begins while they are standing in line, a claim which acknowledges the profoundly formulaic nature of the horror film business (Derry 1977:123–124). Innumerable film critics of the traditional horror film have identified its original manifestation in the psychological trauma and suspense of Hitchcock's **Psycho**. As for the less respectable face of horror – the slasher movie – the narrative foundations for this highly ritualized and formulaic tale are laid for the first time in 1963, in the story of Fuad Ramses and his Blood Feast.

The slasher plot is perhaps the most predictable narrative form in contemporary cinema. The audience of such films is generally highly "slasher-literate", and competent in recognizing and anticipating its narrative conventions. Andrew Britton has described how watching a contemporary slasher film in a downtown cinema with a slasher-literate audience can be akin to participation in a kind of ritual:

"The film's total predictability did not create boredom or disappointment. On the contrary, the predictability was clearly the main source of pleasure, and the only occasion for disappointment would have been a modulation of the formula, not the repetition of it."

—Britton 1979: 2-3

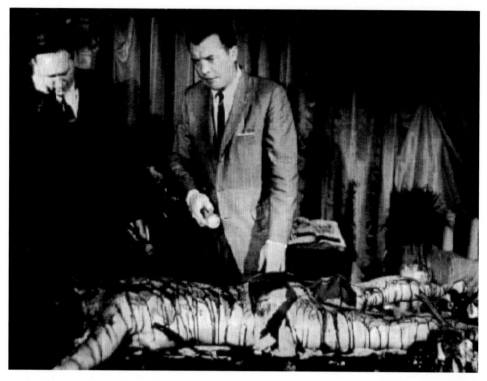

Blood Feast

Blood Feast has been neglected in the slasher genre to which it belongs, just as (and partly because) it has been ignored by academic as well as popular film theory. But – at least in terms of narrative structure and symbolic form – the story of Fuad Ramses and his Blood Feast has been highly influential in what is a long tradition of "disrespectable" slasher and stalker films, from **Halloween** to **Frankenhooker**[5]. To pick up once again on the psychoanalytic metaphor, **Blood Feast** is the "primal scene" of the slasher film genre. Put in its simplest narrative terms, **Blood Feast** is the story of a bloodthirsty fiend who sets about killing and mutilating a series of sexually attractive, pubescent females one by one until only a single girl in the chain remains alive. This highly ritualized and formulaic narrative structure has been analyzed in all its potential variations by numerous critics of the slasher film, notably Carol J. Clover and James Iaccino. Despite countless possible thematic and structural variations, however, certain constraints remain in place. Virtually Aristotelian in structure[6], the slasher narrative regularly adheres to the unity of time (usually taking place on one night), the unity of place (almost invariably small-town America) and unity of action (each killing takes a unique but similar form). The terrible place in which all the victims sooner or later find themselves usually takes the form of a house (or similar building), from Fuad Ramses' Exotic Catering Shop in **Blood Feast** (lit by candles and containing a number of menacing-looking cooking implements), to the Myers house in **Halloween**, to Freddy's boiler room in **Nightmare On Elm Street**. Ramses' set of carving knives are an early version of the terrible weapons which play such a significant part in so many subsequent slasher movies: ice picks, chainsaws, hammers, axes, pitchforks and crossbows.

Carol J. Clover (1992) points out that the slasher film's harvest always reaps an inordinate number of victims. **Blood Feast** claims five (that we are aware of, at any rate), **The Texas Chain Saw Massacre** also claims five, and there are four in **Halloween**. The archetypal slasher film victim is in her late teens and always "guilty" – at least, in the terms set out by the filmic narrative – of some form of sexual aggression, or else is depicted in a sexual context, or drawn in overtly sexual terms. In **Blood Feast**, Ramses' first victim is murdered when she is naked in the bath, the second when making out with her boyfriend on the beach and the third in a motel room hired by her boyfriend. A property of the later slasher film cycles of the 1970s is what Clover has described as the "final girl" – a masculinized tomboy who is resourceful in stopping the murderer, and a character that allows male horror spectators to experience the thrill of identifying with a woman. Significantly, however, none of these traits are true of Suzette Fremont in **Blood Feast**, an attractive, feminine woman identified most clearly as Pete Thornton's girlfriend. In fact, it is Suzette's giggly ignorance that saves her life when Ramses tries to slaughter her in the kitchen.

Ultimately, the slasher film is characterized by its use of cinematic shock relating to body horror. Typically, the serial murders of the slasher film are distinguished by the opening up of the body and the shocking revelation of the taboo insides. In **Blood Feast**, this involves the removal of the brain and tongue, the "hacking away" of the face, the dicing up of body parts and, in the memorable words of the newspaper headline following Ramses' initial murder, "Legs Cut Off!". This making vivid of our bodily reality through the revelation of internal organs and fluids evokes the trauma of the abject on display. Or, in the words of Joseph Conrad, "the fascination of the abomination".

In *Men, Women And Chainsaws*, Clover acknowledges the critical importance of the **Blood Feast** recipe. "It may be argued", she writes in a footnote, "that **Blood Feast** (1963), in which a lame Egyptian caterer slaughters one woman after another for their bodily parts (all in the service of Ishtar) provides the serial-murder model" (Clover 1992:32). Other writers, including cult movie critics like Michael Weldon, the Phantom of the Movies and Joe Bob Briggs all agree that **Blood Feast** occupies the primary position in the narrative history of the slasher movie.

To participate (as audience) in the slasher film narrative is to take part in a ritual ceremony, a public practise in which, as necessity arises, at the proper season, or in certain circumstances, the communal magician or myth-maker – in his modern guise as film director – is under an obligation to perform his magic, to keep the taboos intact, and to exert his control over the entire enterprise, just as Fuad Ramses, high priest of the murderous cult of Ishtar, is compelled to re-enact the sacramental feast of the dark goddess.

Louise Krasniewicz, in her anthropological reading of the slasher film genre, makes the argument that the failure of the filmic protagonist to learn the lessons encoded by these narratives (don't go into the cellar, don't answer the phone, don't leave your little sister alone, don't go into the woods) are paralleled by the slasher film's compulsive tendency towards remakes, sequels and new chapters (Krasniewicz 1992). The **Friday The 13th** series, for example, "finished" with Joseph Zito's **Friday The 13th Part 4 – The Final Chapter** in 1984, which was rapidly followed by Danny Steinmann's **Friday The 13th Part 5 – A New Beginning** in 1985, leading to three additional sequels. Wes Craven's original **Nightmare On Elm Street** in 1984 has spawned a whole array of offspring, from cinematic sequels, to TV mini-series, to video spin-offs and Freddy Krueger gloves ("you too can be the bastard son of ten thousand maniacs!"). The slasher film's function as a rite of passage for adolescents of the media generation means that such sequels are a necessary accompaniment to the original ceremony. Each "new" manifestation of the slasher narrative has its own spin-offs, sequels and by-products, leaving its audiences with the sense that Jason will always rise up from the swamp, Michael Myers will always return on Halloween night and Freddy will never – really – be dead.

Like myths, fairy tales and folklore, the slasher movie is a fixed tale type that has generated an endless stream of what are in effect variants. "Basically, sequels mean the same film", observes John Carpenter, director of **Halloween** (1978). "That's what people want to see. They want to see the same movie again". Carpenter makes the suggestion that, like the purveyors of folklore, the makers of slasher movies operate more on instinct for formula than conscious understanding. Clover agrees that the entire horror genre is structured around unconscious re-enactment:

"What makes horror 'crucial enough to pass along' is, for critics since Freud, what has made ghost stories and fairy tales crucial enough to pass along: its engagement of repressed fears and desires and its re-enactment of the residual conflict surrounding those feelings."

—Clover 1992:11

Throughout cultural history – to return once again to the metaphor of psychoanalysis – we are destined to repeat, from generation to generation, the primal deeds of our forefathers. This repetition-compulsion may serve the function of helping us to struggle through a cultural rite of passage (in the case of the Oedipus complex or the incest taboo), or a ceremonial performance of an ancient act (in the case of the sacramental meal of the Catholic communion, for example). In either case, the occasion of the original deed, and whether it happened in fact, myth or fiction, has ceded its importance to the ritual re-telling of the tale, from age to age, in its various cultural forms and manifestations.

Herschell Gordon Lewis's **Blood Feast** is, in psychoanalytic terms, the original narrative prototype impelling both the repetition-compulsion of the slasher genre in its endless litany of remakes, spin-offs and sequels, as well as the horror film's obsessive interest in cannibalism, whether this be cannibalism averted, cannibalism as an act, or cannibalism as a metaphor relating to the way in which films in the slasher genre "feed off" one another, helping themselves to "parts" and "pieces" of different narrative manifestations. But just as the original blood sacrament was never fulfilled, its various narrative re-enactments, accordingly, are destined never to be completed or resolved.

CANNIBAL CARNAGE

Lewis and Friedman's money-making formula for **Blood Feast** was swiftly and predictably followed up by a second tale of violent carnage, **Two Thousand Maniacs** (1964), (also "Gruesomely Stained in Blood Color!"), a psychotic ghost story. One hundred years ago, or so the story goes, a group of Union soldiers passed through a small town in the Southern states, and laid it to waste. A century later, the town reappears, populated entirely by vengeance-seeking ghouls eager to get their own back on the Yankees, who are murdered one by

Two Thousand Maniacs

one by a variety of gruesome methods, including dismemberment, mutilation, torture as a fairground attraction, and – of course – the traditional cannibal barbecue, speciality of the deep south[7]. This eventful story of "A Town of Madmen... Crazed for Carnage!" ("Brutal... Evil... Ghastly Beyond Belief!") equalled the success of the earlier **Blood Feast**, but had a slightly harder time finding an audience. Although there were no current regulations against violence in the cinema, and although the film was neither sexually explicit nor profane in its language, many States had introduced local legislation prohibiting explicit screen violence as a result of the phenomenal success of **Blood Feast**, nervously anticipating the next blood-drenched offering from the Freidman-Lewis stable.

      Spider Baby (a.k.a. **The Maddest Story Ever Told**, a.k.a. **Cannibal Orgy**, a.k.a. **The Liver Eaters**), directed by Jack Hill in 1965, is a cinematic curiosity – a relatively unknown and critically neglected cannibal-themed B-movie. Hill began his career directing some snippets for Roger Corman's patchwork horror film **The Terror**. In 1968 he directed Boris Karloff in a number of scenes intended to go into a set of four Mexican films, but which turned out to be Karloff's last work. Since then, Hill has been making films for New World. **Spider Baby** stars Lon Chaney Jr. as Bruno, a loyal family retainer who takes it upon himself to look after the rich but congenitally insane Merrye Family. Elizabeth Merrye (Beverly Washburn) is a grown woman who dresses and behaves like an eleven-year-old child, her brother Ralph (Sid Haig) is a bald, sub-infantile freak, and their sister Virginia (Jill Banner), the "spider baby" of the film's title, believes she is a spider, and catches flies to eat. The family are suffering from Merrye's Syndrome – a rare condition that afflicts only the descendants of Ebenezer Merrye, related to dementia and in-breeding, and characterized by mental regression to a pre-human, cannibal stage of evolution, accompanied by homicidal urges. The current generation of Merryes, however, have not yet regressed completely and are cared for during

Spider Baby

their sickness by the loyal Bruno.

The story begins when an unwary postman approaches the creepy mansion and is trapped and killed by Virginia. The postman was delivering a message from the family's Aunt Emily (Carol Ohmart) and Uncle Peter (Quinn Redecker), who are about to arrive for an unexpected visit, accompanied by their lawyer Mr. Schlocker (Karl Schnazer) and his assistant Ann Morris (Mary Mitchel). The scheming Aunt Emily intends to have the rest of the family declared insane so she can claim the Merrye's mansion and their fortune. After an ominous meal, Uncle Peter and Ann Morris go in search of a motel, while Schlocker explores the house, and is trapped and killed by Virginia and Elizabeth, who resent the way in which he squashes spiders. Aunt Emily is alarmed by the lust-crazed Ralph and flees the house with the baldly goonish Ralph in pursuit; when Ralph catches up he strips her down to her black underwear and rapes her until she becomes as insane as the rest of her family.

Meanwhile, Uncle Peter and Ann Morris, unable to find a motel, return to the mansion. Uncle Peter is caught by Virginia, tied up, and made the victim of a teasing game of spider and fly, before the three siblings decide to drain Ann Morris of her vital juices. However, they are interrupted in the process by the arrival of Bruno, and the eruption of the hideously mutated older generation of Merryes from the cellar. Peter and Ann manage to escape, and Bruno dynamites the house. Years later, Peter refuses to admit that the curse has been passed on to his strange little daughter.

Spider Baby was re-released on video in 1985 as the second part of a double-bill, along with the archaic anti-drugs tract **Reefer Madness**, apparently in the hope of appealing to camp sensibilities. The film does have a number of camp

elements to it, such as the cartoon credits accompanied by Lon Chaney Jr. singing a gravelly rock-and-roll theme song. But as Kim Newman has pointed out (1985:354–355), the film is really too artful and witty to be enjoyed as wholly camp.

The Undertaker And His Pals, directed by David C. Graham in 1967, is a Z-gore story in the tradition of Herschell Gordon Lewis. Two bikers murder women for their pal, an undertaker (played by one Ray Dannis), who for some reason serves up their bodies in a diner. The detective investigating these crimes has secretaries with food names, who are duly butchered and eaten (eg: Miss Lamb, whose cooked body parts are presented as 'leg of lamb', etc).

We return to the redneck-rotisserie theme in **The Folks At The Red Wolf Inn** (dir. Bud Townshend, U.S, 1972), in which co-ed Regina (Linda Gillin) wins a vacation and leaves school without informing any of her family or friends where she is going. As part of her free vacation, she is taken by charter plane to The Red Wolf Inn and greeted by the host, retard Baby John (John Neilson), and his grandparents Henry (Arthur Space) and Evelyn (Mary Jackson). Also vacationing at the Red Wolf Inn are two attractive female guests, Pamela (Janet Wood) and Edwina (Margaret Avery), who leave mysteriously very early the next morning. Naturally, Regina becomes suspicious and decides to explore the back quarters of the inn, eventually coming across the dismembered torsos and decapitated heads of the two guests in the walk-in freezer just off the kitchen. Her escape attempt is foiled when she is caught on the road to town by Henry, Evelyn and Baby John, who has fallen in love with her. In the vague and muddled assault that follows, Henry chases Regina down and attempts to attack her with a meat cleaver. The film ends with John and Regina in the kitchen of the Red Wolf Inn, taking things up where the older generation left off. Before the credits roll, Grandpa's decapitated head grins and winks from a shelf in the walk-in freezer.

As contemporary reviewers pointed out, this is a film which seems quite confused in its direction and intent, seemingly unable to make up its mind which way to go. It begins very seriously with a lengthy dinner scene, where the classical background music and the meticulous enjoyment of food suggests that the filmmakers intended the scene to be a serious one. As the story progresses, however, it seems to grow more and more parodic, vacillating between gentle satire and downright slapstick. By the end of the film the original tone has been lost in a confusion of tasteless parody, intensified by the overuse of repetitive camerawork – all either medium shots or claustrophobic close-ups.

1972 also brought us Ivan Reitman and Dan Goldberg's amateur exploitation movie **Cannibal Girls**, filmed in the winter snows of the East Canadian border. Clifford Sturges (Eugene Levy), a musician, and his girlfriend Gloria Wellaby (Andrea Martin) run into car trouble in the deserted town of Farhamville, and check into a motel run by old Mrs. Wainwright (May Jarvis). Left with time on their hands, they decide to check out a nearby farmhouse which used to be inhabited, or so local legend has it, by the infamous Cannibal Girls – sisters Anthea, Clarissa and Leona – and their "keeper", a demonic preacher. According to legend, the Cannibal Girls seduced men back to the farmhouse, killed them, and either ate them on the spot, or else had their faithful servant Bunker butcher them in the basement storehouse.

When Clifford and Gloria arrive, they discover that the farmhouse has been bought out by the Reverend Alex St. John (Ronald Ulrich) and turned into a "theme" restaurant, and they are the only customers in sight. The Reverend joins them at their table, and they are served the "house speciality", free of charge, by three lovely waitresses, Anthea (Randall Carpenter), Clarissa (Bonnie Neilson) and Leona (Mira Pawluk). Rumours of an escaped maniac on the loose cause them to decide to stay the night at the farmhouse, and it is at this point that the film descends into a confusing and unsavoury mixture of legend, flashback, dream and present actuality. The couple are woken in the middle of the night to discover that they have been handcuffed to the bed and are surrounded

Cannibal Girls

by the Reverend and his Cannibal Girls. Gloria manages to escape and find a doctor, who gives her a sedative. Clifford joins her and tries to persuade her that it was all a dream, but she is not convinced and wants to leave town. Clifford insists that they return to the restaurant with the doctor and the sheriff to prove that nothing is amiss. On arriving, however, the Reverend welcomes Clifford to "the fold", and when Gloria learns that Clifford has brought her to the cannibals in order to save his own skin, she kills him by smashing his head in with an ancient mace. The Reverend and the Cannibal Girls then proceed to dine on Clifford's body, and a dazed Gloria – about to become a Cannibal Girl herself – gradually joins in. As the sheriff, doctor and other townsfolk sit down to a similar meal, another couple are checking into Mrs. Wainwright's motel.

Cannibal Girls was made from an improvised idea, on a low budget and in a rush for the 1972 Cannes Film Festival, and this is reflected in the film's low production values and confused narratives. Perhaps the film's most notable feature on its theatrical release was the inclusion of the William Castle-style gimmick of a buzzer on the soundtrack with the intention of warning audiences of any upcoming scenes of horror, followed by a loud chime for the "all-clear" signal, which seems somehow beside the point. For those who chose to cover their eyes for these scenes of horror, there can hardly have been much left worth watching.

After delighting his fans and disgusting his critics with movies like **Mondo Trasho** (1969) and **Multiple Maniacs** (1970), John Waters introduced a cannibal theme to perhaps his best-known film, the memorable **Pink Flamingos** (1973). Overweight transvestite Divine starts as a trailer-park fleshpot, housemother to a

Bloodsucking Freaks

caravan full of geeks, including Waters's familiar bit-part fat-lady Edie Massey as the grotesque Egg Lady. Although the film includes a cannibal barbecue as well as a varied selection of other perverted acts, it is perhaps best-known for its climactic scene in which Divine eats a handful of steaming dog shit, freshly produced by her obliging pet poodle. And at the climax of Waters' darkest film, **Desperate Living** (1977), the Queen of Mortville (played by Edie Massey) is roasted alive and eaten by her revolting (!) subjects.

      Shriek Of The Mutilated (1974) was directed by Michael Findlay, a former sexploitation filmmaker who, with his wife Roberta, also made the legendary **Snuff** (1976). It tells of a group of students in search of the "abominable

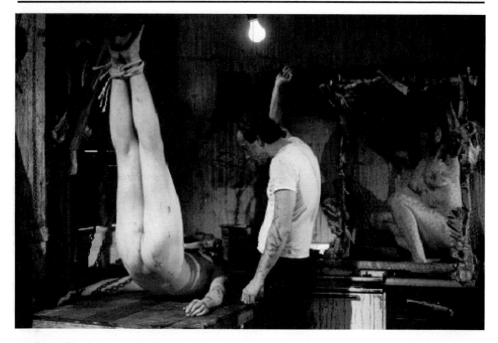

Roadkill: The Last Days Of John Martin

snowman". Two of them are viciously murdered by a white beast, which turns out to be one of two cannibal professors in disguise.

In 1976, Joel M. Reed directed a tongue-in-cheek, Grand Guignol-style shocker called **The Incredible Torture Show,** a film that would later gain cult popularity in its 1982 release under the title **Bloodsucking Freaks**. The story concerns an off-taste, off-Broadway "Theater of the Macabre" run by a sadistic impresario known only as Sardu (Seamus O'Brien), with the assistance of Ralphus (Louie DeJesus), his malevolent dwarf assistant who keeps a harem of cannibal girls locked up in cages. Sardu's tastes run not only to pain but also include necrophilia and cannibalism. He specializes in the presentation of brutal tableaux, including nude women being guillotined, drilled in the head, and violently tortured and decapitated – brains are sucked out through drinking straws, limbs amputated, and women used as human ashtrays and dartboards. Sardu is intent on legalizing his backstreet "theater" – actually a front for a lucrative Gotham-based white slave trade – by integrating its tableaux into a ballet format, with plot and music, involving kidnapped New York State Theater dancer Natasha (Viju Krim). Sardu's efforts eventually land him in trouble with the police, however, who are searching for the missing dancer. The film's grand finale, in which the cannibal women are released and fall upon their captors in a feeding frenzy, tearing them to shreds and devouring them (including the eating of a penis sandwich), provides plenty of gore and violence served up with the macabre black humour typical of the cult late-night video classic, which **Bloodsucking Freaks** quickly became. In a similar vein – though even more inept – is **The Long Island Cannibal Massacre** (Nathan Schiff, 1980), a low-budget gore offering in which a gang of delinquents who prey on sunbathers and tourists are discovered to be procuring food for an ancient cannibal.

Jim Van Bebber's intense **Roadkill: The Last Days Of John Martin** (1989) is a short independent movie about a grave-robbing psychopathic cannibal, with obvious overtones of the Ed Gein case. The psycho, who eviscerates dead animals and eats their raw entrails, and lives in a hovel strewn with empty beer bottles, rats and unidentifiable body parts, progresses to human meat after picking up a stranded man and woman and incapacitating them with a stun gun. The woman awakens to find herself naked in a cage atop the psycho's oven. She is forced to watch him dismember and dissect her dead boyfriend; as her screams subside into sobbing, he turns on the gas rings... Cut to the psycho slumped in front on the TV, eating from a plate of raw offal. The end.

CANNIBAL CARNAGE: SPANISH STYLE

In 1972, Spanish director Eloy de la Iglesia released **Cannibal Man**, the tale of Marcos (Vincente Parra), an impoverished slaughterhouse worker whose vocation has resulted in the brutalization of his mind and his senses. His character is vivified even before the opening credits have rolled, when graphic scenes of cattle having their throats sliced open, meat and entrails being pushed around and workers wading in rivers of blood are juxtaposed with the figure of a quiet character standing to one side, silently eating a meat sandwich.

The film has a curious, rank atmosphere of destitution and decay. Many scenes are shot in the dark or the twilight, with stray cats and dogs always hanging around the squalid adobe huts and the constant sound of street children playing football outside. A clock ticks loudly in the otherwise silent background during scenes of sex and scenes of murder. Elsewhere, the soundtrack consists of indefinite mechanical noises, a Spanish guitar plucked moodily, loud cicadas chirping, bullfighting music and the slow beat of a drum.

Marcos lives with his brother, a truck driver, in a three-room adobe hut on a stretch of waste land surrounded by a new development of luxury high-rise apartment buildings. The nearby slaughterhouse is owned by Flory, a meat soup company whose trite, singalong commercials, played repeatedly on the television in Marcos's local café, provide a stark and ironic contrast to the savage scenes inside the abattoir. Rosa, the waitress at the café, is also a prostitute who is keen to offer Marcos her services, but he prefers lying at home on his matted sofa masturbating to the pornography which is plastered all over the walls, or else dating a schoolgirl Paola (Emma Cohen), whose family are unaware of their clandestine relationship. Marcos also has a silent admirer, a wealthy male neighbour in one of the high-rise buildings who seems to have a strange fascination with him, watching his comings and goings through binoculars, and even watching his sex life through the glass roof of his hut.

Marcos takes Paola out for the evening and they embark on some heavy petting on the back seat of a taxi. An argument ensues when the taxi driver tries to throw them out, and Marcos refuses to pay him. During the scuffle, Marcos smashes the driver's head with a brick and he falls to the ground, comatose. The following day, they learn from a newspaper of his death. Paola wants them to go to the police, but Marcos feels that he won't get a fair deal because he is so poor. They argue, and when Paola insists on going to the police on her own, Marcos strangles her, rolls her body up in a sheet and puts it in his bed.

Marcos's brother, Steve (Ismael Merlo), arrives home from his trip a day early and, after a few drinks, Marcos confesses what he has done and shows Steve the dead body. Steve also insists that Marcos turn himself in, so Marcos brains him with a huge spanner and puts the body on the bed, next to Paola's. By now things are getting a little rancid in the hovel, so Marcos takes a walk, bumping into his mysterious neighbour from the high-rise (Eusebio Poncela), who's out walking his boxer dog, which is on heat. The neighbour, Nestor, has decided to let his dog run loose with the strays for a while to get some action. Marcos is worried that the boxer will be torn apart, but Nestor reminds him cryptically that "a well-fed dog is always more powerful than a hungry one".

The next to die is Steve's fiancée Carmen (Vicky Lagos), who was supposed to be marrying him the following week. Waiting for Steve in the brothers' house, she comments on the dirt and the noxious smell; meanwhile, Marcos chain-smokes nervously. When she goes into Steve's room and finds the two decaying bodies, Marcos cuts her throat slowly with a long razor, then lifts her body on to the pile accumulating on his brother's bed, his wedding sheets now soaking in blood. Marcos goes for a walk and meets Nestor again, and they go to the café for a drink and a chat. The neighbour uses a sophisticated vocabulary that Marcos has trouble understanding, and when the police turn up for an ID check, they overlook the fact that Nestor has no ID because of his obvious wealth. When Nestor asks to see inside Marcos's house and Marcos refuses to invite him in, he is advised to "bury the memories".

The next morning, Carmen's father turns up searching for his missing daughter, and discovers the bodies, now decaying rapidly, and surrounded by flies. Marcos dispatches him graphically with a meat cleaver between the eyes. With the same cleaver, he then sets about chopping up the bodies into offal, which he stuffs into a sports bag and takes to the slaughterhouse to dispose of in the meat soup-mixing machine. He repeats this ritual every day until the bodies are almost gone. Meanwhile, however, a pack of stray dogs have gathered around his house, sniffing and yelping, and when one of them nearly gets inside the gym bag, Marcos visits the chemist for six bottles of air freshener, and ten bottles of a perfume called "Flesh". That night he eats with Rosa, who comes on to him, but he has started to prefer the company of his neighbour Nestor, who has by now become the subject of his erotic fantasies. He visits Nestor's fancy health club for a midnight swim and some homo-erotic scenes in the showers to the accompaniment of a romantic Spanish guitar.

Back at the slaughterhouse, Marcos's work colleagues have taken to mocking the fact that he seems to have taken on a new lifestyle, going to a health club and wearing cologne. They claim he's "not one of them" any more, and his supervisor begins to suspect him of stealing meat. On Sunday, Rosa comes round to visit him, and they have sex. As Rosa is cooking him breakfast, however, she begins to notice the house's fetid smell fused with the stench of the cologne, notices Marcos's tool collection, the bloodstains on the walls and the flies congregating around the door of Steve's bedroom. She tries to leave but Marcos gets hold of her and kills her by beating her head against the wall, a scene which is intercut with footage of the street children kicking a ball around outside. He then eats a meat sandwich and goes outside. In the street, a crowd has gathered around a dog which has been hit by a car but is not yet dead.

When Marcos gets back from the city, he is unable even to enter his house because it is by now literally surrounded by a massive pack of sniffing stray dogs. Instead, he visits Nestor who shows him the binoculars and that he can see into Marcos's living room, where most of the murders have taken place. Marcos suddenly realizes that Nestor is aware of everything he has done; he grabs a glass, breaks it and holds it to Nestor's throat, but is unable to kill him and collapses weeping instead. Finally, as daylight breaks over the squalid hovel, Marcos phones the police and confesses to his crimes, whilst Nestor sits alone, fingering the shards of broken glass.

There are a number of closely linked themes running through this uneasy film, the most obvious of which are the social hypocrisy and bigotry that trigger Marcos's psychotic behaviour. Appetite and hunger, both for sex and for food, cannot be completely satisfied without crossing some dangerous social boundary. For example, when Rosa tells Marcos that the soup he is eating is made by Flory, we are shown a horrendous close-up of pink flesh quivering on the end of a dirty spoon, and Marcos staggers outside to vomit in the gutter, where he lives, at the foot of the luxurious new high-rise. Rosa claims she is going to confession, but she actually goes to have sex with Marcos instead. Nestor claims that Marcos's work in the slaughterhouse is vital for people like him, who enjoy eating meat but not preparing it. But none of these themes seems to be carried through to any kind of closure; threads are left hanging in the air, and the implications of much of the imagery are never explored in their entirety.

Legendary sex/horror director Jésus Franco, who had flirted with cannibalistic imagery in such films as **La Comtesse Perverse** (1973) and **Greta, The Mad Butcher** (1977), turned to the cannibal movie full-scale with **Mondo Cannibale** (a.k.a. **White Cannibal Queen**, 1979). A little girl's parents are attacked by a tribe of cannibals; she ends up in the river and is finally washed up on the jungle banks, where the cannibals take her and adopt her as their goddess. Years later, the girl's father (played by Fulci actor Al Cliver) leads an expedition back to the area in search of his long-lost daughter and encounters the cannibals. Though fairly unexciting in terms of both nudity and gore, **Mondo Cannibale** is an interesting companion piece to Franco's superior cannibal effort, **The Devil Hunter**.

Laura Crawford (Ursula Fellner [Ursula Buchfellner]), a film star, is out scouting locations for her next movie in an unspecified third world country. The opening scene of **The Devil Hunter** (a.k.a. **The Man Hunter**, a.k.a. **Mandingo Manhunter**, dir. Clifford Brown [a.k.a. Jésus Franco], Italy, 1980) is shot as rough, hand-held camera, cineverité-style footage, possibly to give yet another feeble Deodatoesque stamp of "reality" to the entire film, though it would certainly need more than this to convince even the most gullible of red-eyed cannibal cinephiles. Laura is kidnapped by a gang of criminals who take her to their island hideaway of Puerto Santo and demand a $6 million ransom for her release. Before the ransom demands are ever responded to, however, one of the kidnappers, Chris (Werner Pochath) freaks out in an attack of jungle fever and sadistically slices away at Laura's breasts. To make matters worse, she is also raped by the leader of the kidnappers, Thomas (Antonio de Cabo).

A rescue party, consisting of Peter Hunt (Al Cliver [Peter Luigi Conti]) and his Vietnam-veteran colleague Jack (Robert Foster [Antonio Mayans]) arrives by helicopter to rescue Laura, and as the rescuers and kidnappers attempt to double-cross one another, Laura escapes into the jungle. At this point, the action starts to heat up, with some eerie heavy breathing, deep groans on the soundtrack and a vaseline-stained camera lens to give the point of view of cannibals, who kidnap Laura (again) and prepare to sacrifice her to their god. When they actually appear, however, the cannibal tribe are more laughable than terrifying, being composed of a mixed group of black actors and actresses who are clearly from a variety of different ethnic backgrounds, although they all seem to share a taste for chomping on steaming entrails in graphic close-up.

Back on the kidnappers' boat, Jack and a female gang member are killed

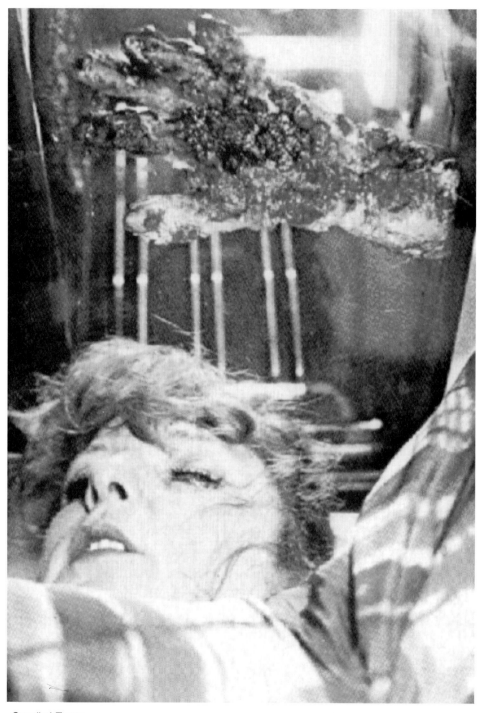

Cannibal Terror

by a huge cannibal, the "devil" of the film's title (Claude Boisson), while they are making love. He next murders another of the kidnappers, Jane (Gisela Hahn), by bashing her over the head with a rock. In the film's climax, Peter Hunt battles with the "devil" in a cliff-top brawl in which Peter inevitably gains the upper hand and sends the cannibal king hurtling to his death on the rocks below.[8]

Julio Perez Taberno's French production **Cannibal Terror** (1980) largely utilised the set of **Mondo Cannibale** but delivered an inept film far below even Franco's standard. The story concerns a bungling kidnap gang on the run from the police who hide out in a forest, where they fall prey to a tribe of cannibals. The cannibals are unconvincing, the gore far too sporadic.

In 1980 Jacinto Molina (a.k.a. Paul Naschy) directed the Spanish-Japanese production **El Carnaval De Las Bestias** (a.k.a. **Human Beasts**). The film is a somewhat unusual variation on the cannibal movie, more an adventure in which a bandit on the run from the Japanese cohorts he has betrayed, seeks refuge in a house which just happens to be infested by man-eaters. The climax is gory but uninspired.

CANNIBAL CARNAGE: UK

Pete Walker's 1974 British film **Frightmare** (a.k.a. **Once Upon A Frightmare**), from a script by David McGillivray, features Sheila Keith as the sweet and gentle old Dorothy Yates, an affectionate little old lady whose character has one unfortunate flaw: she cannot survive without feeding on human flesh. Her special diet is provided for her by her devoted husband Edmund (Rupert Davies), who, despite his feelings of guilt, is compelled to indulge his wife's "special needs", and with hideous consequences. Condemned in reviews as "yet another of the rather detestable spate of films emphasizing graphic depictions of perverse brutality", it is referred to by Robin Wood in his seminal 1979 essay "An Introduction To The American Horror Film" as "revoltingly gruesome and ugly", but at the same time Wood notes its considerable significance as one of those rare British horror films that lie outside the main tradition of the decade, as generally represented by Hammer Productions.

The film begins with a black-and-white flashback of a middle-aged man walking through a deserted funfair somewhere in London in 1957. The man approaches one of the caravan trailers and knocks tentatively on the door, which is opened by an unseen hand. The man begs desperately for help, and is let into the trailer. After some more footage of the deserted funfair the camera pans slowly around the dirty interior of the caravan – the sink full of washing-up, the walls stained with what looks like blood. The middle-aged man is sitting on a bench, apparently waiting for something or someone, until his body gradually begins to sag to the left, his head falls down to his chest and we suddenly realize that the right side of his face is missing, replaced by a bloody mess of gore. The frightmare has begun.

We next cut to a scene in the Old Bailey, still part of the black-and-white flashback sequence. A stern judge is sentencing a husband and wife for some unnamed series of despicable crimes. "Normally", he claims, "I would have no hesitation to impose the death sentence on you both", but since the nature of the crimes imply that the couple are obviously insane, the judge commits the couple – who are shown only as a pair of tightly clasped hands – to a lunatic asylum ("and let the members of the public be assured that you will remain in this mental institution until you are fit and able to take your place in society again").

Back in the present day, colour footage of tarot cards being turned over to the accompaniment of creepy organ music provides the setting for the film's titles. This footage is immediately contrasted with scenes of seventies disco music as a gang of bikers roll up outside a seedy club. A bartender refuses to serve one of the biker girls, Debbie (Kim Butcher), who's recently been released from either a convent or an orphanage (we're not sure which). Debbie gets the bikers to wait around after the club closes and beat the barman up for her. She is the last to leave the fight, obviously relishing every moment of it, and tells her friends she'll hitch a ride home. The following morning, she is questioned by the police about the man's death.

It turns out that Debbie, who is under the impression that her parents are dead, lives with her older sister, Jackie (Deborah Fairfax). Jackie leaves the house at 2AM every night to drive out to deliver a small, brown paper parcel to an old castle out-building, where her father, the chauffeur to a Lord, lives with his ailing wife. The loopy mother Dorothy (Sheila Keith), lurking in the shadows, is a self-confessed "night person". She seems pleased with her special package, but becomes a little disturbed when it leaks blood on to her hands. We learn that she's been in an asylum for the last fifteen years, but gets a migraine whenever they come to discuss the subject. That night, Jackie dreams she is reading in a train carriage. Blood drips on to the pages of the book. Looking up, she sees her mother leaning towards her, offering her a blood-soaked parcel, and drooling blood....

The next day, when Jackie is at work (as a make-up artist for the BBC), her father phones and says he has to meet her immediately. They meet outside the BBC studios. The father, terribly anxious, claims that his wife has "started again", and shows Jackie a glimpse of a severed head wrapped in a blanket in the trunk of Sir Joseph's car. Part of the power of this film is built up by the contrast between scenes like this one – in the modern world of pubs, discos, cinemas, industrial machinery and police sirens – and the tense sequences in the fairy tale cottage, with its flickering fire and creaky doors. Traditional haunted-house-style sequences of howling winds and squeaking bats are juxtaposed with the familiar world of London, Tower Bridge, the BBC studios at Shepherd's Bush and afghan-wearing bikers, which allows the film to seem plausible even in its most deranged sequences, and therefore all the more fascinating.

Back at the castle, Mother has a visitor, a middle-aged woman who "saw the ad in *Time Out*". It turns out that Mother reads Tarot cards – "a fascinating, fascinating subject" – but the woman's future doesn't look good at all. "Swords, swords, swords, swords – it's all strife, isn't it? Strife, heartache and loneliness", claims Dorothy portentously. Once it has been established that the visitor has neither family ties nor close friends, the Death card is turned over – and what a death. Out in the barn, Mother experiments in some serious cranial DIY, her eyes rolling grandly, her face splattered with blood as she bores into the woman's skull with an electric drill. When Jackie gets to the castle that night, Mother claims she's simply been doing a bit of fortune-telling in her spare time. "They come and go, lonely people – all of them, lonely people, without a friend in the world", she claims. "I just try to help them... it's so lonely here all day. Can't I have any of my own interests? You know how I look forward to your visits Jackie, with your little parcels. You will keep on bringing them, won't you Jackie? Just to please me?"

While Jackie is out her boyfriend, Graham (Paul Greenwood), a psychiatrist (resplendent in thick black glasses, a polo neck, and a jacket with gigantic checks and enormous lapels), goes round to her house and meets Debbie for the first time. Suspicious about her behaviour, he tries to analyse her, and she refuses to

Frightmare

admit she needs help, and attempts to seduce him. The next day, Graham visits the asylum to learn the history of the sisters' parents – and is horrified by what he learns. It turns out that their mother, Dorothy, experienced a terrible trauma as a child, when a pet she loved and cared for was killed and eaten by the family during the depression years. When Dorothy found out what had happened she never recovered, and started eating the brains of animals. After she married Edmund Yates (who already had a child, Jackie, by a previous marriage), she progressed to "cannibantropy", or pathological cannibalism, and killed and ate six people. Edmund, the doctors suspected, was innocent of the crimes, but feigned madness so he wouldn't be separated from his wife. Fifteen years later, they were released, and now "they're as sane as you or I". Cut to a shot of Edmund and Dorothy hiding severed heads in the haybarn.

Debbie goes to meet her biker boyfriend, Alec, in an industrial warehouse. She gleefully shows him the severed head of the barman in a car boot. One eye is missing, half the face has been eaten away, and all the signs point to Debbie. Meanwhile, Mother gives another Tarot reading to a woman whose husband has recently passed away. This time she seems quite mad, gibbering about "the little animals – they come to see me during the day". The woman tries to escape but the door is locked. Dorothy grabs a poker out of the fire and stabs the woman with it, who drools copious quantities of blood before collapsing on the floor. When Edmund comes home she pleads with him not to send her back to the asylum ("you're not angry with me – not angry?"), and he helps her clean up the mess. It turns out that Dorothy's been killing people all along, ever since she was released from the asylum, and the little packets of brain Jackie's been bringing her from the abattoir in an attempt to persuade her that she's been doing the killing on her mother's behalf haven't convinced Dorothy at all. It also turns out that Debbie is aware of her mother's existence, and has been helping her with the murders. She brings her boyfriend Alec to the castle on his motorbike, and leads him to the hayloft where he is shocked to find a selection of assorted severed heads in the hay before being stabbed in the face by Dorothy with a pitchfork.

Back in London, Jackie tells Graham about the death of the barman, and her suspicions that Debbie might have had something to do with it. When they find out that Debbie has disappeared, Graham decides to go out to the castle and pretend he is interested in having a Tarot reading. When he does so, however, Debbie peeps through the door and lets her mother know he is lying. Next, Debbie phones her sister and asks her to come out to the castle, where she is confronted by her father, with a heavily bruised face. "Your stepmother's a very sick woman, Jackie", he tells her. "She's had a serious relapse". The buzz of the electric drill from upstairs leads to a shot of Dorothy drilling like a maniac into Graham's head, clutching the Death card in her hand. When Debbie grabs a meat cleaver and approaches her sister with it, Father does nothing to stop her. The film closes with an ironic reminder of the words of the judge: "And let the members of the public be assured that you will remain in this mental institution until you are fit to be able to take your place in society again".

"GHOUL: Person of Revolting Tastes". This definition, thrust on the screen before us, provides a highly promising opening to Tyburn Productions' film. With his son Kevin as producer, **The Ghoul** is directed by Freddie Francis, well-known for his stories of killer bees, creeping flesh and deadly skulls. Unfortunately however, like many similar British efforts, **The Ghoul** fails to live up to its potential, mainly due to the weak script by John Elder, and the film's failure to do more than resurrect a number of old Hammer-horror style cinematic clichés.

The Ghoul begins with a society party some time in the 1920s, where a group of rich young flappers indulge in some vicious party games. One couple, Billy (Stewart Bevan) and Daphne (Veronica Carlson) challenge another couple, Geoffrey (Ian McCulloch) and Angela (Alexandra Bastedo), to a midnight car rally to Land's End. The challenge is accepted. During the race, Billy runs out of petrol and goes in search of a garage. Meanwhile, Daphne is waylaid by a dishevelled youth, Tom (John Hurt), who claims he is a gardener from a nearby country house. Escaping from Tom, Daphne ends up at the country house and is taken in by Dr. Lawrence (Peter Cushing), a violin-playing ex-clergyman who lost his faith after apparently witnessing some "savage heathen practises" in India. Daphne goes to bed and Tom is sent out to search for Billy, but instead of helping him, he pushes both Billy and his priceless car over a cliff. In the middle of the night, Daphne is stabbed to death by a mysterious, sandal-wearing figure with bloodstained feet summoned from the top of the house by the Indian Ayah (Gwen Watford), the housekeeper who periodically lets this flesh-famished ghoul out of his bedroom for a midnight forage.

The next morning, Geoffrey and Angela are shown Billy's missing car by the typically inept, bicycle-riding, curse-muttering village bobby. In an attempt to solve the mystery, Geoffrey goes to Dr. Lawrence's house, leaving Angela behind to be abducted by Tom. When Angela is found to be missing, Dr. Lawrence tells Geoffrey that he saw he getting on a bus, but Geoffrey, an ex-army officer, refuses to believe him and tries to assert his military status over Tom, an ex-army deserter. Finally, Tom tells the truth: Angela is still somewhere in the house, and Dr. Lawrence, torn between the Christian and the Infidel, keeps a ghoulish

Motel Hell

creature in the attic that feeds on human flesh. Geoffrey confronts Dr. Lawrence, who admits that the cannibal is his own son – another casualty of the "heathen rites" witnessed in India. When Geoffrey tries to break into the son's room, the whole ghoul lurches into view – he has so far appeared from the waist down, as nothing more than a pair of bloodstained legs loping down the stairs in sandals. Geoffrey is quickly dispatched by the cannibalistic fiend, followed by Tom, who is on the verge of raping Angela. Finally, and not before time, Dr. Lawrence decides to shoot the ghoul before it can cause any further mayhem.

CANNIBAL CATERERS

Kevin Connor's film **Motel Hell** (a.k.a. **Nuits De Cauchemar** 1980), takes us back to the deep south of the United States, home of country music and strange goings-on in the hills. An incestuous couple, Vincent (Rory Calhoun), a quiet megalomaniac who sometimes believes he is God and sometimes God's manager, along with his sister (Nancy Parsons), run a motel where the speciality of the house, known all over the area, is smoked meat. The plot revolves around the couple's attempts to look for a successor to their business who is able to make the delicacy of the kitchen – half pork, half human flesh. During their search, Vincent comes to believe that he has been charged with a mission from God.

Most critics and reviewers regarded **Motel Hell** as just another cannibal B-movie that didn't even manage to get a rating. Others, however, saw it as the supreme statement of capitalism – a social manifesto that is many times more powerful than any number of dull treatises on political economy. In a simplified

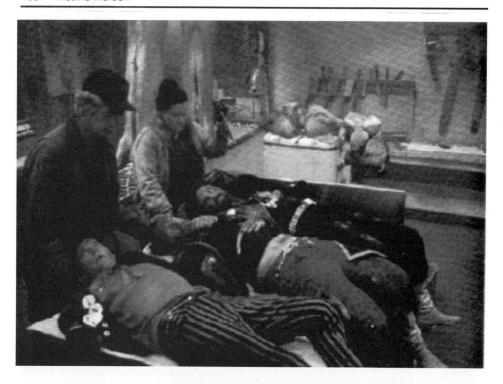

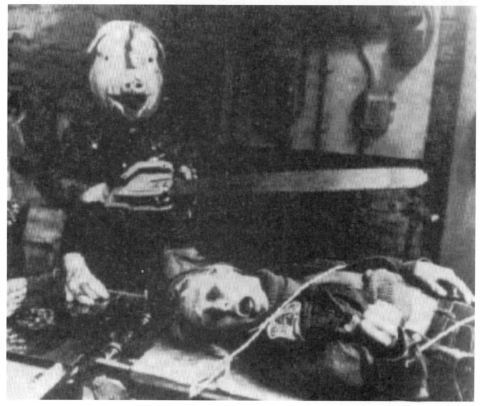

The German Chainsaw Massacre

and straightforward way, **Motel Hell** illustrates the ultimate circle of capitalist production, distribution, and consumption which goes along without a hitch. The people who work in the motel seem like completely normal people with absolutely nothing unusual about them at all. The peaceful facade of daily rituals turns out not to be a facade at all, but the simple ordinary routine of daily life, without the slightest sense of horror about it. With a steady tone and quiet humour, Connor presents us with an intelligent story of two people who are simply going about their business with a sense of order, decorum and pleasure in their work. Details of production and consumption are shown clearly and straightforwardly.

One of the most interesting aspects of **Motel Hell** is the film's presentation of a form of cannibalism that is anything but regressive. The cannibalism in this film signifies not a brutal return to savagery, nor an escape back into barbarism, nor nature wreaking its horrible revenge on the over-saturation of culture, but simply the latest stage of that neurosis known as civilization – a difference of degree but not of nature. The normality and legality of the economic system is maintained, and its efficiency is established beyond doubt. The French found Connor's film particularly engaging. According to the reviewer for *Cahiers du Cinéma*, **Motel Hell** "has the tone of a short story by Ambrose Bierce – healthy and tonic, like a dose of humour, but possessed of a cynical and cutting detachment. Few other films have captured the conscience of America, an America built on death, and, after living alongside the dead, finally beginning to live *off* them" (see "Motel Hell", 1981:58).

In 1991, German director Christoph Schlingensief produced **Das Deutsche Kettensägenmassaker** (aka **The German Chainsaw Massacre**), in which a demented cannibal family from East Germany migrate to the West with the collapse of the Berlin Wall. Here, in a rather obvious "social comment", they proceed to butcher and feed off the capitalists who had formerly oppressed them.

Also in 1991, Danny Lee – star of John Woo's **The Killer** – directed a Hong Kong movie of his own entitled **Bun Man: The Untold Story**. The film tells the allegedly true tale of a restauranteur who murders his partner and family over a game of Mah Jong, then slices them up and serves them to his customers. In typical Hong Kong fashion, it contains scenes of graphic and gruelling violence, including much torture aimed at women. To Western sensibilities, the worst moments must be those where the madman's children, bound and gagged, await the fall of the cleaver. The Bun Man also employs a circular saw to carve up his victims, and piles of severed limbs, caved in heads and other anatomical ephemera proliferate.[9]

CANNIBAL CAPRICE

Jackie Kong's **Blood Diner**, released in the U.S. in 1987, is a kitschy parody of Herschell Gordon Lewis's exploitation classic **Blood Feast**. Two crazed young children, locked up for exhuming and eating the brains and eyeballs of their certifiable uncle, are released from the asylum as adults and open up a diner. The brothers, Michael and George Tutman (played by Rick Burks and Carl Crew, both mimicking Mal Arnold as the bug-eyed Fuad Ramses), intend to assemble a variety of body parts from an assortment of young girls, in order that "Sheetar", a "500,000-year-old goddess", can be restored to life. They go about their business with the unknowing assistance of LaNette La France (Sheba Jackson playing Lyn Bolton playing Mrs. Fremont), and Connie Stanton (Lisa Guggenheim playing Connie Mason playing Suzette Fremont), spilling plenty of gore in the process, including a mass murder at a nude aerobics class. *Variety*, in its inimitable style, slammed the film as "more gore bore lore", commenting that "the parody of blood lust is a pathetic bust", and concluding that "the only way **Blood Diner** could possibly reach its high camp intentions is if it had been filmed in a lean-to on Mount Everest" (see "Blood Diner", 1987:16).

Lucky Stiff is a genuinely amusing cannibal comedy full of black humour and off-beat one-liners directed by Anthony Perkins – his first directorial effort since **Psycho III** – with a modest budget and a thirty-day schedule, and released in 1988. Originally entitled **Mister Christmas Dinner**, the film was advertised as "an outrageous and bizarre comedy about a man who treats women too tenderly, and a woman who prefers her men tenderized through and through". From a script by Pat Proft, **Lucky Stiff** revolves around the overweight Ron Douglas (Joe Alaskey) who has just been jilted at the altar. Alaskey is spotted by the alluring and sophisticated Cynthia Mitchell (Donna Dixon) and her brother Ike (Jeff Kober), who decide he would make the ideal meal ticket for their family of inbred cannibals. In a Lake Tahoe ski lodge, the slow-witted Ron is seduced and picked up by the seductive Cynthia, who takes him back with her to the remote family homestead where the whole family devote themselves to fattening him up for their next meal. The film fell victim to poor distribution, but gained a significant cult following when it was released on video in 1989.

Lucky Stiff is first and foremost a comedy, and plays up its genteel humour at the expense of the taboo-breaking subject-matter. Apparently, Perkins sat through a lengthy barrage of cannibal films – including Connor's recent **Motel Hell** – before filming began, and found them generally too violent and too serious. Such films, according to Perkins, are representative of "a dangerous trend, as well as bad movie-making". "I think if there's a trend in horror films right now, it's that the gross-out film has had it. They went too far", he claimed in an interview with *Cinéfantastique* to publicize the film's video release in 1989. "There's a numbing quotient that comes in when people can sit and watch decapitations while chewing popcorn. In a way they are unmoved. There's something definitely wrong. I'm hoping the more suggestive elements of the genre will be on the rise in the next decade, and the explicit violence and horror will be on the wane". Ironically, Perkins went directly on to star in **Edge Of Sanity**, Gerard Kikione's steamy and gore-drenched reworking of the Jekyll and Hyde theme filmed in Czechoslovakia, followed by **Psycho IV** for Universal.

The Microwave Massacre (Wayne Berwick, 1979) is an alleged "satire" on gore movies, a quasi-comedic effort in which a man kills his wife, stores her body parts in the freezer, and finally eats her; he acquires the taste for human flesh and goes out in search of more victims.

CARNAL CANNIBALS

Aldo Lado's Italian film **Love Ritual** was released in Japan in 1990 as an obvious attempt to make money out of the Japanese public's continual obsession with cannibal killer Issei Sagawa (see chapter 2). In this film, a Futura production, a sinister "inscrutable" Oriental man meets a beautiful blonde Western woman, and persuades her to come to his flat for dinner. She is fascinated by his stories of Japanese culture and the total union of man and woman promised by "the ancient Oriental love rituals". After they make love, she tells him to do whatever he wants, and he eats part of her arm. She wants the ritual to continue, so he kills her and eats the rest of her body raw. Sagawa himself saw the film, and when asked to give his comments on the movie, he reported that it had aroused him sexually to the extent that he had had three erections. He preferred, however, the German film **Trance** directed by Eckhart Schmidt "about the very beautiful girl who kills her boyfriend when he wants to leave her, and ate him up". He also reportedly enjoyed a 1987 Belgium film called **Adoration**, directed by Olivier Smolders, again based directly on the facts of his case.

Marco Ferreri's 1991 film **The Flesh** (a.k.a. **La Carne**), on a virtually identical theme, achieved a rather wider audience than Lado's, causing something of a minor scandal at the 1991 Cannes Film Festival. Ferreri's self-indulgent erotic fantasy from his own script stars the popular Italian comic Sergio Castellitto as Paolo, a hypochondriac nightclub singer and pianist whose marriage has recently ended in divorce. Paolo is lonely – he can only see his two children on visiting days, and he is over-attached to his dog. One night, in the club, he meets the sexy Francesca (Francesca Dellera), who tells him all about the tantric sex she indulges in with her young Indian guru. When Paolo takes Francesca back with him to his beach house, the film fades into a confused blur of sex games, philosophical discussions and arbitrary dialogue and incident, including brief interludes with a nursing mother on the beach, a lesbian, and Paolo's children. The final section involves more tantric sex in unusual positions, empty symbolism of storks and sunsets, and crazed behaviour from Francesca leading to a climax of erotic murder and arbitrary cannibalism. Meanwhile, Paolo's dog dies from neglect.

CANNIBAL CHARISMA

In Jonathan Demme's classic thriller **The Silence Of The Lambs** (1991), a young FBI

agent, Clarice Starling (Jodie Foster), is sent to interrogate an imprisoned serial killer, Dr. Hannibal Lecter (Anthony Hopkins), to see if he possesses any information or insights which could help the FBI in its pursuit of a second serial killer, Buffalo Bill[10]. Lecter, known as "Hannibal the Cannibal" for obvious reasons, was also, in his time, a brilliant psychiatrist. Hopkins plays Lecter as a decadent aesthete and a connoisseur of exquisite cuisine: he collects copies of *Bon Appetit*, and describes to Clarice how he ate the liver of one of his victims "with some fava beans, and a good Chianti". Based on a combination of cannibal killer Eddie Gein and charmer Ted Bundy, Lecter is given much of his own character, too. Not only an Epicurean, he is also a classical music aficionado and an artist capable of rendering a Florence street scene from memory. He also has a macabre sense of irony. One of his first tasks for Clarice is to send her to explore a storage facility called "Your Self Storage": clearly a metaphor for her unconscious. Moreover, the encounters between Lecter and Clarice are staged in close-up, bringing that heightened sense of intimacy and concentration that we associate with the psychoanalytic therapy session.

There has been much written, in academic film theory and elsewhere, on Jonathan Demme's fascinating film and the issues and themes that it involves. The majority of this critical engagement, however, centres around the film's complex treatment of gender and sexuality. Some gay critics have taken offense at the character of Buffalo Bill, a transvestite dressmaker, rejected for transsexual surgery, who sets about killing large women for their skin, to make himself a "girl suit" like Eddie Gein's – with all the attendant implications that homosexuality must stem from a mother complex like Gein's, and carry the social stigmata of psychosis. Some critics have applied to the film Carol J. Clover's conclusions about the contemporary horror film (1995), that the "killer as feminine male and the main character as masculine feminine" may be a product of "massive gender confusion" unique to contemporary society[11].

Silence Of The Lambs

Certainly, the character of Buffalo Bill exploits an enormous amount of contemporary anxiety over gender and sexuality, and his confusion and dissatisfaction are sometimes expressed in extremely violent terms. Other have made much of the fact that the actress who plays Agent Starling – Jodie Foster – also has a media and a personal image which consistently refuses to adhere to conventional gender boundaries[12]. It strikes me, however, that the film negotiates some far more interesting issues, and those are the issues surrounding the notion of an accomplished psychiatrist who is also a cannibal, and a serial killer. As Judith Halberstam has pointed out[13], the serial killing spree, like the psychoanalytic therapy session, promises interminable chapters, promises to serialize, to keep one waiting for an ever-deferred conclusion. Serial murders have something of a literary quality to them: they happen regularly over time, and each new one gives further information, and creates further expectations.

In his role as cannibal, we witness Lecter committing bone-crunching, flesh-ripping murder with his teeth and bare hands in the most brutal and primitive of ways. He is a cannibal, a vampire and a psychopath. We are told of him mutilating the face of a nurse, we witness him killing and skinning two police officials, and we know that he plans to have Dr. Chilton "for dinner". The film also implies that Lecter is so powerful and has such unlimited access to the unconscious that he can make a person do anything at all. Merely by whispering to him, Lecter persuades a fellow inmate, Miggs, whose behaviour has offended him, into committing suicide by self-cannibalism (swallowing his own tongue).

As both a cannibal and a psychiatrist, Lecter has made a career out of drawing out and ingesting – even nourishing himself upon – other people's pain. Demme equates Lecter's physical hunger for human flesh with his more-than-professional hunger for details of other people's lives, especially their unconscious

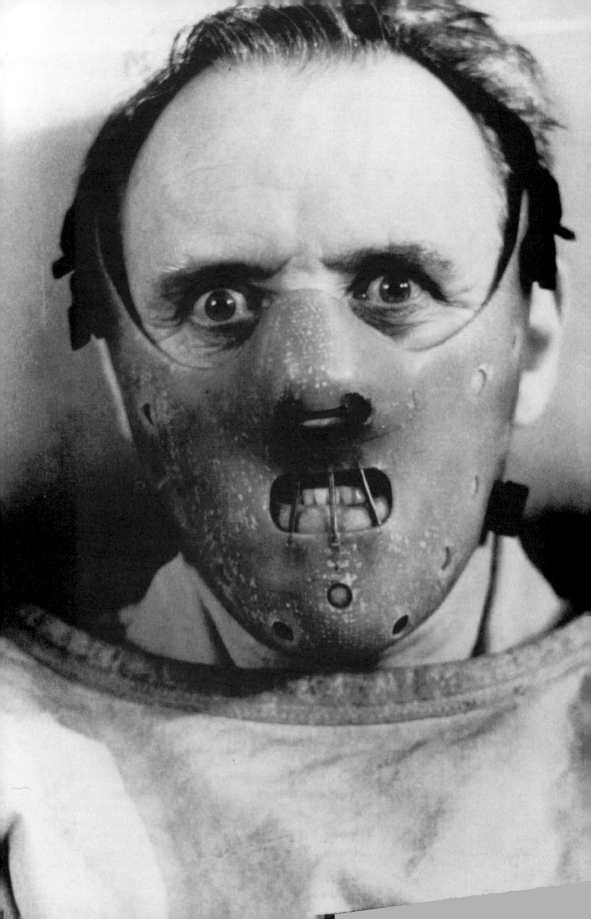

lives. As a practising psychiatrist, the film implies that Lecter gained the utmost pleasure from draining the minds of his patients, such as the transvestite Benjamin Raspail – Buffalo Bill's lover – before he drained and consumed their bodies. Lecter is, as Crawford warns Starling, somebody "you don't want... inside your head", but Lecter is an expert at getting into other people's heads, as well as – like Buffalo Bill – getting under their skin, as he does literally with the police officer whose face he temporarily "borrows". He eats both minds and bodies – his cannibal tendencies reach to not only the removal of the skin of the face, but the ingestion – both literal and symbolic – of what lies beneath it. The bargain he strikes with Clarice is a reciprocal one: she receives the power of his knowledge, and he gains a glimpse inside her unconscious mind. During Clarice's confession, Lecter savours every single word she utters as though it were some exquisite delicacy from the pages of *Bon Appetit*. And to Clarice, Lecter becomes the all-powerful therapist, the fairy-tale father, and Clarice his special child, the only child that the all-powerful father does not eat, whose purity and love redeem him from his usually savage ways.

Hannibal Lecter is a psychopath for the twenty-first century: a unique combination of savage and sophisticate, both connoisseur and cannibal, who dismembers and eats his victims to the music of Bach. His ferocious oral appetites find their release in the complexities of language, as well as the textures of human flesh. He combines the stone-age appetites and magical thinking of the savage butcher with the genius of the artist-scientist. In Hannibal Lecter, body and soul are both filled with stolen power. Art, magic and religion come together, and the sacrifice of the communion is made flesh[14].

When producer Dino de Laurentiis offered the manuscript of the new movie **Hannibal** to director Ridley Scott – at the time shooting **Gladiator** in Malta – Scott apparently replied impatiently that he was already doing Romans, that he'd had his fill of Romans, and was in no mood for going over the Alps. To a generation younger than Ridley Scott's, however – perhaps even to the majority of westerners – the name "Hannibal" has nothing to do with Romans and elephants, and everything to do with a charismatic serial killer who likes his human organs washed down with a cheeky little red wine.

Hannibal, the long-awaited sequel to Jonathan Demme's immensely successful **Silence Of The Lambs**, was released in February 2001 with Julianne Moore as Clarice Starling, and Hopkins reprising his role as Dr Hannibal Lecter. Also featured is Gary Oldman – unrecognisable behind truly hideous make-up – as the man hell-bent on revenge against Lecter, who once fed him an overdose of LSD and convinced him to slice off his own face with broken glass. And although he may give psychiatry a bad name, Hannibal Lecter has achieved the rare feat of making cannibalism fashionable. No longer the rather distasteful hobby of unappealing lower-class serial killers (could you imagine Jeffrey Dahmer subscribing to *Gourmet* or *Bon Appétit*?), cannibalism is now the sideline *de rigueur* of the postmodern serial killer.

The final scene in **Hannibal**, for example, shows Lecter (Hopkins again) during a plane journey, unwrapping a Dean and DeLuca takeout lunch he's brought on board with him, which includes plenty of the kinds of gourmet treats one might expect from the upmarket delicatessen. In the box, however, is something rather less appetizing - a plastic container containing a human brain. Did the gourmands at Dean and DeLuca condone this ghoulish example of product placement? Apparently so. According to Dean and DeLuca's Pat Roney,

Hannibal

who agreed to the collaboration, the gourmet food company liked the idea of being identified with a "hip, edgy" movie like **Hannibal**.

And **Hannibal** is, of course, simply a fairy-tale for grown-ups. Like Beauty, Clarice Starling makes a pact with the Beast, who's so smitten by her charm and virtue that not only does he protect her from the fate that meets his other victims, but he allows her a glimpse at the vulnerable man behind the mask. She gives him her trust, and he gives her his power. Moreover, both **Hannibal** and **Silence Of The Lambs** are full of classic fairy tale motifs: the ogre in the dungeon, the terrible house, the captured princess, the magic skin, people being thrown into dungeons and fed to the pigs.

There's something about Hannibal Lecter, however, that makes him particularly appealing. Unlike his slasher-movie counterparts (Freddy Krueger, Jason Vorhees, Michael Myers), Lecter isn't just a masked boogieman bent on revenge but an individual in his own right – even something of a hero. Unlike the masked killers of **Scream**, **Scary Movie** and the recent **Valentine**, Lecter doesn't disguise his identity, so we can come to know him as an individual personality, and not just a man behind a mask. And unlike your dime-a-dozen cannibal killers, Lecter is an anthropophage *and* a gentleman: a brilliant doctor, decadant aesthete and bon vivant with a stylish wardrobe and a morbid taste in irony.

Hannibal is perhaps most memorable for the "dinner party" scene where Ray Liotta, the top of whose skull has been removed by Lecter, is spood-fed his own cooked brains by the doctor, who slices off bits of the bloody, exposed cerebellum while Liotta burbles incoherently.

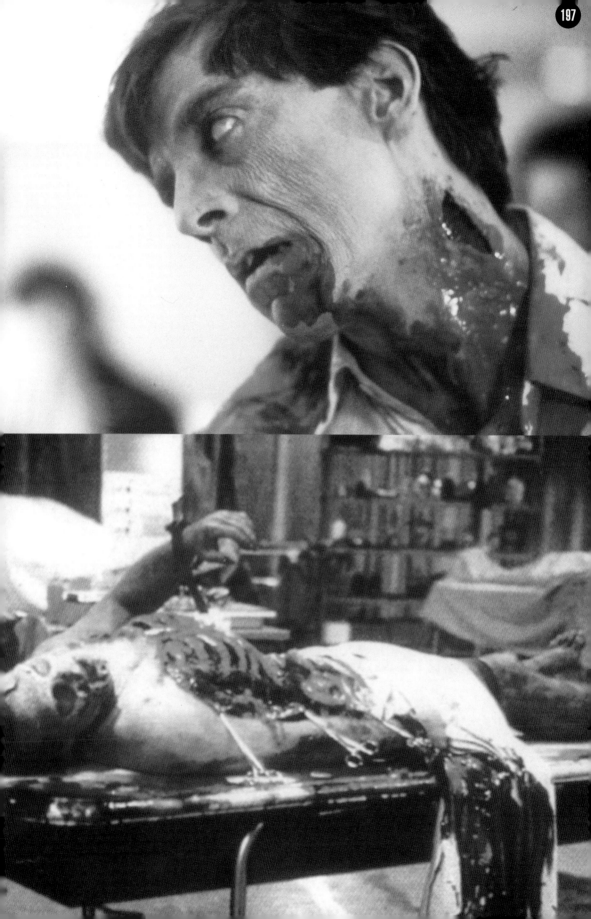

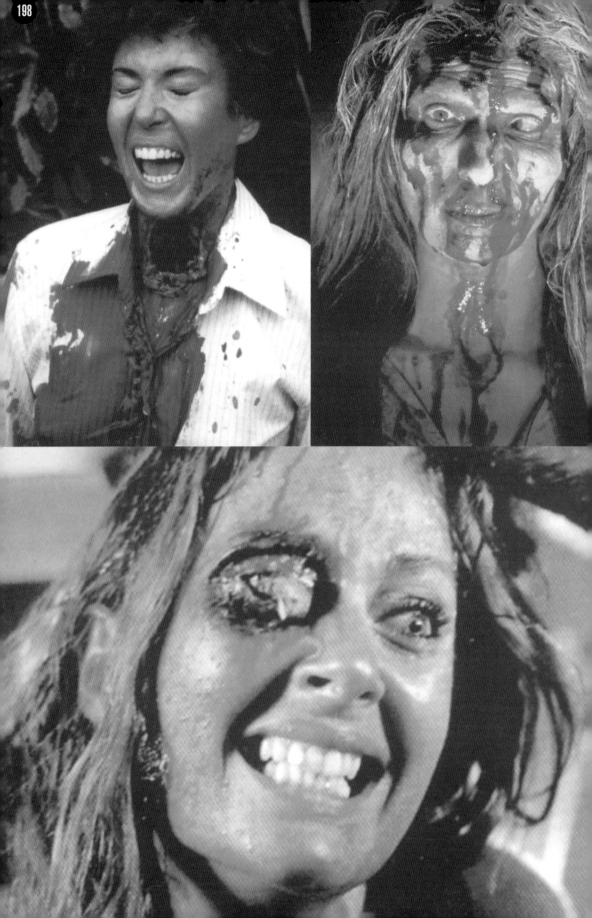

Hannibal closes with Lecter offering a fastidious young boy a taste of his cerebral snack, urging him to try something new, with the implication that a taste of Lecter's brain food will transform the child into a fledgling flesh-eater. Clearly, there's more going on here than an admonition against accepting candy from a stranger. This scene may help to shed some light on why the last few years have brought an unprecedented glut of cannibal films to the big screen.

Significantly, the food contamination paranoia resulting from the outbreak in Europe of "mad cow disease" (transmitted specifically through brains) is especially relevant to a culture increasingly dependent on fast food, where contamination folklore is commonplace. Our culinary laziness leaves us wide open to all kinds of paranoia about cheap, easily available, pre-prepared food (earthworms being ground up and used as taco meat is perhaps the most ubiquitous example). Are we all being fed something terrible for the sake of economic convenience, like the unknowing cannibals of **Soylent Green**? Much of the folklore surrounding food contamination reflects the anxiety of the individual in the face of those gigantic corporate franchises that feed us our daily diet of meat from the mother lode – meat that looks nothing like it does in the pictures. The content of these stories can be attributed to American ambivalence toward major changes in society associated with industrialization: manufactured foods, large impersonal organizations, urbanization and new technology. Their plausibility, however, is open to interpretation; anybody who buys live bait could tell you that a pound of earthworms costs far more than a pound of taco meat.

Our increasing anxiety about being fed something nasty is perhaps what lies beneath this recent spate of cannibal films. Like most food contamination stories, modern-day cannibal tales contain a strict admonition against eating out, and cater to our guilt about the fact that it's other people – often anonymous ethnic others – who prepare most of the food we eat, and feed to our children. After all, with pre-packaged lunches, you never know quite what you're going to get. Even when they're from Dean and DeLuca.

NOTES

1. Z-movie director Andy Milligan (**The Body Beneath, The Ghastly Ones, The Rats Are Coming! The Werewolves Are Here!**, etc etc) churned out a no-budget version of the Todd story, entitled **Bloodthirsty Butchers**, in 1970.
2. Astrid Olsen, a bunny girl who worked at Miami's Playboy Club, was selected for the part because she had a mouth large enough to accommodate a sheep's tongue, cranberries, gelatin and Lewis's special blood solution. Lewis recalled that the sheep's tongue was purchased in Tampa, and so spoiled on the day of shooting that it had to be soaked in Pine-Sol. Olsen's "tongue" scene is perhaps the most notorious episode in **Blood Feast** – James O'Neill points out that "the tongue torn from a girl's mouth looks long enough to have come out of a giraffe!" (O'Neill 1994:68). In an interview with John Waters in *Shock Value*, Lewis remembers filming the scene. "We pulled out her tongue and her head lolled to one side and she gagged", he recalls. "It worked out very nicely. That was her part. One take only because it messed up her face. Our one big problem with stage blood was that it would not come out of clothing. Axion in its original formation was great, but strangely enough they changed it so it wasn't as good" (Waters 1991:206–7).
3. Lewis, an ex-college professor with a Ph.D. in English and the self-styled "Wizard of Gore", lost most of his capital in the courts, when he was arrested for his part in a fraudulent car rental agency, along with a series of other mail fraud convictions including a fake abortion referral agency and a phoney gas-saving device. The arrest brought his filmmaking career to an abrupt end, and he now heads a mail marketing service in Fort Lauderdale, Florida. According to John Waters, Lewis's exploitation films are "impossible to defend; thus he automatically becomes one of the greatest directors in film history" (Waters 1991:206).

4.   Capitalizing on the unexpected underground success of the film, in **1988** Herschell Gordon Lewis published the film's story in novel format, extending it into a grim comedy with sardonic overtones. In **Blood Feast** the novel, all references to cannibalism in the screenplay are deliberately embellished and camped up, usually to comic intent.

5.   A brief selection of the slasher films directly influenced by the prototype narrative of **Blood Feast** would include Lewis's own **The Gore-Gore Girls** (1972), John Carpenter's **Halloween** (1978), Sean S. Cunningham's **Friday The 13th** (1980), Kevin Connor's **Motel Hell** (1980), Rick Rosenthal's **Halloween 2** (1981), Tom de Simone's **Hell Night** (1981), Miner's **Friday The 13th Part 2** (1981) and **Friday The 13th Part 3 in 3D** (1982), Tommy Lee Wallace's **Halloween 3: Season Of The Witch** (1983), Zito's **Friday The 13th Part 4 – The Final Chapter** (1984), Wes Craven's **A Nightmare On Elm Street** (1984), Danny Steinmann's **Friday The 13th Part 5 – A New Beginning** (1985), Holder's **Nightmare On Elm Street 2 – Freddy's Revenge** (1985), Jon Kranhouse's **Friday The 13th Part 6 – Jason Lives** (1986), Rubens's **The Stepfather** (1986), Chuck Russell's **Nightmare On Elm Street 3 – Dream Warriors** (1987), Harlin's **Nightmare On Elm Street 4 – The Dream Master** (1988), Buechler's **Friday The 13th Part 7 – The New Blood** (1988), Fischer's **Friday The 13th Part 8 – Jason Takes Manhattan** (1989), Hopkins's **Nightmare On Elm Street 5 – The Dream Child** (1989), Mary Lambert's **Pet Sematary** (1989), Ralph Singleton's **Graveyard Shift** (1990), Henenlotter's **Frankenhooker** (1990) and Talalay's **Freddy's Dead – The Final Nightmare** (1991).

6.   And Lewis himself, of course – however tongue-in-cheek – likens his narrative talent to that of the classical tragedians.

7.   See also, for example, **The Texas Chain Saw Massacre, Motel Hell, Cannibal Girls, The Folks At The Red Wolf Inn**, and so on.

8.   Franco is still making his own peculiar brand of film, the latest being entitled **Tender Flesh** (1996). Franco has described **Tender Flesh** as being – unsurprisingly – a "strange erotic film, mostly insane".

9.   Lee also directed **Dr. Lamb** (1992), again based on a real-life killer. Here, a misogynistic necrophile fulfils his lusts on the bodies of female victims, including eating parts of them. Real corpses were allegedly used in filming these sickening scenes of depravity. The real-life killer was apprehended when he took photos of his victims' remains to be developed at the local drugstore.
        Perhaps the most well-known (in the West) Chinese cannibal film is Tsui Hark's **Diyu Wu Men** (a.k.a. **We Are Going To Eat You**, 1980), in which a government agent pursues a notorious bandit only to end up in a village inhabited by flesh-eaters. The cannibals wear human-skin masks in the manner of Leatherface, and their village is a microcosm of violence and horror. This trend continues with the likes of **Human Sausages, Human Skin Lanterns, Cannibal Mercenaries, Primitives, Ebola Syndrome**, and **Horrible High Heels** (described as "a Chinese Texas Chain Saw Massacre"). Japanese cannibal films include **Luminous Moss**, a science fiction entry, although the subject was dealt with the most seriously in Kon Ichikawa's celebrated anti-war film **Nobi (Fires On The Plain**, 1959).

10.   Ted Bundy, during his years on Death Row, performed a similar function for members of the FBI's crime team (see chapter 2).

11.   See, for example, Tharp 1990:106–113.

12.   See, for example, Young 1991:4–25.

13.   See Halberstam, 1991:26–53.

14.   See Murphy, 1991:32.8.

chapter six:
supernatural cannibals

MOST supernatural cannibals appear in the form of zombies – not the zombies of the traditional, Caribbean-voodoo films of the '30s and '40s (like **White Zombie** and **I Walked With A Zombie**), whose *dramatis personae* tend to be necrophagic (rather than anthropophagic) in nature – but the post-Romero, Italian and American zombies of the zombie new wave, which tend to be bigger, better, blanker, and (at times) more aggressively cannibalistic than their predecessors. In these more recent zombie films, the supernatural origins of the cannibalistic appetite tends to be draped in fashionable sci-fi trappings. These vengeful, man-eating zombies are cannibals as a result of atomic radiation from a space satellite, a lethal chemical toxin or even dubious chemical weaponry used on G.I. subjects in Vietnam, rather than voodoo ceremonies or ancient magical rites.

NIGHT OF THE LIVING DEAD

The premise of **Night Of The Living Dead**, George A. Romero's groundbreaking and now classic 1968 zombie epic, is that atomic radiation from a space satellite has the power to animate the recently deceased, and these mindless cannibal ghouls thereupon prey indiscriminately upon the living, eating their warm bodies. These zombies can be stopped only when their warped brains are completely destroyed.

      Night... has been analyzed in a variety of different ways by a range of different critics, who've generally paid most attention to the film's ideological content. Richard Dyer, for example, writing in the film journal *Screen*, is particularly interested in the racial elements of the film and the specifically white dimension of the relationship between these zombies and the American society that has created them. He writes:

"If whiteness and death are equated, both are further associated with the USA. That the film can be taken as a metaphor for the United States is established right at the start of the film. It opens on a car driving through apparently unpopulated back roads suggesting the road tradition of 1950s American movies... with its idea of the 'search for America'. When the car reaches the graveyard (the U.S.?), a stars-and-stripes flag flutters in the foreground."[1]

In a similarly ideological vein, Jane Caputi in *The Journal Of Popular Film And Television* takes a look at **Night...** with reference to the nihilism of much post-1950s American cinema, which, Caputi speculates, tends to reflect the anxiety of the nuclear age. She studies the film's imagery for its nuclear elements, relating the psychic experience of zombiedom to the partial shutdown of mental facilities and emotional responses experienced by the survivors of nuclear war. According to Caputi:

Night Of The Living Dead

*"**Night Of The Living Dead** offers not only a symbolic description of the landscape of a post-nuclear world: it provides a powerful metaphor for the psychic numbing that characterizes general consciousness in the Nuclear Age."[2]*

Others, including Steve Beard, are more interested in the role of the zombie as surplus human capacity processed through the system as grotesque human waste, and conscious fears about mass unemployment in the recessionary climate of the time. In other words, the heterogeneity of Romero's zombies contains the implication – and one that has become more transparent since 1968 – that "nobody is immune from the social restructuring of post-Fordism... Everybody's job is potentially at risk"[3].

Romero himself helped to back up this ideological interpretation of the living dead. "Zombies are the real lower-class citizens of the monster world, and that's why I like them", he says. Individually, as Beard has pointed out, they are slow, stumbling and weak. Collectively, they're a rampaging mob of clawing hands and gnashing teeth[4]. What's special about Romero's zombies, however, is their cannibalistic appetite. Romero is almost entirely responsible for the now-familiar incarnation of the zombie as ghoulish cannibal, as bloodthirsty anthropophage who adds to his numbers by feeding on living human flesh.

Taking the cultural taboo of cannibalism as a starting point, it seems evident that there are a number of important psychoanalytic issues in **Night Of The Living Dead** which haven't been widely discussed, which seems unusual for a film which has managed to earn such an established critical reputation. But both

Night Of The Living Dead

psychoanalysis and anthropology can bring a lot to our understanding of Romero's zombie epic, and the nature of the supernatural cannibal.

Both psychoanalysis and anthropology have a lot to say, for example, about western cultural taboos surrounding the burial of the dead. In Romero's film, John and Barbara have come to Maryland to lay a wreath on their mother's grave. When we first meet John, he's impatient and irritated that Barbara spends so long kneeling by the grave. "C'mon Barbara, praying's for church", he tells her on a number of occasions. He also complains that it's a waste of money to buy a new wreath every year, and they'd be better of recycling the old ones. Later on, while the survivors are watching television, a medical authority warns of the dangers to any delay to the destruction of corpses:

"No, you're right, it doesn't give them time to make funeral arrangements. The bodies must be carried to the street and... and... and burned. They must be burned immediately. Soak them with gasoline and burn them. The bereaved will have to forego the dubious comforts that a funeral service will give... They're just dead flesh, and dangerous."

High levels of radiation from a malfunctioning space probe have led to the revival of recently-deceased corpses. This is a film about the dead returning to life, and our collective cultural fears surrounding improper funeral rituals and inadequate bereavement. Images of the unburied dead fill the screen repeatedly – corpses that are seemingly bent on avenging a culture that has casually broken this most sacred of western taboos. According to traditional anthropology, anxieties surrounding burial neglect relate to a society's fear of their deceased ancestors' jealousy of the living, and their need to avenge that jealousy upon those who remain alive. In psychoanalytic terms, however, the dread of improper burial is quite clearly connected to our fears surrounding the notion of repression – the dread that whatever terrifying anxieties and taboos lie hidden in the unconscious have been inadequately buried, and may revive any moment, breaking through into the conscious world of logic and reason. And as anthropology has established, that which fails to fit into traditional cultural characters – such as the living, walking dead – is always regarded by a culture as abject and contaminating.

The pathological dimensions of this incomplete repression are symbolically embodied in the architectonics of the house, with its front façade (under attack by the unburied dead), its upstairs (where the dead body of the previous tenant lies half-eaten), and the cellar (representing the dark nether regions of the human body, sexuality and repression). In **Night Of The Living Dead,** much of the final section of the film is taken up with an angry debate between Ben and Mr. Cooper about whether they are safer staying upstairs, confronting the marauding cannibals head-on, or else barricading themselves in the cellar. Mr. Cooper wants to get together everything they might need and hole up in the cellar. The cellar, he claims, has only one door, which can be locked from the inside, but upstairs there are too many doors and windows. Cooper argues that the cellar is the safest place to hide; Ben thinks it's a death-trap. "If you've locked yourself in the cellar and those things get in the house, you've had it", he claims. "At least up here, you've got a fighting chance". Unknown to the survivors, however, the cellar is already inhabited by a zombie of its own. Karen, Mr. Cooper's young daughter, has been bitten by one of the ghouls and is about to revive in the form of a zombie. In an added irony, it's only Ben who survives the night – and only then by barricading himself up in the cellar.

The psychological dimensions of this analogy are obvious. Like the besieged survivors in Hitchcock's **The Birds** (1963), another film about inadequate repression[5], the characters in **Night Of The Living Dead** try to barricade themselves in the house whilst the menace proliferates outside. As in **The Birds,** attacks occur at moments of mounting social tension in the narrative. Surplus repression reveals itself in the form of the gathering undead, and social traumas and conflicts manifest themselves in the form of inexplicable paranormal mayhem. The temporary makeshift barriers constructed by Ben represent the barriers of repression we build to separate conscious from unconscious neurosis, to defend our unstable egos against the return of the repressed.

The breaking down of these barriers by the inexplicable threat is a symbolic re-interpretation of that which we, as human beings, fear the most: mental breakdown, neurotic collapse, or the process of becoming caught, like Barbara, in that liminal, terminal no-man's land between the conscious of logic and stability and the unconscious of unreason, repression and neurosis. It seems somehow right, then, that the zombies can be killed only by aiming a gun or other implement at the physical embodiment of their minds. As the radio announcer says, "kill the brain and you kill the ghoul". But one question remains. What terrifying trauma lying buried somewhere in the unconscious does this inexorable assault represent?

Night Of The Living Dead is the story of a night when the whole world turns upside-down. Much is made, in the opening sequence, of the fact that this is the first day of winter, the day when the clocks go back, giving an extra hour of daylight before night falls with shocking suddenness. John and Barbara have

Night Of The Living Dead

somehow accidentally driven into a topsy-turvy world, a world in which the dead re-animate mysteriously, roam the earth, and seek to devour living human flesh.

The first taboo to be broken is that of bodily control. The zombies stumble and drool in their clumsy quest for human flesh, often with intestines spilling out or broken limbs dangling. Brains splatter against the walls; zombies collapse groaning to the ground. The human body – even your own body – is out of control, and you're no longer able to understand or relate to it.

The second broken taboo is that of incest. Barbara's obsession with her brother's death leads her to remain in a catatonic state throughout the remainder of the movie, but the psychic numbing she so obviously manifests is a version of the psychic state that is more subtly and powerfully represented by the cannibalistic zombies themselves, including her beloved brother John, who returns from the dead at last to claim her for his own.

The third and most significant broken taboo is that of cannibalism, especially intra-familial cannibalism (endophagy). The inversion of traditional feeding behaviour is first made manifest when Ben and Barbara take refuge in the kitchen, whose table is laid out neatly for a meal. Ben gathers together the plates and crockery in the tablecloth, pushes it all to one side, upends the dining table and dismantles it to make boards for the windows while Barbara takes the lace tablecloth, folds it and cradles it, hanging on uselessly to this symbol of traditional eating behaviour. Ben, who tells Barbara that he was first attacked in a nearby diner, kills the intruding zombies one by one then throws the bodies outside to appease the hunger of the others, at least temporarily, while Barbara listens transfixed to the radio broadcast constantly emphasizing the predatory nature of these cannibalistic ghouls, and their unsavoury appetite for human flesh:

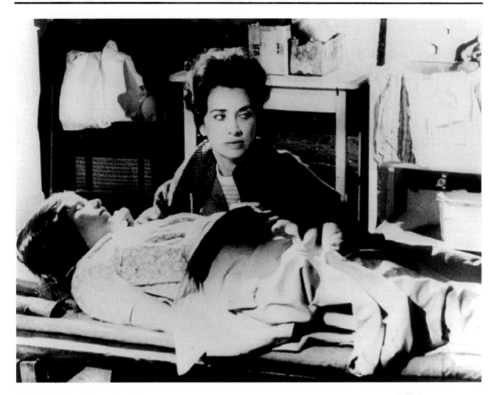

Night Of The Living Dead

"...consistent reports from witnesses of people who acted as though they were in a kind of trance who were killing and eating their victims prompted authorities to examine the bodies of some of their victims. Medical authorities in Cumberland have concluded that in all cases the killers are eating the flesh of the people they murder... Civil defense authorities have told newsmen that murder victims show evidence of being partially devoured by their murderers. Medical examinations of the victims' bodies show conclusively that the killers are eating the flesh of the people they kill..."

Barbara sits stunned, staring at the radio in utter incomprehension and disbelief, trying to make some sense of what she's heard. Meanwhile, the zombies move in, stumbling slowly and clumsily towards the house, motivated solely by the desire to find and devour living human flesh.

The film ends in a nightmare of chaos. The lovers, Tom and Judy, are roasted to death when their truck blows up, and they're graphically consumed by the cannibalistic ghouls who move in on them like a pack of hyenas. The explosive nuclear family ends up eating itself – Mr. and Mrs. Cooper bicker and snipe constantly until their dead daughter Karen, kept down in the dark recesses of the cellar, revives only to destroy and eat her parents. Barbara's brother John, who teased and tormented her while she was living, and whose death caused her to revert to a state of catatonic stupor, returns from the dead to break down the kitchen door, seek out his traumatized sister and eat her alive. And the heroic Ben, who alone survives the terrible night, is mistaken for a ghoul by a roving posse, shot in the head and dumped carelessly on a pile of dead bodies. When the

The Living Dead At The Manchester Morgue

improperly buried return from their makeshift graves into the realms of the living, there can be no survivors. No-one remains to greet the morning.

Now regarded as one of the seminal horror films of all time, **Night Of The Living Dead** inspired a whole generation of horror film makers, and its influence is clear in such intriguing movies as Willard Huyck's **Dead People** (1972) and Bob Clark's **Children Shouldn't Play With Dead Things** (1972), as well as a continuing host of ultra low-budget entries including Chuck McCrann's **The Bloodeaters** (1980), Tony Malinowsky's **Curse Of The Screaming Dead** (1982), Glenn Coburn's **Bloodsuckers From Outer Space** (1985), Pericles Lewnes' **Redneck Zombies** (1987), and Donald Farmer's **Cannibal Hookers** (1987)[6]. In 1990 **Night Of The Living Dead** was remade, in colour, with effects-man Tom Savini as director. Although this seemed quite pointless, contractual matters were later cited as the reason for the film's creation.

THE LIVING DEAD AT THE MANCHESTER MORGUE

Also known as **No Profanor El Sueno De Los Muertos** and **The Living Dead,** and directed in 1974 by Jorge Grau, this overlooked and little-known film is a low-budget classic of the zombie-cannibal genre. The film's storyline is clearly influenced by **Night Of The Living Dead**; George and Edna meet when she accidentally reverses into his motorbike at a petrol station, so feels duty-bound to offer him a lift to the Lake District. Unfortunately for both characters, however, they never arrive, as both are pulled into a series of bizarre events beyond their control.

In **The Living Dead At Manchester Morgue,** the revival of the dead is an unintended by-product of a new form of pest control developed by the

The Living Dead At The Manchester Morgue

Department of Agriculture – an "ultrasonic radiation" device that attacks primitive nervous systems, intended to make insects kill one another, thereby preserving crops. However, several babies in a nearby hospital are born with "homicidal tendencies", proof that the device has been effecting more than the local insects. It also revives the recently deceased, who then animate further corpses by applying freshly spilled blood to their eyelids.

As in the tradition begun by **Night Of The Living Dead,** these zombies are in search of fresh meat. Vivid scenes of cannibalism include some graphic gut-

Dawn Of The Dead

munching and eyeball-chomping – scenes which led the film to be placed on the infamous list of "video nasties", and it wasn't in fact granted an 18 certificate until 1985. As to why specifically a morgue in Manchester, the idea belonged to producer Edmondo Amati, who was obsessed by both Manchester and **Night Of The Living Dead**. Speaking on TV show *Eurotika!*, Grau said, "For him the magic word was Manchester. For him a horror movie had to be set in Manchester"[7]

DAWN OF THE DEAD/DAY OF THE DEAD

The new wave of early '80s zombie films was launched with **Dawn Of The Dead** (1979), George Romero's bloodsoaked sequel to **Night Of The Living Dead**, initiating an upsurge in movies dealing with undead protagonists for whom a cannibalistic appetite is virtually *de rigueur*. **Dawn Of The Dead** continues from where **Night Of The Living Dead** left off – the world is being overrun by zombies whose sheer numbers are multiplying at a terrible rate. A small group of survivors – a couple who work for a television station and two deserting soldiers – take off in a helicopter and make their way to an empty shopping mall, where they decide to stay. Before too long they've cleared the place of trolley-pushing zombies, blocked the exits and are enjoying the pleasures of conspicuous consumption, oblivious to the goings-on in the outside world – a situation that lasts only until the next invasion.

Reviewers and critics have drawn attention to **Dawn Of The Dead** as a wry condemnation of American commodity culture and the media-induced paralysis that turns us all into lifeless zombies. But there's more going on here than a

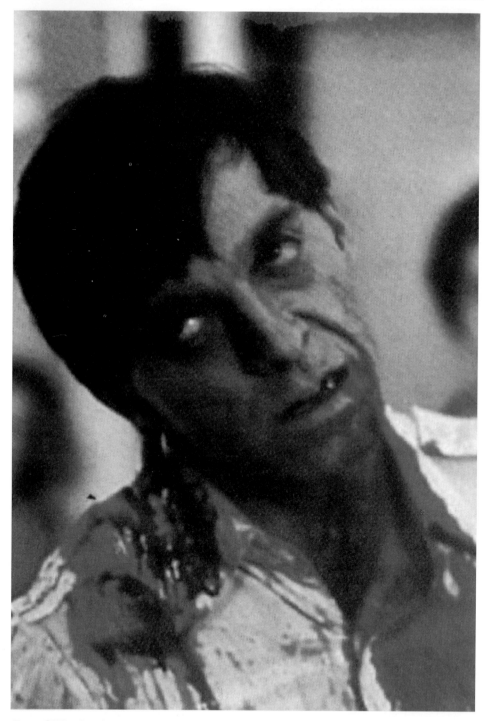

Dawn Of The Dead

critique of capitalism, thanks to Tom Savini's skilful special effects. These zombies are like none seen on the screen before, continuing their relentless attack despite

Day Of The Dead

dangling limbs, hanging viscera and exposed brain tissue. And if that's not enough, the hi-tech weaponry used to fight the living dead allows for plenty of dramatic gunshots to the head, as well as the usual throat rippings and bodies torn in half.

Day Of The Dead (1985), Romero's follow-up, isn't quite as well-loved as **Dawn...**, but has some notable moments nevertheless. As in **Dawn...**, rampaging zombies have taken over the world. Deep underground in a secure bunker hide a ragtag crew of survivors, presided over by a doctor obsessed with experiments designed to domesticate the zombies, and a maniacal bloodthirsty soldier intent on gunning down as many of the living dead as he possibly can. When the soldier

Day Of The Dead

finds out that the doctor's been using the corpses of his dead companions as food for his pet zombie, all hell breaks loose, and the pet zombie is soon serving up innard appetizers.

Unlike **Night...** and **Dawn...**, **Day...** brings a certain amount of closure to Romero's trilogy with a happy, Hollywood-style ending which is rather disappointing after the nihilism of the two prequels. The plot is a little loose – the point of Dr. Logan's bizarre experiments is never really made clear. However, Tom Savini does another excellent job of creating the goriest zombies ever seen on screen, with the help – for the scene in which Captain Rhodes gets ripped apart in the hallway – of a pile of real pig intestines.

THE ITALIAN NEW WAVE

The Italian New Wave of ultra-violent cannibal zombie movies was initiated by zombie *auteur* Lucio Fulci, whose own series of thoughtfully atmospheric yet sporadically graphic films begins with **Zombie Flesh Eaters** (1979), also sometimes known as **Zombi 2** – an attempt to pass itself off as a sequel to George Romero's **Dawn Of The Dead**, which Fulci claimed as one of his greatest influences. Like all Fulci's films, **Zombie Flesh Eaters** is most memorable for its haunting mood and memorably violent set-pieces, which led to it being heavily cut by the BBFC for its British release.

When her father goes missing, a young woman and a reporter she meets along the way make the journey to a remote tropical island where her father was involved in research. After further investigation, she discovers that her father died after falling afoul of an ancient voodoo curse that seems to be bringing the dead back to life to avenge themselves upon the flesh of the living. Before long, the island is overrun with zombies, and the small group of survivors are caught in a

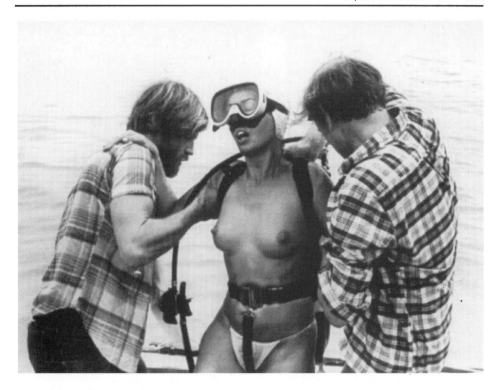

Zombie Flesh Eaters

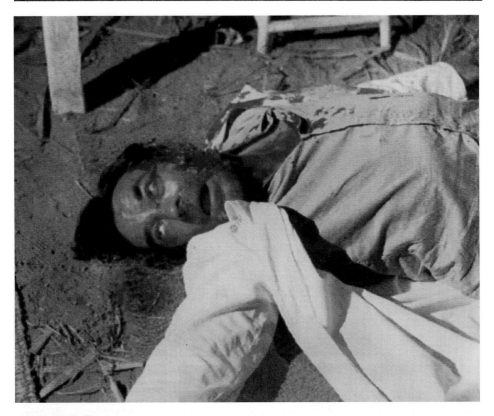

Zombie Flesh Eaters

desperate and futile struggle to fight off the maggot-riddled undead. The film is particularly notorious for a sequence in which a woman has her eye skewered on a wooden splinter, but such moments of violence – of which there are many – are nicely counterbalanced by its suspenseful atmosphere and evocative images, especially the crewless vessel adrift off the coast of a besieged New York.

Fulci's next film was 1980's **Gates Of Hell**, also known as **City Of The Living Dead** or **Paura Nella Citta Dei Morti Viventi**. Again, as in **Zombie Flesh Eaters**, the motivation behind the cannibalistic appetites of the living dead has a magical origin. By hanging himself, a priest mysteriously opens up the gates of hell in the Lovecraftian setting of Dunwich, a small American town. Elsewhere, in New York, a woman is pronounced dead after her dabblings in witchcraft go horribly wrong. Her coffin is placed in the ground, and she wakes up right on the verge of being buried alive.

The woman is saved by a local reporter whose investigations show that the couple must travel to Dunwich to destroy the body of the suicidal priest in order to prevent an apocalypse caused by the revival of the dead. As in most of Fulci's work, infelicities of plot are smoothed over by stylish atmospherics, nightmarish settings, and – in this case – some crafty photography (by Sergio Salvati). Whilst never quite attaining the status of some of Fulci's other work, **Gates Of Hell** makes use of witchcraft in a very interesting way, displays the requisite piles of writhing viscera, and – as usual – involves a cast of zombies so putrescent and maggot-ridden they actually seem to be rotting right before the eyes.

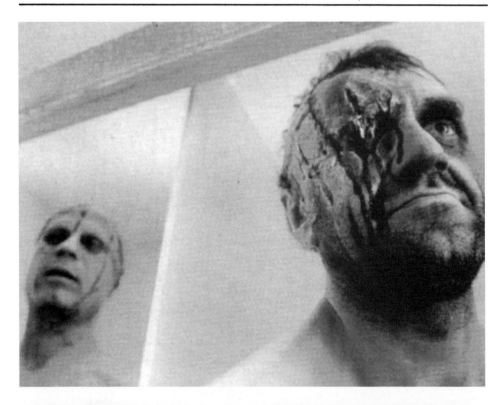

The Beyond

The Beyond

One year later came Fulci's zombie classic – and perhaps his best-known film – **The Beyond** (1981), (also known as **The Seven Doors Of Death** and **...E Tu Vivrai Nel Terrore!**). In 1927 Louisiana, an artist residing in a small hotel discovers one of the seven gateways to hell, is branded as a warlock and dispatched by a torch-bearing lynch mob. Many years later, the hotel is purchased by a young woman who, unwittingly, re-opens the gateway to hell in room 36, with predictably gruesome consequences. The town slowly becomes populated by an army of reanimated corpses, and the protagonists escape from the zombies only to find themselves trapped in a hellish landscape painted by the unfortunate artist.

Some find the plot of **The Beyond** too confusing and convoluted to remain coherent; Kerekes and Slater argue that "**The Beyond** trips over its own confusion. It almost tries to be too clever with its esoteric mystery and unexplained characters and as a result the film's pace is adversely effected"[8]. Others argue that the plot is deliberately ambiguous. Michael Grant, for example, claims that "[Fulci] has taken narrative beyond itself, as a condition of its existing, and it is only because the being of the characters can be doubled into the beyond that he finds their actions worth narrating at all"[9]. For most, however, the film is memorable for its slick atmospherics and some of the best set-piece eye-poppings in the entire zombie-cannibal genre[10].

Zombi 3 (1987), a film whose storyline is almost identical to that of Bruno Mattei's **Zombie Creeping Flesh** (1981) – the dead are reanimated by means of a chemical virus – is also attributed to Lucio Fulci, but most of what happens on screen was actually handled by Bruno Mattei, who took over production when Fulci fell ill.

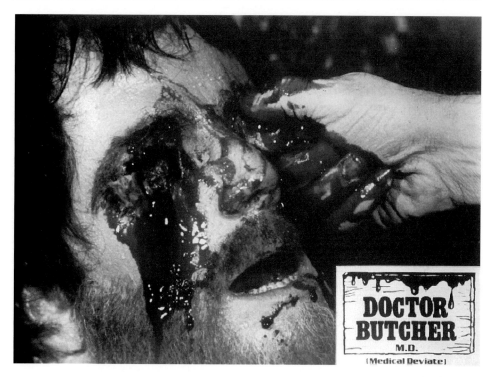

Dr. Butcher, M.D.

Dr. Butcher, M.D. (Frank Martin, 1980), also sometimes known as **Zombi Holocaust** or **La Regina Dei Cannibali**, revolves around a hospital where the body parts of corpses are going missing. We are shown scenes of an Asiatic-looking character called Toran robbing and eating the hearts from corpses in a number of local morgues. Doctor and anthropologist Lori Ridgeway (Alexandra Cole) becomes personally involved when she has a ceremonial knife stolen from her collection, and by matching its inscription with those of the tattoos of the corpse robbers, deduces that these rituals are part of an ancient native ceremony involving human sacrifice and cannibalism. When Toran makes a suicide leap from a hospital window – making a nasty mess on the ground – Lori catches his dying words, one of which is "Kito", meaning – apparently – "Divine Island".

Consequently, Dr. Ridgeway, a fellow scientist, Peter Chandler (Ian McCulloch), a reporter, Susan Kelly (Sherry Buchanan) and her boyfriend George (Peter O'Neal) mount an expedition to the Pacific Island of Kito to investigate a local cannibal cult. Only here does the blood really start to flow. On the island the scientists encounter the mad Dr. Abrera or "Dr. Butcher" (played by Donald O'Brian). Lori removes her clothes for bed only to find a maggot-covered, rotting, severed head under the sheets; she is later attacked by one of the natives, and plants a machete in his forehead. George has his intestines and eyeballs yanked out and eaten, and Susan is kidnapped.

It turns out that "Dr. Butcher" is a crazed dictator à la Dr. Moreau, whose mad experiments in human transplants have created an island full of disfigured zombies. Beset by scalp-crazed headhunters and acts of on-camera cannibalism, Peter has to contend with a tribe of gore-crazed savages who have kidnapped and stripped Dr. Ridgeway. Her body is painted with tribal make-up and she is

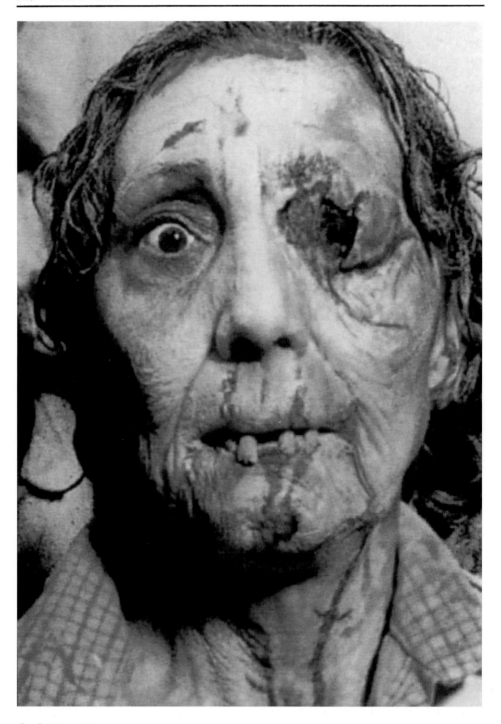

Dr. Butcher, M.D.

prepared for sacrifice, until the cannibals suddenly change their minds and hail her instead as a magical being. Finally, after a smattering of dismemberments, and a tribal battle in which one aggressor is splattered with a whirring outboard motor, Peter manages to escape from the operating table to wipe out the mad Dr. Butcher and his crazed henchmen, with just a little help from the cannibals.

This is perhaps the only film in the genre that features not only cannibal zombies, but zombies *and* cannibals besieging the same island, attacking not just the group of explorers, but the very furthest shores of plausibility.

1980 also brought us the infamous **Cannibal Apocalypse** (a.k.a. **Cannibals In The Streets, Invasion Of The Flesh Hunters, Savage Apocalypse**), directed by Antonio Margheriti (under the name of Anthony M. Dawson). The film begins with a section of claustrophobic jungle footage from Vietnam, where a missing G.I, Charlie Bukowski (John Morghen [Giovanni Lombardo Radice]) is discovered by his commanding officer Norman Hopper (John Saxon) sitting in a pit with his colleague snacking on what is left of an unfortunate Viet Cong soldier. We then cut to Atlanta, where Bukowski is released from a hospital for mental disorders, presumed cured. However, after checking into a seedy hotel room, the first thing he does is to take a huge bite out of a young woman's neck. After hiding out in a local shopping mall (in an idea lifted from Romero's **Dawn Of The Dead**, although Margheriti's interiors were shot in Rome), he is apprehended, and returned to his colleague in the mental hospital. The two cannibals then proceed to run riot, and consume most of the hospital's staff. The cannibalism turns out to be infectious, making it difficult for the local police to curb the city-wide urban panic; indeed, some of the police even become infected themselves.

It turns out that GIs returning from Vietnam have been infected with a rabies-like virus which turns them into flesh-hungry cannibals. However, instead of becoming blank-eyed, shuffling zombies, those infected retain the appearance of relatively normal people, with normal people's problems and hang-ups, including a soap-opera strand of marital infidelity. Captain Hopper, himself bitten, manages to resist the effects of the disease and gathers together a crack troop of Atlanta policemen to stage a number of routine chases and siege shoot-outs, involving plenty of gore effects, biting, the eating of human flesh and spilling of blood on-camera. Finally, Bukowski leads his cannibal horde down into Atlanta's sewers for a last stand against the police with their flame-throwers – a pitched battle which involves the death of the cannibal chief Bukowski, who is blown open by a shotgun. As the cannibals are finally put to rest and the film draws to a close, we are shown a group of kids in another part of the city storing the dismembered parts of their mother in the fridge.

Margheriti's cannibal-zombie narrative has all the metaphoric resonance of Romero's tales of society "eating itself alive" in a rush to consume material goods, as well as all the other sociological implications of zombiedom. In his films, Romero gives us a glimpse of a post-Vietnam American society in which there are no heroes, only realistic characters struggling for self-preservation – often at the expense of others – in a world which has completely fallen apart and collapsed into chaos, panic, and gruesome death and destruction. Margheriti, however, takes this one step further. **Cannibal Apocalypse** takes place in a world whose ruin is our own responsibility.

Cannibal Apocalypse is notable mainly as the first fusion between the Italian cannibal genre and the Vietnam movie, which had recently been revived by Francis Ford Coppola's phenomenally successful **Apocalypse Now**. But **Cannibal Apocalypse** never really does anything with its potentially potent metaphor of cannibal Vietnam vets, and even the cannibalism is thin on the ground (the zombies are unconvincingly human in personality, and tend to shoot people far more often than eating them). The film is perhaps most visually memorable for

Burial Ground

the scene in which John Morghen gets a hole blown right through his abdomen, and people can be seen moving around on the other side. John Saxon claims that working on the film led him to an "almost suicidal despair"[11].

In Umberto Lenzi's **City Of The Walking Dead (Incubo Sulla Citta Contaminata,** 1980), a reporter is assigned to interview a famous atomic scientist as he touches down at the airport. But when the plane arrives there's an ominous radio silence, and when the doors open, out tumble a pile of cannibalistic zombies who proceed to take over the city. As in many similar strains of the genre, the zombies have been created by a mutant strain of radiation which has distorted their cellular structure, leading them to crave human flesh. And since the mutation is contagious, the non-zombies don't stand much of a chance until they manage to escape to the countryside. This city/country divide allows the film to introduce a rather glib sub-theme about the corruption of cities and the misuse of science.

The same year also brought us Andrea Bianchi's **Burial Ground** (also known as **Zombie Horror, Hell Night** and **Le Notti Del Terror**), in which a group of friends vacationing in a Scottish castle are terrorized by zombies, hungry for their flesh. The result is a cannibal gorefest of gut-munching, decapitations, head smashing and the staple of the genre – the requisite eyeball skewering. The only notable element of the film – apart from its rather sudden and anticlimactic ending – is its totally unmotivated overtones of mother-son incest.

In 1981, the zombie-cannibal genre reached a new low with Bruno Mattei's **Zombie Creeping Flesh,** also sometimes known as **Inferno Dei Morti-Viventi,** just as its director is sometimes known as "Vincent Dawn". When an experiment to call an end to overpopulation goes horribly wrong and a man-made nerve gas turns corpses into decomposing flesh-eaters, a crack team of

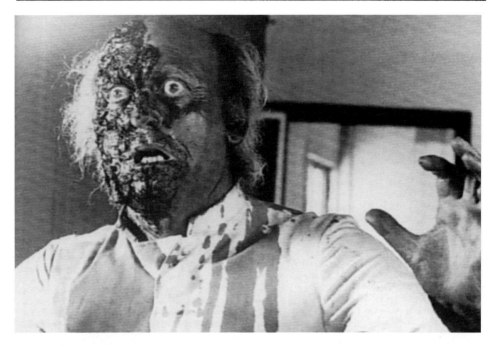

Zombie Creeping Flesh

soldiers is called in to deal with the situation. As they investigate further, they begin to witness horrible acts of mutilation, death and cannibalism. The contamination spreads through the primitive tribe, kills the soldiers and finally reaches America (the film seems to end where Romero's **Night Of The Living Dead** takes off).

Zombie Creeping Flesh has little to recommend it. As with the worst examples of the genre, gory special effects and fleeting scenes of cannibalism are used to distract from weaknesses in plot and character motivation. Zombie-cannibal connoisseurs may be entertained by the film's use of stock footage of real corpses in varying degrees of composition – much of it lifted from Akira Ide's mondo film **Guinea Ama**[12].

Before the creation of his magnum opus **Anthropophagus The Beast**, Joe D'Amato had dabbled in cannibalism in soft-core cannibal smut flicks like **Voodoo Baby** (1979) and **Erotic Nights Of The Living Dead** (1980). The latter is a particularly strange concoction, starring Laura Gemser (from D'Amato's many "Black Emanuelle" movies) and George Eastman (Luigi Montefiore), star of the same director's **Anthropophagus The Beast**, and alternating segments of sex and violence in much the same way as his earlier **Emanuelle In America** (1976), which managed to include both horse masturbation (real) and "snuff" movie footage (fake). Cannibalism and pornography are an uneasy combination, however, and D'Amato's scenes of fellatio culminating in the biting off of organs are just unnecessary and, ultimately, laughable.

Far more successful was **Anthropophagus 2** (also known as **Absurd** and **Rosso Sangue**), a pseudo-sequel to the previous year's **Anthropophagus The Beast**. In fact, however, there's very little to connect **Anthropophagus 2** with D'Amato's earlier film except for the participation of George Eastman, cast once again as the eponymous anthropophage. While freeing from a Catholic Priest, Eastman impales

Erotic Nights Of The Living Dead

himself on a fence outside a family's house. The family send him to a hospital, where he reawakens and goes on a cannibalistic killing spree, eventually returning to the family's house to attack a child and his babysitter. Meanwhile, a bumbling policeman and his deputy drive around endlessly in search of the mysterious cannibal killer, whose preternatural appetites are ascribed to his body continually regenerating from injury at the expense of his brain cells.

As in **Anthropophagus The Beast**, the plot is choppy and disconnected, but any ambiguities fade away into insignificance beside D'Amato's trademark scenes of set-piece gore. A nurse in the hospital gets a drill through her skull; heads are severed, eyes gouged out and guts spilled by the gallon, and the babysitter has her head thrust in the oven and baked – a scene that's actually shot from inside the oven itself. Unsurprisingly, **Anthropophagus 2** was banned by the BBFC and put on the original list of "video nasties" – a fact that apparently made D'Amato rather proud.[13]

Absurd

POST NEW WAVE: MID '80s AND '90S

The zombie-cannibal new wave lasted until the mid '80s, mainly in Italy, then

Return Of The Living Dead

suffered a gradual demise[14], and has only been brought back to life in sporadic bursts, and often in the form of comedy/parody.

Dan O'Bannon's **Return Of The Living Dead** is a very successful example of how the zombie theme can be appropriated for a comedy that still manages to be scary. In this film, which has something of a minor cult following among stoned teenagers due to its punk rock soundtrack and topless zombie punk chicks, a bumbling pair of employees at a medical supply warehouse accidentally release a deadly gas into the air. Inevitably, the vapours cause the dead to re-animate and go on a rampage in search of their favourite snack: human brains. **Return Of The Living Dead** was followed up in 1988 with a less successful sequel, **Return Of The Living Dead Part II**, directed by Ken Wiederhorn, and a much better second sequel in 1993, **Return Of The Living Dead 3**, directed by the much under-appreciated Brian Yuzna.

Yuzna's highly under-rated film **Society** (1992) has no zombies, but relocates the trauma of adolescence into a conspiratorial netherworld of cannibals and shape-shifters where teenage bodies are, quite literally, out of control. Bill (Billy Warlock) just doesn't seem to fit into his family's world of coming-out parties and cocktail engagements. Even though he runs for class president and his girlfriend Shauna (Heidi Kozak) is the foxiest girl in school, he finds it more and more difficult to communicate with his sister and his parents, and he confides to his therapist that he feels alienated from not only his parents, but from society in general. The therapist assures him that this is only natural at his age. However, when his sister's coming-out party degenerates into a mind-boggling cannibalistic orgy, it is clear that it is not Bill who is deeply troubled, but the exclusive society he has been adopted into. Further investigations reveal that Bill's parents, and, indeed, the entire adult society surrounding him, have given in to their Oedipal desires, breaking every one of normal society's taboos: they are incestuous

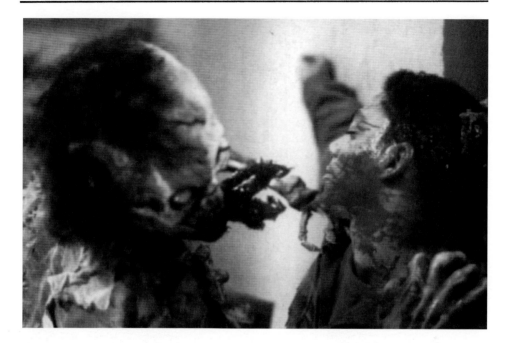

Return Of The Living Dead 3

cannibals who shape-shift, and thus, by failing to repress their adolescent desires, are permanently trapped in adolescence, depicted by their twisting bodies. **Society** is a stunning satire, a radical take on the "rich-as-bloodsuckers" cliché plunged into the realms of visceral horror by Screaming Mad George's special effects, which are unrelentingly surrealistic and grotesque in the tradition of Salvador Dalí's classic vision of mutual assimilation, *Autumn Cannibalism*.

Another comedic zombie film with a significant following is 1992's **Braindead** (also sometimes known as **Dead Alive**) by New Zealand filmmaker Peter Jackson, who first touched on the cannibal theme in his 1987 movie **Bad Taste**. **Braindead** starts with a young man's mother being bitten by a horrifying little "rat monkey", which causes her to die and come back to life as a flesh-crazed zombie. Like **Bad Taste**, **Braindead** features the creative and successful fusion of gore and comic horror, experimenting with every possible permutation on the zombie-cannibal cast (including baby zombies, whining mother zombies, and zombies that have sex). The film is most famed for its climactic gore orgy, as the hero dispatches dozens of zombies with the whirring rotars of a lawn-mower, chopping and mincing them in a blood-storm of flesh, limbs and viscera.

An interesting departure from the typical use of cannibalism as a gimmicky horror theme came with the crafted 1999 movie **Ravenous**, directed by vegetarian Antonia Bird. Set in the old West, **Ravenous** revives the Native American folk legend of the Wendigo – a monster with supernatural strength and an insatiable appetite for human flesh. In **Ravenous**, Captain John Boyd (Guy Pearce) is decorated for his single-handed capture of a command post in the Mexican-American war, where – it's revealed – he was dumped with a pile of dead bodies from the battlefield and inadvertently ends up regaining his strength by drinking human blood. Suspected of cowardice and foul play, he's posted to a run-down fort near the Sierra Nevada mountains to work with a ragtag bunch of

Braindead

cavalry officers and their eccentrically benevolent commander. More to the point, he can't even look at a bloody steak without vomiting.

One day, a half-dead man (Robert Carlyle) staggers into the fort suffering from cold and starvation. He tells a story of settlers taking a shortcut through the Sierras who decided to hole up in a mountain cave to get through the winter. After three months in the cave without food, the settlers begin to feed on the dead bodies of their deceased friends, and once they taste human flesh, they

Ravenous

begin murdering one another in order to survive. Cannibalism has become a compulsion over which the men have no control. The camp commander decides they must go and rescue the remaining men.

Avoiding most of the clichés of the typical cannibal movie, **Ravenous** still manages to deal out a considerable amount of violence and gore. At the same time, much of the film's power derives from its creepy atmospherics – dark colours, far-off cries, chiming bells and a feeling of damp, miserable, bone-chilling cold. And although the film includes a number of tongue-in-cheek puns, **Ravenous** is also interesting in the way it deals with cannibalism in a very serious way, relating it to deep and ancient fears about hunger, strength, virility and the magic powers of human flesh.

NOTES

1.   Dyer, Richard, "Whites In Film", *Screen* XXIX 14: Autumn 1988: 60–61.
2.   Caputi, Jane, "Nuclear Issues In The Cinema", *Journal Of Popular Film And Television* XVI.3, Fall 1988, 103.
3.   Beard, Steven, "No Particular Place to Go", *Sight And Sound* iiv.4. April 1993: 30.
4.   Ibid.
5.   See Brottman, Mikita, "Psycho/The Birds: Hitchcock Revisited", *Necronomicon 1*, ed. Andy Black, Creation Books, London 1996: 84–88.
6.   Donald Farmer's miserable shot-on-video film **Cannibal Hookers** features a pair of sorority girls who pose as hookers as part of a sorority initiation, and end up attempting to escape from a crew of cannibal prostitutes. Again, there's plenty of opportunity for using cannibalism as a metaphor for prostitution, for the condition of women and so on, but the theme is used as no

more than a comedy gimmick for a film that looked as though it was made in somebody's basement. In the same style, Dan Hoskins' **Chopper Chicks In Zombie Town** (1989) features a group of biker women fighting off a rather pitiful bunch of zombies in order to save a busload of blind children.

The 1990s saw no let up in the production of independent, low-budget zombie movies, as characterized by J.R. Bookwalter's messy **The Dead Next Door** (1990) and Scooter McCrae's more considered and original **Shatter Dead** (1995).

7.   Cit in Kerekes and Slater, *See No Evil: Banned Films And Video Controversy*, Critical Vision, Manchester, 2000.

8.   Ibid, 85.

9.   Grant, Michael, "Fulci's Waste Land: Cinema, Horror And The Dreams Of Modernism", *Unruly Pleasures – The Cult Film And Its Critics*, ed. Xavier Mendik and Graeme Harper, Fab Press, 2000: 61–73.

10.   **The Beyond** in fact features several scenes – including a throat-ripping, a head dissolved by acid, and a face blown apart by bullets – which highlight Fulci's cinematic penchant for acts of extreme violence against women, a trend which found its bloody apotheosis in his slasher film **The New York Ripper** (1982).

11.   John Saxon, interviewed in *Is It... Uncut?*, no. 8.

12.   Ibid, 280.

13.   A word should be said here about one notable US film of the time, Joel M Reed's 1981 rarity **Night Of The Zombies** – if for no other reason than that it stars Jamie Gillis in one of his very rare "legitimate" (ie. non-porno) film appearances. Whilst low on the hardcore cannibal gore typical of the zombie new wave, **Night Of The Zombies** has a lurid Nazi theme, and centres somewhat loosely around the imperative to recover canisters of a special experimental gas which the U.S. developed for use on the Germans. As usual, the "chemical experiments" are simply an updated form of voodoo, providing a narrative excuse for the ubiquity of flesh-munching, torso-roasting cannibal zombies. Other films in the zombie-Nazi subgenre include **Shock Waves** (Ken Wiederhorn, 1975), **Zombie Lake** (Jean Rollin, 1980), and **Oasis Of The Zombies** (Jess Franco, 1982). Rollin also made the zombie-ridden **Pesticide** (1978) and the blood-drenched **Living Dead Girl** (1982).

Also of this period is Ignasi P Ferre Serra's Spanish production **Morbus** (1982), in which a scientist revives the dead with a serum, inadvertently creating a crew of flesh-eating zombies. Though the film has a terrible ending – it all turns out to be a joke – Serra manages to indulge in plenty of graphic sex, cannibalism and gore. Another related Spanish production is Frank Agrama's **Dawn Of The Mummy** (1981), a gore film in which ancient Egyptian mummies come to life as shuffling flesh-eaters; essentially, the film is a cannibal zombie movie in (thin) disguise.

14.   The only recent Italian zombie movie of any note was Michele Soavi's **Dellamorte Dellamore** (a.k.a. **Cemetery Man**, 1996), based on the comic strip *Dylan Dog*.

tea with a cannibal

MARCH 2001 saw the New York release of **Keep The River On Your Right**, a documentary directed by brother and sister film-making team Laurie and David Shapiro, and based on the book of the same name by artist, anthropologist and one-time cannibal Tobias Schneebaum (see also pages
1
12–13). The documentary, which won a Critic's Citation Award at the Los Angeles Independent Film Festival, begins by focusing on Schneebaum's life today, as he gives talks at New York City museums and lectures on art and tribal homosexuality against the unlikely background of a cruise ship.

Upon arrival in Indonesian New Guinea, Schneebaum and the film crew leave the cruise ship and head into the remote interior of Asmat country. Here, they run into Schneebaum's former sexual partner and cultural informant, Aipit, whom Tobias had presumed to be dead for many years. Partly as a result of this chance meeting, and after much coaxing by the film's directors, the 78-year-old Schneebaum finally agrees to return to Peru forty-five years after his original trip. The journey back through the Amazon at first seems like a wild goose chase, but after careful detective work by Schneebaum and the filmmaking crew, the trip yields more than any of them could possibly have anticipated. After finding the village where Tobias once lived, the crew come across six members of the original hunting party who remember their western visitor, and are as shocked to see Tobias again as he is to see them.

The documentary was shot under conditions of great difficulty, both physically and psychically. Working in 16mm, Super 16mm and digital video, the Shapiros had to pretend that they were bird watchers so that authorities didn't confiscate their equipment. The finished film, edited down from an original 800 feet of footage, is punctuated with vintage talk-show clips in which Schneebaum chats with Mike Douglas and Charlie Rose about his unique jungle adventures. Former New York neighbour Norman Mailer calls Tobias "one of the most extraordinary people I've ever known".

Schneebaum now makes his living as an artist and lives in Greenwich Village, where in March 2001 I met him for tea to chat about his adventures in the jungle. Schneebaum is a sensitive and articulate man who explained how many people had approached him in the past about making a film of *Keep The River On Your Right*, but he'd never been interested in any of their ideas. It took four years for the filmmakers to gain his trust and to persuade him to return with them to Peru. As the film relates, Tobias was initially a reluctant participant in the journey, mainly because he was still haunted by the horrors he experienced during the moonlit headhunting raids, when he took part in ritual murder and cannibalism. He was unable to talk about his experiences for ten years, and it was fifteen years before he was able to write about them.

The trip back into the jungle, however, has finally put many of Schneebaum's nightmares to rest, as well as reviving a lot of old memories. One memory in particular that haunted his dreams ever since his original trip to Peru was the tune of a tribal hunting song that the Indians would sing before setting out on their cannibal raids. A key scene in the film involves the song being sung for Schneebaum, at his request, by members of the original hunting party. To film this scene, the Shapiros had to use military lenses so as not to anger or disrespect the Indians. But instead of being angered, the Indians were thrilled with the visit. Many westerners since Tobias have been to see their tribe; what they loved about Schneebaum, they claimed, was the fact that "he came back".

Schneebaum explained that he has always been fascinated by tribal cultures after an early experience at Coney Island, when he recalled being sexually aroused by an exhibit called "The Wild Man of Borneo" (an African American, Henry Johnson, who suffered from microcephalus and was dressed in a fur "ape suit"). These feelings of erotic fascination were what first inspired Schneebaum to travel into the jungles of Peru. "I always lusted after the Wild Man of Borneo", he told me.

Keep The River On Your Right at first downplays Schneebaum's experience of cannibalism, and Schneebaum himself is rather sanguine about the enormous amount of publicity attracted by this element of his adventures. As a result of one single episode of flesh-eating, he's now become infamous as a "modern-day cannibal", something he's grown a little weary of. He complained that the most frequent questions he gets asked about his time among the Indians concern what part of the body he ate, and what it tasted like. This public fascination with his one single act of cannibalism has become something of a burden to him. "After all", he said, "the world is full of cannibals. I'd rather be known for my work or my art than known for being a cannibal. But that's what people are interested in, and that's what they always want to know about". But Schneebaum is also realistic enough to realize that his one act of cannibalism will always be more compelling and intriguing to most people than any other aspect of his life, his work or his art. "And in the end", he concludes with a sigh, "I suppose you have to go with the flow."

afterword

"There are odours not alien to beauty in the dung."
—Norman Mailer, *Advertisements For Myself*

T HE act of one human being eating another is so clearly full of ritual and symbolic significance that it is important to conclude this study with a brief attempt to understand, and come to terms with, some of the reasons why cannibalism has come to be such a powerful and meaningful cultural taboo. The cannibal himself, as a grotesque figure of power, threat and atavistic appetites, has played such an important part in the narratives that the members of our culture tell one another, whether oral, written or filmic, that it is necessary to consider why this uncanny practise has the capacity to inspire so much fear, revulsion and dread.

Combining such fundamental elements as human bodies, death, eating and ritual behaviour, cannibalism represents one of the most symbolically laden narratives in the human psychic repertoire. Of course, humans have believed one another to be man-eaters long before the word "cannibal" ever entered the language. As early as A.D. 79, the Roman chronicler Pliny the Elder described Africans as barbaric, man-eating savages. Much later, in the sixteenth century, the historian Winthrop D. Jordan, in his study of the first contact between Africans and whites, refers to the common European belief that Africans eat each other both dead and alive, just as we eat beef or chicken. On the other hand, the Africans believed equally that whites were cannibals, but despite numerous and severe European atrocities against Africans, the evidence suggests that they stopped short of literally eating their captives (see Turner, 1993:11). Explorer Mungo Park describes the common belief amongst captured Africans that they were going to be eaten by their captors, assuming that the slave traders had bought them only to fatten them up and afterwards eat them as a delicacy – an assumption that often led to attempts at rebellion and mutiny amongst the captives.

This sense of mutual threat and suspicion between black slaves and their white captors came partly from the misinterpretation, on both sides, of circumstantial evidence. The blacks observed that whites were buying and selling human flesh, fattening them up with rich foods, and lived off a highly unusual kind of diet. The whites, in their turn, saw how many Africans wore their teeth filed down and pointed, ate with their hands, were ambivalent about clothing, and indulged in unregulated sexual practises. In fact, however, for most of the Africans bought and sold in slavery, cannibalism was as much a taboo as it was for the white traders. Many Africans considered cannibals as threatening as witches, and individuals accused of cannibalism were summarily executed.

It did not take long for this mistaken currency of thought about man-eating, based on fear and ignorance on both sides, to solidify into a community of narrative and legend. The Europeans, in particular, had plenty of reasons for believing such narratives. By exaggerating the physical, behavioral and cultural gulf that existed between themselves and the Africans, they discouraged any doubts or hesitations on the part of those called upon to exploit the "African savages". Minor physical differences were considered aesthetically displeasing by the Europeans, and thereby assessed with negative value, becoming symbolic of moral taints as well. Some Europeans apparently believed Africans were so sexually permissive that black women mated freely with apes. They also supposed that blacks had more in common with the savage, man-eating beasts that inhabited the "dark continent" than with the white men and women of Europe (see Turner, 1993:17) Narratives of cannibalism amongst Africans similarly came into circulation through the transmission of regional enemy images, collective intimidation and ethnological gossip.

Although Arens is obviously overstating the case when he claims that accounts of African cannibalism have been based largely on hearsay, rumour, misunderstandings of ritual behaviour and verbal folklore, and on a Western propensity to believe the worst about a culture as a prelude to exploitation, nor is it true to claim, on the other hand, that there are cannibals hiding in every patch of jungle. However, rumours about cross-cultural cannibalism did not end with the cessation of the slave trade; in fact, the circumstances that influence relations between the two groups have changed only superficially, with an unfortunate legacy of mistrust and animosity persisting between Africans and Europeans (see Turner 1993:21).

Narratives on the subject of cannibalism, whether written or filmic, are taken for granted, committed to memory and passed down through the ages, and thereby qualify as a kind of contemporary folklore. It would be wrong to believe that the prevalence of this kind of folklore has diminished under the influence of technological change. It would also be wrong to identify it necessarily with traditional, archaic, or pre-literate societies. On the contrary, modern folklore is being constantly transmitted and engendered, and thrives in the contemporary media, especially in the cinema, as this study has shown. These are the kinds of narratives that guarantee survival for the individual or group, and guarantee their own status in their eyes. Whether etched in hieroglyphs on ancient scrolls or enacted in "blood color" before us on the cinema or video screen, all folklore involves the telling and re-telling of fantastical, magical, sacred stories about the founding of communities and the origins of things.

These modern stories of ancient behaviour have many and various functions. First of all, they are compensatory and projective stories which tell of that which is absent, unusual or impossible in a culture in an attempt to compensate for that culture's ontological limitations. Compensatory narratives deal with the kinds of things that cause feelings of deprivation and frustration in relation to society's restrictions, often departing from the actual ethic of the society by exaggerating certain actions, as well as the responses to those actions. Stories about cannibal behaviour often also involve sexual promiscuity, for example. Eating humans, the ultimate, taboo-breaking act of human aggression, is closely bound up with the notion of sexual domination. This wanton abuse of living human bodies is the worst kind of behaviour that can be imagined by most of the world's peoples. Clearly, then, these kinds of narratives – stories about departing from the social ethic, about disrespecting precisely what is respectable in the ideal – are a way of taking revenge on an ideal which can be violated with impunity only in narrative or filmic form. Cannibal stories which edge towards the obscene, or which feature unscrupulous savages violating social and sexual taboos, are projective attempts to compensate for a culture's social and moral limitations. They also work to engender and relish extreme sensations within a controlled and safe environment – a "laboratory-style" test condition. These conditions of safety allow such narratives to rationalize some extremely horrible and disturbing kinds of behaviour, revealing that our prosaic contemporary life is capable of producing some shocking and amazing occurrences, but in ways are always contained, somewhat, by "rational" explanations. These terrifying stories thereby reduce anxiety in the face of threat by revealing the terrible consequences of social, moral and sexual transgression.

These narratives of cannibalism also have a justifying and validating function, serving to vouch, give warrant, and provide testimonial for our culture's rituals, customs and practises. The Italian "jungle-rescue" cycle, for example, presents blacks behaving like savages, placing no restrictions on satisfying their basic human appetites and urges. Films like these may vouch and give warrant for European racist attitudes, and renew the status of racist rituals, cultures and practises amongst Europeans and other whites. They may also serve to reconcile, in a dramatic form, otherwise irreconcilable conflicts of value and practises. For example, it was the white Europeans and Americans, metaphorically speaking, who were the large-scale "consumers" of African peoples, and the whites who exhibited an insatiable appetite for African bodies. In these "jungle-rescue" cannibal films, perhaps, this cultural cannibalism is projected on to its victims in the more vivid and intelligible notion of individual cannibalism.

Films like **Cannibal Holocaust**, **Last Cannibal World**, and **Eaten Alive** present us with tales of misbehaviour on the part of both "civilized" whites and "savage" cannibals. Such stories work to serve a pedagogic function in that they inculcate examples of behaviour that a society and a culture finds valuable by summing up and giving guidelines to examples of right and wrong behaviour, and social and moral attributes. Films like **Cannibal Ferox** and **Cannibal Holocaust**, where no-one is quite sure "who the true cannibals are", serve as dilemma tales indicative of some form of conflict in the social code, highlighting areas in which a society is not as clear as it might be about what constitutes acceptable or unacceptable behaviour. Both of these films, for example, involve ambiguous behaviour on the part of the "decent" protagonists, from cruelty to animals and the use of cocaine, to fabricating the results of a Ph.D. thesis. On the scale of acceptable and unacceptable behaviour manifested in both these films, it is unclear quite how such transgressions should be treated. And the more a society is in doubt about its sanctioned codes of behaviour, the more such dilemma tales are told. Often there is no solution to such dilemmas – they are retold in filmic form simply to highlight a particular site where cultural values seem to be in conflict. In narratives where the line between sanctioned and unsanctioned behaviour is much clearer, like **Dr. X** or **Blood Feast**, the function served is more likely to be one of induction. Films like these exert pressure or imply some kind of moral threat in order to induce conformism within social norms, or to provide excitement directed against deviancy. In dramatic form, such stories disapprove of, deride or condemn aberrations or transgressions, or involve sanctions against some cultural prohibition that has quite clearly been violated. In other words, films like these act as behavioral sanctions telling of a culture's organization and its prohibitions, endorsing certain kinds of social relationships and counselling against others. They commend and celebrate such conformist behaviour as Suzette Fremont's giggly ignorance and Joanne Xavier's fear of the dark, and provide correctives to unreasonable expectations or excessive demands.

In psychoanalytic terms, these stories of moral transgression and broken taboos could be considered to represent the enactment of a series of repressed ideas, bringing them back into the forefront or consciousness of a culture, but in a censored form, in symbolic disguise. According to psychoanalysis, films operate according to the same kind of symbol-based associative logic of dreams, where each image is an indicator of something other than itself, and the images are strung together in not entirely arbitrary patterns. The imagery of films like **Spider Baby** and **Frightmare** have a lot in common with the imagery of dreams, especially in the loose but not unsystematic way they are connected. Narratives like these, dominated by their powerful symbols and striking images, seem to be structured according to the magical ways of thinking characteristic of childhood, and could thereby be said to articulate in repressed form the unconscious anxieties of all human beings. By appropriating the logic of substitution, displacement, condensation and fusion, a film like **Spider Baby** both obscures, hides and yet at the same time restates hidden relationships. This symbolic coding allows things to be both hidden and expressed simultaneously. Narratives like these thereby present the disguised gratification of repressed desires, a fact which may help to explain the residue of their appeal, and the popularity of such narratives beyond timing and history. According to some psychoanalysts, such as French theorist Jacques Lacan, the internal consistency of a narrative is itself evidence of psychic censorship. Coherence and smoothness are indices of repression. This argument, if followed, would suggest any narrative filled with gaps and missing pieces is a highly accessible text for psychoanalytic interpretation. Stories full of inconsistencies, like Reitman and Goldberg's **Cannibal Girls**, or stories full of omissions like **Karamoja**, are narratives whose abruptness and incoherence provide a direct means of access to the unconscious netherworld of anxiety, neurosis and taboo.

Anthropologists such as Claude Lévi-Strauss and Mary Douglas, as well as psychoanalysts such as Freud and Lacan, have studied how patterns of cultural behaviour reflect individuals' anxieties about their own bodies, and, in particular, anxieties concerning bodily boundaries and orifices. Stories like **Prisoner Of The Cannibal God** and **Anthropophagus, The Beast** are stories about groups of people who do not seem to share such anxieties, who are not disgusted by situations that would disgust "us", and therefore people who do not seem to share "our" terms of repression. We, however, remain fascinated and appalled by what cannibals do because we are afraid of cannibalism. This fear has its foundation in our knowledge, however unconscious, that the widespread violation of these moral taboos would lead, in the end, to the disintegration of our society.

According to Freud, emotions like shock and disgust are simply one way of coming to terms with that which is repressed in the human unconscious. If Freud is right, then we are all cannibals at heart. Our shared human fascination with cannibalism is connected to infantile needs and desires arising in the oral-sadistic phase of childhood development, by virtue of which it becomes a powerfully repressed element of the human unconscious. To act on such needs and desires, however, would be to subvert the very foundations of human society. Taboos are created because they sanction against such possibilities. The greater the repression, the stronger the fascination, and the stronger the fascination, the more powerful and prohibitive the taboo. Whenever the taboo is broken – either vicariously, in narrative form, or horribly, in reality – we are allowed a brief glimpse into human society without civilization, without boundaries, without limitations. The knowledge that this could actually happen, that it *has* happened, that it might be happening somewhere now, that human beings are really capable of such behaviour, is the ultimate cause of the fear of social, psychological and bodily disintegration/collapse – the very fear that makes us human.

BIBLIOGRAPHY

Note: Where relevant information is available sources are fully referenced, however given the nature of various cuttings, archives and sources this has not always been possible.

Adamides, Andrew; "Angster's Paradise: Psychoanalysis Of Depictions Of Male Teen Adolescence Throughout Eighties Film Comedies". Unpublished paper, University of East London, 1997.
Apostolou and Greenberg, eds; The Best Japanese Science Fiction Stories. New York: NYU Press, 1989.
Arens, William; The Man Eating Myth. New York: Oxford University Press, 1979.
Artaud, Antonin; Selected Writings (trans. Helen Weaver). New York: Farrar, Straus and Giroux, 1976; Collected Works. New York: John Calder, 1991.
Beard, Steve; "No Particular Place To Go". Sight & Sound III/4, April 1993:30–31.
Bettelheim, Bruno; The Uses of Enchantment: The Meaning And Importance Of Fairy Tales. London: Thames and Hudson, 1976. Reprinted, Penguin 1978, 1988; Peregrine, 1982; Random House, 1988.
Bloch, Maurice & Jonathan Parry, eds; Death And The Regeneration Of Life. Cambridge: Cambridge University Press, 1982.
"Blood Diner" (review), Variety CCCXXVIII, Sept. 2nd, p16, 1987.
Boar, Roger and Nigel Blundell; The World's Most Infamous Murderers. London: Hamlyn, 1990.
Boukhabza, D. and J. Yesavage; "Cannibalism And Vampirism In Paranoid Schizophrenia". Journal Of Clinical Psychiatry 42 (1981).
Briggs, George William; Goraknath And The Kanphata Yogis. Calcutta: YMCA Publishing House, 1938.
Briggs, Joe Bob; The Cosmic Wisdom Of Joe Bob Briggs. New York: Random House, 1981.
Brite, Poppy Z.; Exquisite Corpse, London & NY: Phoenix, 1996.
Brittain, Robert P.; "The Sadistic Murderer", Medicine, Science And The Law, 10:4 (1970).
Britton, Andrew et al, eds; The American Nightmare: Essays On The Horror Film. Toronto: Festival of Festivals, 1979.
Brown, Geoff; "Fried Green Tomatoes" (review), Sight & Sound I/II, March 1992:46.
Brown, Norman O.; Love's Body. Berkeley, CA: University of California Press, 1966. Reprinted 1992.
Brown, Paula, and Donald Tuzin, eds.; The Ethnography Of Cannibalism. Washington D.C.: The Society for Psychological Anthropology, 1983.
Burroughs, William; The Soft Machine. London: Flamingo, 1986.
Burton-Bradley, B.G.; "Cannibalism For Cargo", Journal Of Nervous And Mental Disease, 163 (1976).
Calhoun, John B.; "Plight Of The Ik And Kaiadilt Is Seen As A Chilling Possible End For Man", Smithsonian, Washington D.C.: Smithsonian Institute, 1972.
Campbell, Joseph; The Hero With A Thousand Faces. London: Fontana, 1988.
"Cannibal Holocaust" (review). Variety, June 19th, 1985.
Caputi, J.; "Nuclear Issues In The Cinema", Journal Of Popular Film And Television XVI.3, Fall 1988:100–107.
Catullus, Gaius; Selections From Catullus, ed. R.O.A.M. Lyne. Cambridge: Cambridge University Press, 1973.
Cleckley, Hervey Milton; The Mask Of Sanity. St. Louis: C.V. Mosby, 1982.
Clover, Carol J.; "Her Body, Himself: Gender In The Slasher Film", Representations 20 (Fall):187–228, 1987. Reprinted in Fantasy In The Cinema, ed. James Donald. London: BFI Press, 1989. Men, Women And Chainsaws. London: BFI Press, 1992.
Conrad, Joseph; Heart Of Darkness. London: Penguin, 1989.
Conradi, Peter; The Red Ripper. London: True Crime Books, 1982.
Cornwell, Tim; "Eat, Drink, Man, Woman?", The Times Higher Education Supplement, May 1997:23:17.
Cros, Jean-Louis; "Cannibal Holocaust" (review), Image et Son: Revue du Cinéma 361:39–40, May 1981.

Dante, Aligheri; *The Inferno*. Berkeley: University of California Press, 1992.

De Certeau, Michel; *Heterologies: Discourse On The Other*, trans. Brian Maasumi. Minneapolis and London: University of Minnesota Press, 1995.

Defoe, Daniel; *Robinson Crusoe*. London: Penguin Popular Classics, 1994.

De River, J. Paul; *The Sexual Criminal – A Psychoanalytic Study*. Springfield, Illinois: Charles C. Thomas, 1950.

Derry, Charles; *Dark Dreams – A Psychological History Of The Modern Horror Film*. London: A.S. Barnes, 1977.

"Destins Du Cannibalisme", (special issue), *Nouvelle Revue De Psychanalyse* 6 (Autumn), 1972.

Douglas, Mary. *Purity And Danger – An Analysis Of The Concepts Of Pollution And Taboo*. London: Routledge and Kegan Paul, 1966. Reprinted London: Routledge, 1984, 1989; *Risk And Blame – Essays In Cultural Theory*. London: Routledge, 1992, 1994; *Implicit Meanings: Essays In Anthropology*. London & Boston: Routledge and Kegan Paul, 1978.

Drury, Nevill; *The Occult Experience: Magic In The New Age*. New York: Avery Publishing Group, 1989.

Durkheim, Emile; *Sociology And Philosophy*. Hemel Hempstead: Free Press, 1953.

Dyer, Richard; "Whites In Films", *Screen* XXIX/4, Autumn 1988:44–64.

Ellis, Bret Easton; *American Psycho*. London: Picador, 1981.

"Emanuele E Gli Ultimi Cannibali" (review), *Variety* CCCXV/6, June 6, p20, 1984.

Fitzhugh, George; *Cannibals All, Or, Slaves Without Masters*. Harvard: Harvard University Press, 1960.

Flaubert, Gustave; *Salammbo*, trans. A.J. Krailsheimer. London: Penguin Classics, 1977.

Fogelson, Raymond D., "Psychological Theories Of Windigo 'Psychosis' And A Preliminary Application Of A Model Approach", *Context And Meaning In Cultural Anthropology*, Melford E. Spiro, ed. New York: The Free Press, 1965.

Frazer, Sir James George; *Totemism And Exogamy – A Treatise On Certain Early Forms Of Superstition*. London: Macmillan, 1910.

Freud, Sigmund; "Beyond The Pleasure Principle", *Standard Edition*, 18:1–64, 1923; "From The History Of An Infantile Neurosis", *Standard Edition*, 17:7–122; "The Uncanny". *Standard Edition*, 17:219–52, 1919; "On Sexuality", *Collected Papers*, volume 7, Standard Edition; *The Standard Edition Of The Complete Works Of Sigmund Freud*. James Strachey, trans. London: Hogarth Press, 1950; *Totem And Taboo*, New York: W.W. Norton, 1962.

Friedman, David; *Confessions Of A Youth In Babylon*. Essex: Prometheus Books, 1991.

Frome, Donald; *The Complete Essays Of Montaigne*. Stanford: Stanford University Press, 1958.

Furst, L.R. and P.W. Graham, eds.; *Disorderly Eaters*. Philadelphia: Penn State University Press, 1992.

Garsault, Alain; "Cannibal Holocaust" (review). *Positif* 243:65, June 1981.

Genet, Jean; *The Complete Poems Of Jean Genet*. Boyes Hot Springs, CA: Manroot Press, 1988.

Gere, F.; "Cannibal Holocaust" (review). *Cahiers Du Cinéma* 326:63, July/August 1981.

Girard, René; *Violence And The Sacred*. New York: Johns Hopkins University Press, 1977. Reprinted Athlone, 1988.

Gollmar, Robert; *Edward Gein: America's Most Bizarre Murderer*. Delaven, WI: Hallberg, 1981.

Grant, Barry Keith, ed.; *Planks of Reason: Essays On The Horror Film*. Metuchen, New Jersey: Scarecrow Press, 1984.

Halberstam, Judith; "Skinflick: Posthuman Gender In Jonathan Demme's The Silence Of The Lambs", *Camera Obscura* 27, September 1991:38–52.

Hamilton-Parker, Craig; "Cannibal Castaways". *Fortean Times* 92 (1996), 32–33.

Harris, Marvin; *Cannibals And Kings: The Origins Of Cultures*. New York: Random House, 1977.

Heckelthorn, Charles William; *The Secret Societies Of All Ages And Countries*. New York: University Books, 1965.

Heimer, Mel; *The Cannibal: The Case of Albert Fish*. New York: Xanadu Publications,

1986.

Heinlein, Robert; *Farnham's Freehold*; *Stranger in a Strange Land*.

Heraclitus; *Fragments*, ed. Charles H. Kahn. Cambridge: Cambridge University Press, 1981.

Hesiod; *Theogony & Works And Days*, trans. M.L. West. Oxford: Oxford Paperbacks, 1988.

"The Hills Have Eyes Part II", review, *Variety* CCCXXII/4, Feb 19, p12, 1986.

Hillberg, Raul; *The Destruction Of The European Jews*, Chicago and London, 1961.

Homer; *Odyssey IX*, ed. J. Muir. Bristol: Bristol Classic Press, 1980.

Horner, Martin; "Jivaro Souls", *American Anthropologist* 64:258–272, 1962.

Hughes, Ted; *The Hawk In The Rain*. London: Faber Paperbacks, 1957.

Huizinga, Johan; *The Waning Of The Middle Ages*. London: Harmondsworth, Penguin, 1974, reissued 1955.

Hulme, Peter (ed); *Cannibalism And The Colonial World*. Cambridge, UK: Cambridge University Press, forthcoming 1998.

Iaccino, James; *Psychological Reflections On Cinematic Terror: Jungian Archetypes In Horror Films*. Greenville, N.C: Greenwood, 1994.

Juvenal; *Satires*, ed. John Ferguson. London: Nelson, 1979.

Jung, Carl G.; *The Archetypes And The Collective Unconscious*. 2nd edition, Routledge 1991; *Symbols Of Transformation*. Bollingen Series, Princeton: Princeton University Press, 1960.

Kekes, John; "Disgust And Moral Taboos", *Philosophy* 67: 1992:431–446.

Kerekes, David & David Slater; *Killing for Culture: An Illustrated History Of Death Film From Mondo To Snuff*. London: Annihilation Press, 1993. Reprinted Creation Books, 1995.

Kilgour, M.; *From Communion To Cannibalism: An Anatomy Of Metaphors Of Incorporation*. Princeton: Princeton University Press, 1990.

King, Stephen; "Survivor Type", *Skeleton Crew*.

Klein, Melanie; *The Selected Melanie Klein*, ed. Juliet Mitchell. London: Penguin, 1986.

Koch, Stephen; "The Texas Chain Saw Massacre" (review), *Harper's*, November 1976.

Komatsu, Sokyo; see Apostolou and Greenberg.

Krafft-Ebing, R.; *Psychopathia Sexualis*. Philadelphia, PA: F.A. Davis, 1892. New edition: Velvet Publications, London, 1997.

Kraniauskas, J.; "Death Line" (review), *Sight & Sound* V/1, p41, Jan 1995.

Krasniewicz, Louise; "Cinematic Gifts: The Moral And Social Exchange Of Bodies In Horror Films", *Tattoo, Torture, Mutilation And Adornment: The Denaturalization Of The Body In Culture And Text*, ed. Frances E. Mascia-Less and Patricia Sharpe. New York: SUNY Press, 1992.

Lacan, Jacques; *Écrits*. London: W.W. Norton, 1980, reissued 1983.

Lapouge, Gilles; "Mangez-vous Les Uns Les Autres", *La Quinzaine Littéraire*, March 1973.

Lévi-Strauss, Claude; "Structure And Form: Reflections Of A Work By Vladimir Propp", *Vladimir Propp, Theory And History Of Folklore*, ed. Anatoly Liberman, trans. Ariadna Y. Martin and Richard P. Martin. Minneapolis: University of Minnesota Press, 1984. *The Raw And The Cooked: Introduction To A Science Of Mythology*, trans. John & Doreen Weightman, London: Penguin, 1964.

Lewis, Herschell Gordon; *Blood Feast*. New York: Epics International, 1988.

Lewis, Matthew Gregory; *The Monk: A Romance*, ed. Howard Anderson. Oxford: Oxford Paperbacks, 1980.

Leyton, Elliot; *Hunting Humans: The Rise Of The Modern Multiple Murderer*. London: Penguin Books, 1986.

Lloyd, Georgina; *One Was Not Enough: True Stories Of Multiple Murderers*. London: Bantam Books, 1989.

Lourie, Richard; *Hunting The Devil: The Search For The Russian Ripper*. London: Grafton Books, 1993.

"Lucky Stiff" (review), *Variety* CCCXXXV/4, May 10:52, 1989.

MacCannell, Daniel; "Cannibal Tours", *Visual Anthropology Review* 6 (2):14–24, 1990.

Mailer, Norman; *Advertisements For Myself*. Harvard: Harvard University Press, 1992;

An American Dream. London: Flamingo, 1992; The Short Fiction Of Norman Mailer. New York: Tor Books, 1981.

Mandeville, Phillip; The Fable Of The Bees (4th & 5th Dialogues), ed. F.B. Kaye. Oxford: Clarendon Press, 1966.

Marriner, Brian; Cannibalism: The Last Taboo. London: Arrow Books, 1992.

Masters, Brain; The Shrine Of Jeffrey Dahmer. London: Hodder and Staughton, 1993.

Martingale, Moira; Cannibal Killers: The History Of Impossible Murderers. New York: Carroll & Graf, 1993.

Maturin, Charles Robert; Melmoth The Wanderer, ed. Douglas Grant. Oxford: Oxford Paperbacks, 1989.

Melville, Herman; Moby Dick, ed. Tony Tanner. Oxford: Oxford Paperbacks, 1988; Typee, ed. Ruth Blair. Oxford: Oxford Paperbacks, 1996.

Mishima, Yukio; The Sailor Who Fell From Grace With The Sea, trans. John Nathan. London: Penguin, 1970.

Montaigne; see Frome, Donald.

Money, John; "Forensic Sexology: Paraphilic Serial Rape (Biastophilia) And Lust Murder (Erotophonophilia)", American Journal Of Psychotherapy, Vol. XLIV, 1:26–36, January 1990; with H. Mustaph, Selected Personal And Social Issues Vol. IV, Oxford & New York: Elseveier, 1978.

"Motel Hell" (review), Cahiers Du Cinéma 319:58, January 1981.

Muensterberger, Warner; Man And His Culture: Psychoanalytic Anthropology After "Totem And Taboo". London: Rapp & Whiting, 1969.

Newman, Kim; Nightmare Movies. London: Bloomsbury 1988; New York: Harmony Books, 1989.

"Spider Baby, Or, The Maddest Story Ever Told" (review), Monthly Film Bulletin LII/622:345–355, November 1985.

Nicholson, Mervyn; "Eat Or Be Eaten", Mosaic 24:3/4 (1991), 191–210.

"Magic Food, Compulsive Eating", Furst, L.R and P. W. Graham, eds., Disorderly Eaters. Philadelphia: Penn State University Press, 1992.

Nietzsche, Friedrich; Ecco Homo, trans. Walter Kaufmann and R.J. Hollingdale. New York: Vintage, 1967. Reissued, Penguin 1992.

Norris, Joel; Serial Killers – The Growing Menace. New York: Doubleday, 1988.

O'Neill, James; Terror On Tape. New York: Billboard, 1994.

Ovid; The Metamorphoses, trans. Arthur Golding. London: Penguin, 1955.

Park, Mungo; Travels In The Interior Of Africa. London: Eland Books, 1983.

Parker, Seymour; "The Wiitiko Psychosis In The Context Of Ojibwa Personality And Culture", American Anthropologist 62:603–23, 1960.

Parry, Jonathan; "Sacrificial Death And The Necrophagus Ascetic", in Bloch & Parry, eds.

Peary, Danny; Cult Movies: The Classics, The Sleepers, The Weird And The Wonderful. New York: Dell, 1981; Cult Movies 2. New York: Dell, 1983.

Plath, Sylvia; Ariel. San Bernardino: Borgo Press, 1991.

Pliny, Gaius (Pliny the Elder); Natural History, ed. Turner; trans. Holland. Arundel, Sussex: Centaur Press, 1962.

Plutarch; Essays, ed. Ian Kidd, trans. Robin Waterfield. London: Penguin, 1992.

Poe, Edgar Allan; The Narrative Of Arthur Gordon Pym. Oxford: Oxford Paperbacks, 1994.

Prins, Herschel; Bizarre Behaviours. London & New York: Routledge/Tavistock, 1990.

Radcliffe, Ann; The Mysteries of Udolpho, ed. Bonamy Dobrie and Frederick Garber, Oxford: Oxford Paperbacks, 1980.

Ramasse, Francois; "La Chair Est Fade, Hélas!", Positif 337, March 1989:66–68.

Raschke, Carl A.; Painted Black. San Francisco: Harper & Row, 1990.

Read, Piers Paul; Alive. Tennessee: Avon Books, 1992.

"Regina Dei Cannibali, La" (review), Variety CCCVII/1, May 5th:21, 24, 1982.

Ressler, Robert K. et al.; "Murderers Who Rape And Mutilate", Journal Of Interpersonal Violence, September 1986.

Rochester, John, Earl of; The Works Of The Earl Of Rochester. London: Wordsworth Editions, 1995.

Rodowick, David N.; "The Eyes Within: The Economy Of Violence In "'The Hills Have Eyes'" in Barry Keith Grant, ed.

Roheim, Geza; "Fire In The Dragon" And Other Psychoanalytic Essays On Folklore, Alan Dundes, ed. Princeton: Princeton University Press 1992.

Roy, Jean; "Cannibal Holocaust" (review), Cinéma 81 270:125–6, June 1981.

Sade, Marquis de; Justine, Philosophy In The Bedroom, & Other Writings. Tennessee: Grove Press, 1990; 120 Days Of Sodom, London: Arena, 1991. Selected Writings. Watchung, N.J.: Albert Saifer, 1987.

Sagan, Eli; Cannibalism: Human Aggression And Cultural Form. New York: Harper Torchbooks, 1974.

Sahlins, M.; "Raw Women, Cooked Men And Other 'Great Things' Of The Fiji Islands", P. Brown and D. Tuzin, eds., The Ethnography Of Cannibalism. Washington: The Society for Psychological Anthropology, 1983.

Sanday, Peggy Reeves; Divine Hunger: Cannibalism As A Cultural System. Cambridge: Cambridge University Press, 1986.

Schneebaum, Tobias; Keep The River On Your Right. Tennessee: Grove Press, 1969. Reissued, 1988.

Seneca, Lucius; Moral And Political Essays, ed. John M. Cooper and J. F. Procope. Cambridge: Cambridge University Press, 1995.

Shakespeare, William; Othello, The Moor Of Venice, ed. M.R. Ridley. London: Routledge, 1965; Titus Andronicus, ed. J. C. Maxwell. London: Routledge, 1968.

Sharrett, Christopher; "The Idea Of Apocalypse In 'The Texas Chain Saw Massacre'" in Barry Keith Grant, ed.

Sheldon, Alice; see James Tiptree Jr.

Smith, Gavin A. & A. Murphy; "Identity Check. Communion", Film Comment Jan–Feb 1991:28–34, 36–37.

Sophocles; Fragments, ed. & trans. Hugh Lloyd Jones. Harvard: Harvard University Press, 1996.

Stam, Robert; Subversive Pleasures: Bakhtin, Cultural Criticism And Film. Baltimore: Johns Hopkins University Press, 1992.

Stanbrook, Alan; "Invasion Of The Purple People Eaters", Sight & Sound LX/1, Winter 1990–91:48–50.

Stekel, Wilhelm; Sexual Aberrations. London: Liveright Books, 1992.

Storr, Anthony; Human Destructiveness. London: Routledge, 1991; Jung. London: Fontana 1973. Reissued, 1986.

Strathern, Andrew; "Witchcraft, Greed, Cannibalism And Death" in Bloch & Parry, eds.

Straus, Frédéric; "Faire La Fete", Cahiers Du Cinéma 416, February 1989, 52–55.

Sundelson, David; "The Demon Therapist And Other Dangers: Jonathan Demme's 'The Silence Of The Lambs'", Journal Of Popular Film And Television 1, Spring 1993:12–17.

Swift, Jonathan; A Modest Proposal And Other Satire. Essex: Prometheus Books, 1995.

Symington, Neville; "The Response Aroused By The Psychopath", The International Review Of Psychoanalysis 7:291–298 (1980).

Tannahil, Reay; Flesh And Blood – A History Of Human Cannibalism. London and New York: Stein and Day, 1975.

Tatar, Marie; Off With Their Heads! Fairy Tales And The Culture Of Childhood. Princeton: Princeton University Press 1992.

Taubin, Amy; "Killing Men", Sight & Sound I/1, May 1991:14–19.

Teicher, Morton I.; Windigo Psychosis. Proceedings Of The 1960 Annual Spring Meeting Of The American Ethnological Society. Seattle: American Ethnological Society, 1960.

Telotte, J. P.; "Faith And Idolatry In The Horror Film" in Barry Keith Grant, ed.

Terry, Maury; The Ultimate Evil. New York: Doubleday, 1987.

Tharp, Julie; "The Transvestite As Monster: Gender Horror In 'The Silence Of The Lambs' And 'Psycho'", Journal Of Popular Film And Television 3, Fall 1991:106–113.

Thirard, Paul Louis; "I Cannibali", Positif 139:63, June 1972.

Tiptree, James Jr. (Alice Sheldon); "Morality Meat" in Crown Of Stars.

Tolstoy, Leo; Resurrection, ed. Richard F. Gustafson, trans. Louise Maude. Oxford: Oxford Paperbacks, 1994.

Turner, Bryan; The Early Sociology Of Religion. London and New York: Routledge,

1984. Reissued 1996.

Turner, Patricia; *I Heard It Through The Grapevine: Rumor In African-American Culture*. Berkeley: University of California Press, 1993.

Vale, V. and Andrea Juno, eds.; *Re/Search #10: Incredibly Strange Films*. San Fransisco: Re/Search Publications, 1986.

Virgil; *The Ecologues*, trans. Guy Lee. Leeds: Francis Cairns, 1980.

Walens, Stanley; *Feasting With Cannibals*. Princeton: Princeton University Press, 1981.

Walpole, Horace; *The Castle Of Otranto: A Gothic Story*, ed. W.S. Lewis and Joseph W. Reed. Oxford and London: Oxford Paperbacks, 1982.

Waters, John; *Shock Value*. New York: Delta, 1991.

"Whatever Happened to Showmanship?", *American Film* 9 (December) 55–8, 1983.

Watson, James L.; "Of Flesh And Bones: The Management Of Death Pollution In Cantonese Society", in Bloch & Parry, eds.

Weldon, Michael; *The Psychotronic Encyclopaedia Of Film*. New York: Ballantyne Books, 1983.

Wells, H.G.; *The Time Machine & The Island Of Dr. Moreau*, ed. Patrick Parrinder. Oxford: Oxford University Press, 1996.

Williams, Tennessee; *The Theatre Of Tennessee Williams*. London: W.W. Norton, 1994.

Wilson, Colin, and Donald Seaman; *Encyclopaedia Of Modern Murder*. London: Pan Books, 1986.

Wittig, Monique; *Les Guerillères*, trans. David Levay. New Jersey: Farrar, Strauss & Giroux, 1985. *Le Corps Lesbien*. Boston, MA: Beacon Press, 1994.

Wood, Robin; "The Return Of The Repressed", *Film Comment* 14:25–32, 1978. "An Introduction To The American Horror Film", *American Nightmare: Essays On The Horror Film*, ed. Andrew Britton et al. Toronto: Festival of Festivals, 1979. Reprinted, *Movies And Methods* vol.2, ed. Bill Nichols. Berkeley and Los Angeles: University of California Press, 1989.

Woods, Paul Anthony; *Ed Gein: Psycho*. New York: St. Martin's Griffin, 1995.

Young, Elizabeth; "'The Silence Of The Lambs' And The Flaying Of Feminist Theory", *Camera Obscura*, 27, September 1991:4–53.

Zimmer, J.; "Cannibal Holocaust" (review), *Image Et Son* (hors serie) 25:49–50, 1981.

Zheng Yi; *Scarlet Memorial – Tales Of Cannibalism In Modern China*, T.P. Sym, ed. & trans., Oxford: Westview Press, 1996.

INDEX OF FILMS

Page numbers in italics indicate an illustration

www.creationbooks.com